Great Medieval Castles of Britain

Great Medieval

Castles of Britain

James Forde-Johnston

THE BODLEY HEAD
London   Sydney   Toronto

Frontispiece
Tantallon Castle: Crown
Copyright, reproduced
by permission of the
Department of the
Environment.

Forde-Johnston, James
    Great medieval castles of Britain.
    1. Castles – Great Britain
    I. Title
    728.8′1′0941   NA7745

ISBN 0 370 30236 2

© James Forde-Johnston 1979
Produced by Guild Publishing,
the Original Publications Division of
Book Club Associates

Designed by Harold Bartram

Printed in Great Britain for
The Bodley Head Ltd
9 Bow Street, London WC2E 7AL
by Lowe & Brydone Printers Ltd
Thetford, Norfolk
set in 10 on 12 Times New Roman
First published 1979

Contents

Acknowledgements

The publishers wish to thank the following for granting permission to use their illustrations.

Aerofilms: 42–3, 64, 81 (bottom), 86, 88, 101, 110, 114. British Tourist Authority: 10, 150, 184. Cambridge University Collection: 61. Commissioners of Public Works in Ireland: 198, 200. Crown Copyright, reproduced by permission of the Department of the Environment: 30, 140, 149, 163, 172, 175, 176, 196. Mary Evans Picture Library: 76. Robert Harding Associates: 104, 182 (bottom). Michael Holford: 13, 16, 20, 26–7, 36, 41, 52, 119, 120 (both), 155 (both), 170, 180–1. Picturepoint: 44 (top), 48, 75, 134, 137, 168, 179, 182 (top), 197. Scottish Tourist Board: 32, 62.

Plans prepared by Harold Bartram.

All other illustrations: James Forde-Johnston.

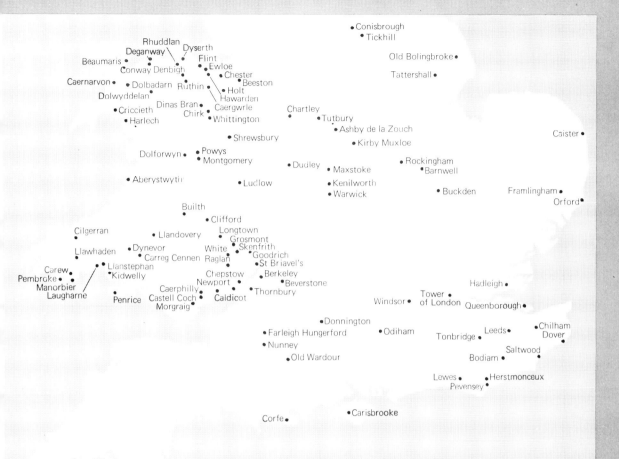

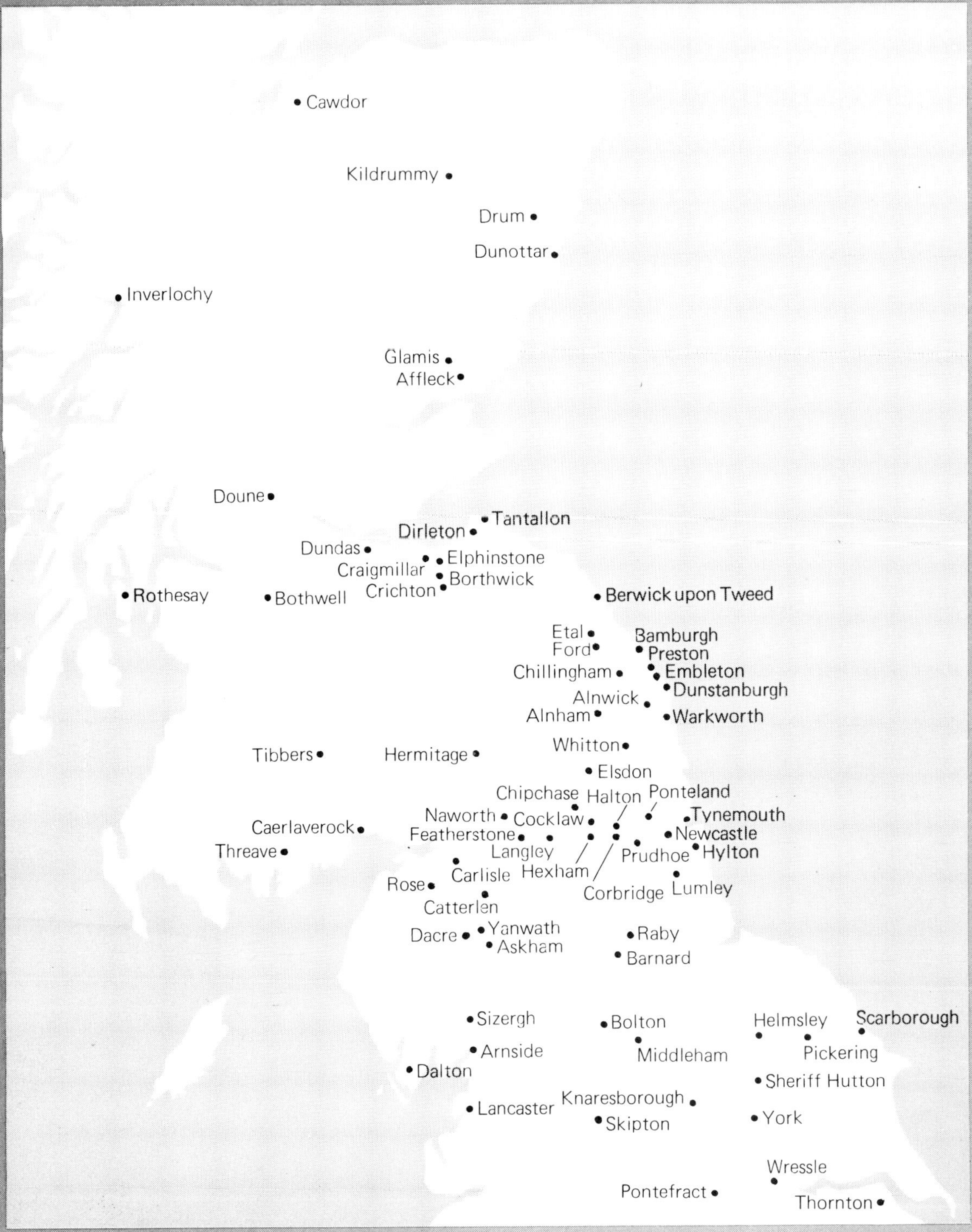

- Cawdor

Kildrummy •

Drum •

Dunottar •

• Inverlochy

Glamis •
Affleck •

Doune •

• Tantallon
Dirleton •

Dundas •
Elphinstone •
Craigmillar • Borthwick •
• Rothesay   Crichton •
• Bothwell

Berwick upon Tweed •

Etal •   Bamburgh •
Ford •   • Preston
Chillingham •   • Embleton
Alnwick •   • Dunstanburgh
Alnham •   • Warkworth

Tibbers •   Hermitage •   Whitton •

• Elsdon

Chipchase • Halton • Ponteland •
Naworth • Cocklaw •   • Tynemouth
Caerlaverock •   Featherstone •   • Newcastle
Threave •   Langley •   Prudhoe • Hylton
Carlisle Hexham •
Rose •   Corbridge • Lumley

Catterlen
Dacre • Yanwath •   • Raby
• Askham   • Barnard

• Sizergh   • Bolton   Helmsley •   Scarborough •

• Arnside   Middleham •   Pickering •
• Dalton
• Sheriff Hutton
• Lancaster   Knaresborough •
• Skipton   • York

Wressle •
Pontefract •
Thornton •

Dunluce

Kilclief •

• Ballymote   Castleroche •

                             Roodstown •

Ballintubber •

Roscommon •

                                        Trim •
                              Donore •
Athlone •   Dunsoghly •

                              • Lea
• Newtown
            • Terryglass

                 • Nenagh
• Quin   • Carlow
• Bunratty
    • Limerick   • Ballynahow
                   Kilkenny • • Clara
                                    Ferns •
              Burnchurch •   Ballyloughan
                                 Enniscorthy
         Kiltinane •

• Liscarroll   Reginald's Tower •   Wexford •

   Blarney •

1
After the Conquest

Castle building in Britain began with the Norman Conquest in 1066 and continued thereafter for about four centuries, as a major preoccupation of both the ruling king and his barons. The native Anglo-Saxon population of England had no castles and this is usually given as the reason for the comparative ease with which the Norman occupation was accomplished. The English were not, however, entirely without fortifications. Under Alfred the Great (AD 849–99) and his successors had grown up a system of *burhs* (fortified towns), as a means of communal defence against the fierce raiding by the Danes. Nevertheless, it remains true that the English had no tradition of castle building, and the great medieval strongholds which are still such a striking feature of the English landscape owe their origins to Norman military architecture, brought in by the invaders to consolidate their hold on newly acquired territories.

These Norman castles continued to be built for a little over a century after the Conquest. Their dominant feature was the great rectangular stone tower or keep which is virtually the hallmark of Norman military building. Towards the end of the twelfth century new ideas of fortification led to new types of stronghold in which the keep had no place, and it is these 'later' castles which form the main subject of this book. There is, in fact, an overlap between the two periods. In spite of the new ideas mentioned above, keeps, in one form or another, survived until the middle of the thirteenth century, so that 'early' castles can be said to have endured for about two hundred years (1066–1250). However, the first signs of the 'later' castles appeared about 1170–80, so that for about seventy or eighty years the two traditions existed side by side. The later tradition as a whole lasted from the dates just mentioned until the end of the medieval era (1485), a period of some 300 years, and it is the fortifications built in these years on which attention will be concentrated in the following pages.

Castles were built either by the king or by his barons, at their own expense. The differences between royal and baronial castles were not differences in style or type. They were rather political differences, arising out of the feudal system which the Normans introduced into this country after 1066. Castles were a necessary part of this system, so that the great castle-building activity which followed the Conquest was not simply the normal military precaution to be expected in newly acquired territory but an integral and necessary part of the political and administrative structure of the country. The word feudal is derived from the medieval Latin *'feodum'*, meaning a fee or payment, but in the form of land rather than actual money. The system was widespread in Europe but not in Anglo-Saxon England, and was introduced here only by the Normans. In its train came inevitably the feudal castle. The system was an acknowledgement of the difficulty of running and defending a large country without a well-developed administrative system, without efficient communications, and without a standing army. These deficiencies were made good, at least in part, by granting land, in greater or lesser quantity, to men (barons) in return for services. In theory at least, all land belonged to the king and was held as a fee or payment from him in return for various political, administrative, and military services. It was, in fact, the use of land as a means of exchange rather than money, although quite clearly it was a question of buying services rather than goods. In the absence of a developed monetary system land was undoubtedly the most secure form of payment.

The system in broad terms worked like this: the king retained a large section of the country under his own direct control; the rest he parcelled out among his barons in return for agreed services to the crown. In turn, the barons, or tenants-in-chief, retained a certain amount of land for their own use and distributed the rest among their followers, who thus became sub-tenants. At the lowest level of the system were the peasants (this term covering a wide range of minor classes), the people who actually worked the land. They held what may be termed smallholdings, in return for which they worked so many days on the land of the lord from whom they held it. The system can be likened to a great pyramid embracing the whole of society, with the king at the apex and the peasantry at the base.

Castles were an integral and essential part of the feudal system. Without a castle (or castles) no baron could exercise the power placed in his hands by the king, and if he could not exercise power then the whole system could break down into anarchy, as indeed it did from time to time when that power was abused. The castle was the local base which provided law enforcement, justice, defence, and all the functions which in another system would be provided by the central government. When strong central government did come to England (under the Tudors, from 1485 on), the day of the feudal castle was finally over. As can be imagined, the system was wide open to abuse. Many of the great barons behaved, at times, like independent princes and carried on petty warfare against each other, extending their land and power as they saw fit. Weak kings, such as Henry III (1216–72), had endless trouble with them. Strong kings, like his son, Edward I (1272–1307), kept them firmly under control and at such times the system worked as well as any such system could be expected to work.

In so far as the king himself was a baron he too had castles, from which his estates were controlled in the same way as any other medieval landowner. The royal castles, between 50 and 100 in number, depending on the period, were less numerous than the baronial castles as a group, but far more numerous than those held by any one baron. From them, through the constable in charge, who was often also the sherriff of the county, the king was able to exercise some sort of general control of the country as a whole, although still falling a long way short of complete central authority.

The castles of the greatest barons differed little, if at all, from those of the king, either in size, magnificence, or type. Nor were the barons limited to a single stronghold. If their domains were scattered, as they often were, they could have a stronghold in each area where they held land. Between them, royal and baronial castles (great and small) are represented by several

Previous page:
Carisbrooke Castle (Isle of Wight) showing the shell-keep which was the Norman nucleus of the original stronghold.

hundred surviving ruins, most of which are accessible, in one way or another, to the general public. Many hundreds of others have been destroyed, leaving little or no trace on the present-day landscape. Those that remain, however, are more than enough to illustrate fully the history of the castle in the medieval period, particularly in the 'later' medieval period as defined earlier.

Although the most enduring marks of the Norman occupation are the great rectangular stone keeps, the Normans brought with them a range of fortification methods which they used as local needs dictated. In a still

A detail from the Bayeux tapestry showing the structure of the motte at Hastings.

hostile, newly conquered land one of their most urgent requirements was the speedy construction of a network of castles through which strict control could be exercised by the new Norman overlords. To this end they made great use of timber-built structures, which could be erected in a matter of months, as well as the more durable stone-built castles, the construction of which might be spread over several years. In the decades immediately following the Conquest, however, stone-built castles must have been heavily out-numbered by the timber-built types, and the balance shifted only gradually in favour of stone.

The arrangement of timber castles is generally described as of the 'motte-and-bailey' type, although the same arrangement can be used also for stone castles. The motte is a flat-topped conical mound, with a surrounding ditch, except where a steep natural slope made one unnecessary. Attached to it were one or more baileys or lower enclosures, surrounded by their own ditches which were linked to the ditch around the motte. The earth from the ditch was thrown inwards to form a bank or rampart around the bailey. These are the earthwork parts of the motte-and-bailey castle and it is the earthwork parts which have survived and indicate for us the numbers (c. 2,500), and distribution, of this type of construction. No timber work has survived and we depend on medieval illustration (notably the Bayeux tapestry), and on a few excavated sites, for our knowledge of medieval timber castles.

The timber work on the flat summit of the motte consisted of two main parts. Around the edge was a timber fence or palisade, perhaps 10 or 12 feet high, with a rampart walk along the inside and, in the larger examples, perhaps supplemented by wooden towers or turrets. Within this circular timber curtain wall (from c. 30–100 ft in diameter) was the central feature of the castle, a wooden tower, the timber equivalent of the rectangular stone keeps. Not a great deal is known from excavation about the structures on mottes, but the wooden tower at Abinger (Surrey) was c. 16 x 12 ft in ground area and this must be one of the smaller ones. There must have been larger towers, about 20–30 ft square, and possibly even larger. There is little evidence as to height but based on the pattern of stone towers they were probably of three storeys. In a country such as England a tower would need a sloping roof to shed the rain and the whole structure would need to be maintained by regular painting.

The defences of the bailey consisted of an earth bank surmounted by a timber fence or palisade, possibly in some cases strengthened by wooden towers or turrets. Communication between the bailey and the motte was by means of a drawbridge, and between the bailey and the exterior by the same means. Buildings within the bailey would have included a barn, stables, accommodation for the lord's followers, and possibly a chapel. They might also include the lord's house or hall in which he would live in peaceful periods, reserving the wooden tower on the motte as a refuge in times of unrest. The 2,500–3,000 timber motte-and-bailey castles mentioned earlier were probably not all in use together. Many of them were probably short-term structures. Nevertheless, at any one time there must have been many hundreds of timber motte-and-bailey castles in use, making them by far the commonest type of early medieval fortification, even if their present-day earthwork remains are relatively insignificant as compared with the remains of the less numerous but more striking stone castles.

The stone equivalent of the timber castle on a motte is the so-called shell-keep which likewise surmounts a mound. Shell-keeps are, in fact, the stone counterparts of the palisade around the top of the motte. The arrangements did not include a stone replacement of the timber tower, possibly for structural reasons, a massive stone tower probably being considered dangerously heavy on top of an artificial mound. Instead, accommodation was provided in one- or two-storey buildings against the inner face of the stone curtain, leaving an open courtyard in the centre. The bailey accompanying the shell-keep was also now defended by a stone curtain wall.

There is no doubt that the most impressive, durable, and formidable Norman strongholds are the great rectangular stone towers or keeps which formed the centrepiece of so many castles built, or rebuilt, in the twelfth century. Because of their sheer size and weight stone keeps were not normally sited on mottes unless these were largely or entirely natural and could therefore withstand the tremendous thrust of such massive structures. The largest were 100 ft or more square in ground area and up to 120 ft high, with massive walls, 12–20 ft thick, and often stood on a colossal, solid stone plinth to make undermining by an attacker more difficult. The entrance was

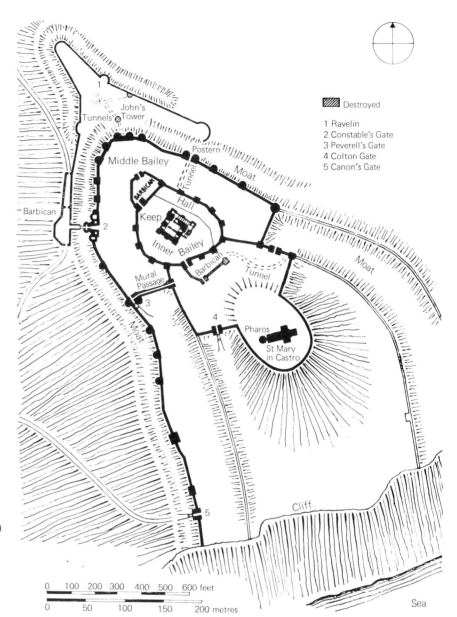

Destroyed

1 Ravelin
2 Constable's Gate
3 Peverell's Gate
4 Colton Gate
5 Canon's Gate

Plan of Dover Castle (Kent) begun under Henry II around 1170. Henry's work consisted of the keep, the Inner Bailey, and a section of the outer curtain wall to the north-east.

usually at first-floor level via a flight of stone steps, often protected by a building against the keep known as a forebuilding. Internally there were three or four storeys and on the upper levels additional rooms were contrived in the thickness of the massive walls. The first floor (entrance level), probably housed the servants and followers, with the main living room, the hall, on the second floor. There might also be a private family room on this floor, unless there was a fourth storey where this could be housed. In most cases the keep also contained a chapel and a number of smaller, personal rooms for members of the family and the more important retainers. Associated with the keep was a stone-walled bailey, the same sort of arrangement as in a timber-built castle. In some cases the keep stood entirely within the bailey, in others it straddled the wall, half in and half out,

The keep at Dover, built about a century after the Conquest, and one of the last rectangular examples to be built, still dominates the remaining defences built by Henry II, John, and Henry III.

so that if the bailey were captured by an enemy and the keep looked as if it might fall also, the defenders could still make their escape beyond the castle walls.

There are many surviving examples of stone keeps, some large, of the dimensions given earlier, some of more modest size, perhaps 40 or 50 ft square in ground area. Two outstandingly preserved examples of large keeps are the Tower of London and Dover Castle. Although the majority of stone keeps were built in the twelfth century, the Tower of London was started very soon after the Conquest as a fortress, palace, and seat of government for the new king. Its subsequent history forms part of the story of the later medieval castle (below pp. 115–17). Dover, on the other hand, was not built until about a century later and was one of the last such structures to be built. Between them, the Tower and Dover bracket the main building period of the rectangular stone type which lasted for about a century from about 1080 to 1180. This was not, however, the end of the keep. Rectangular keeps were replaced briefly by polygonal and then circular ones which prolonged the story for another seventy or eighty years.

The final phases of rectangular keeps fall within the reign of Henry II (1154–89), first of the Plantagenet kings, who came to the throne after nearly twenty years of unrest which followed the death of his grandfather Henry I (1100–35). The thirty-five years of his reign occupy the end of the century or so of stone-castle building characterised pre-eminently by the great rectangular keep. But as the period of the rectangular keep was coming to an end, new trends in military architecture were already apparent. Appropriately, Henry's greatest work, and one of the greatest castles in England, Dover, provides a link between the earlier and the later medieval castles. Its keep, one of the finest and best-preserved of all the rectangular examples, and one of the last of its kind to be built, stands within a range of outer defences, built at the same time, which display clearly many of the features characteristic of the later medieval castle. To a lesser degree the same characteristics appear in one or two other sites of the same date as Dover and this group of castles (Dover, Windsor, Carisbrooke, Framlingham) forms an appropriate starting point in the survey of the new trends towards the later medieval castle.

Dover Castle as it exists today is substantially the work of Henry II, his son John (1199–1216), and his grandson Henry III (1216–72). Henry II's work consisted of the great square keep, the curtain wall of the inner bailey surrounding it, and a section of outer curtain wall to the north-east. The centre piece was, of course, the keep, one of the finest ever built in Britain and one of the last of its kind to be undertaken. It stands at the end of a long tradition of such structures which, more than any other feature, characterise the early medieval castle. The Dover keep is virtually a cube in shape, 98 ft x 96 ft in plan, and 95 ft high. The walls are 17 to 21 ft thick and this allowed for a large number of mural chambers, some twenty in all, in addition to the four main rooms on the first and second floors, each about 50 x 20 ft in area. Dover is unusually complete and well-preserved and ends the century-old tradition of the rectangular keep on a high note.

If Henry's keep at Dover marked the end of one castle-building tradition, then his other works there marked the beginning of another in which, very soon, the keep had no place—at least not in its rectangular form. The Dover keep stood within an oval bailey (c. 350 x 300 ft), surrounded by a curtain wall with entrances to north and south. Thus far there is nothing new in the arrangement. Keeps had always stood within a bailey surrounded by a stone wall, usually quite plain. At Dover, however, the curtain wall of the inner bailey was, from the beginning, strengthened by a series of regularly-placed rectangular towers, ten in number, apart from those at the entrances (below). Curtain wall towers were not new, although in earlier castles they tended, if they existed at all, to be few in number and rather haphazard in arrangement. The curtain wall of the inner bailey at Dover, however, is probably the earliest example of a system of regularly-spaced wall towers, planned as such from the beginning; it stands at the head of a long tradition of regular curtain wall towers which are one of the characteristic features of later medieval castles. In its Dover form (with rectangular towers), it was not to continue for long: like the keep itself, the rectangular shape was about to be superseded. Nevertheless, in their regularity, if not in their shape, the Dover curtain wall towers are a strong indication of the new trends in castle building at the end of the twelfth century.

There were, in fact, fourteen towers in all on the Dover inner curtain wall, ten of which have been mentioned already. The remaining four were grouped in two pairs, one each at the north and south entrances, forming two twin-towered gates, the King's Gate to the north and the Palace Gate to the south. Again this is probably one of the earliest uses of pairs of flanking towers which was to become a regular and, in many cases, a dominant feature in later castles; in the more developed form of the gatehouse it took over many of the functions of the keep as the strongest part of the castle. The rectangular form was not to survive for long, but the principle of twin flanking towers took firm root as one of the characteristic features of the later medieval castle.

In addition to the protection provided by its two towers, each of the entrances had in front of it an outer defence or barbican. A barbican is a small, curtain-walled enclosure built in front of a main entrance, so that an enemy breaking through the outer, barbican entrance would find himself in a very confined space, under attack from the rampart walks on all sides, with the main entrance still intact. Barbican or double entrances became a regular part of late medieval castle planning and were sometimes of great complexity. However, there is no doubt that their beginnings in Britain are to be found in the fairly simple, straightforward examples built by Henry II at the north and south entrances of his inner bailey at Dover. The south barbican was destroyed in the late eighteenth/early nineteenth century, but the northern one is intact.

So much for Henry's work on the inner bailey and the new fortification techniques it exemplifies (regular wall towers, twin-towered entrances, and barbicans). As completed by his grandson, Henry III, Dover Castle had an outer curtain wall as well. But this outer curtain wall was, in fact, begun by Henry II, and the north-eastern sector, from near the Fitzwilliam Gate to the ruined Penchester Tower, a distance of some 500 ft, was his work, built at the same time as the keep and the inner bailey wall. This stretch of outer curtain runs parallel to and about 130 ft in front of the north-eastern section of the inner curtain wall. Since it is highly unlikely that such a length of curtain wall would have been built in isolation it is reasonable to assume that Henry intended it to surround the inner bailey completely. Had it been finished, the result would, in fact, have been a concentric castle, an outstanding type of late medieval castle, built nearly a century ahead of its appearance elsewhere. Henry's (presumed) intention had not been realised at the time of his death in 1189. Little or nothing was done under Richard I, and it was left to his brother, John, to complete the concentric plan. One noticeable difference is that John's wall towers are D-shaped, in contrast to his father's rectangular towers, and this is consistent with the general change in style taking place around the turn of the century.

Why did Dover display so many new ideas in fortification, particularly when it was also an outstanding restatement of the long-standing tradition of the rectangular keep? The answer must be that it was a royal castle, and an important one. As such it would call for the best military engineers available and the most up-to-date ideas on fortification. The man in charge of the works under Henry II, and responsible, therefore, for the great innovations which Dover Castle displays, was Maurice the Engineer. No doubt the keep was still regarded at this time as indispensable, at least by the king and possibly even by Maurice himself. But he, as a professional military engineer, would also have been aware of whatever was new in fortification techniques, and would certainly have wanted to incorporate them in such a prestigious undertaking as the royal castle of Dover. Maurice's commission at Dover was opportune: the time was ripe to try out new ideas, and the undertaking was large enough to give them full scope. The eventual result, dating from the time of Henry III, but on lines firmly laid down by Henry II, was Dover Castle as we see it today.

In addition to his work at Dover, Henry II also carried out very considerable building work at Windsor Castle (Berks.), and although many changes and additions have been made since his day, he established the shape of the castle as it exists today, a large motte or mound, surmounted by a shell-keep, with two large triangular baileys, one to the east and one to the west.

The earliest mention of a castle at Windsor was in 1067, only a year after the Conquest, when land was exchanged in order to obtain the present site, including the hillock which, suitably scarped, now forms the motte. There was at that time a single bailey, to the east of the motte. The fortification may at first have had a timber superstructure, but before Henry II's time the motte had been crowned with a stone shell-keep or curtain wall, more or less circular in plan and some 120 ft in overall diameter. In spite of this, Henry built an entirely new shell-keep inside the existing one, and the earlier structure now forms the terrace which surrounds the present tower. Only the lower half of the latter, below the clearly defined horizontal moulding, is Henry's work; the upper half was added early in the nineteenth century when Windsor Castle was extensively remodelled by Sir Jeffry Wyatville.

However, it was not Henry's work on the motte which was significant for later medieval castle building but the changes he made in the baileys, both the existing east bailey (Upper Ward), and the new west bailey (Lower Ward) which he added. Whatever the defences of the east bailey had been before, Henry built a new stone curtain wall around it, and did the same around the new west bailey which he created on the opposite side of the motte. The most notable feature of both of these curtain walls was that, like Dover, they were equipped with a series of regularly-spaced rectangular towers, again looking ahead to what was to become standard late medieval practice. The treatment of the angles in the east bailey is interesting and shows an awareness of the particular problem they create. The south-east angle has been obliterated by later, post-medieval work, but it presumably followed the pattern of the one on the north-east. Here, instead of the single-angle tower as at Dover and as in most late medieval castles (although in circular form), there are two adjacent towers, one at the end of each wall, forming a re-entrant angle instead of the usual salient angle. Each tower guarded the other and there was no unsupervised salient angle.

Carisbrooke Castle (Isle of Wight) also displays special treatment of the angles, virtually to the exclusion of other parts of the circuit. Like Windsor, Carisbrooke has a shell-keep surmounting a motte, and two baileys, east and west. The west bailey is more or less rectangular since it follows the lines of an earlier Roman fort of the Saxon Shore. Its medieval defences consisted of a stone curtain wall, originally with rectangular towers at three of the angles,

Windsor Castle is dominated by the great shell-keep standing on the motte. The lower half of the keep is the work of Henry II (1154–89), but the upper half was added early in the nineteenth century.

the fourth angle being occupied by the motte. The pattern of angle towers linked by straight curtain walls which they command by means of their projection is a typical late medieval one. At Carisbrooke, however, the arrangement falls short of this. The two southern angles of the curtain wall are bevelled and the towers project from the bevelled sections. The result is that their view along the adjacent sections of curtain wall is very limited. None the less they are angle towers, deliberately sited at the corners, and to this extent they anticipate the regular angle towers of later castles, which were likewise not infrequently the only towers on the curtain wall. In many

ways the most interesting of this group of four castles is Framlingham in Suffolk. Dover has a rectangular keep, and Windsor and Carisbrooke shell-keeps, putting all three firmly within the early castle tradition. Framlingham, however, simply has a great curtain wall and towers. The existing structure dates from about 1200, thus only a little after Henry's work at Dover and Windsor—but it appears to be a rebuilding of an earlier timber-built castle, following the same lines. The significant point is that even as originally built, probably about 1100, it had no keep. It was one of a small group of castles defended by curtain walls, with or without towers, but with only domestic buildings, principally a hall, within. It does indicate that even within the early period of castle building it was possible to conceive of a keepless castle, and to that extent Framlingham, and a few strongholds like it, anticipate the later medieval castles in which keeps have no place.

The original Framlingham (the timber and earthwork castle) was the work of Roger Bigod who received the manor from Henry I. Roger's son, Hugh Bigod, who was created the first Earl of Norfolk, rebelled against Henry II and the king had the castle dismantled in 1175. The existing structure was the work of the second earl, around the year 1200. It is oval in plan (c. 300 x 200 ft), somewhat smaller than the Inner Bailey at Dover (c. 360 x 300 ft), but following the same general plan. The curtain wall is 44 ft high and 8 ft thick. Regularly-spaced around the circuit are thirteen towers which rise another 15 ft or so above the curtain. Apart from the tower at the south-west angle (the corner of which was bevelled), the towers are rectangular and open-backed. One of them housed the only staircase by which the rampart walk could be reached, and another formed the entrance. The hall associated with the stone castle stood against the north curtain wall on the site still occupied by the later almshouse, built about 1640. Externally there were extensive earthworks forming several baileys, surrounded and separated by wet ditches formed by damming a stream.

Between them Dover, Windsor, Framlingham, and Carisbrooke provide a clear indication of the direction in which medieval castle building was heading in the years around 1180–1200. At Framlingham, the original castle of 1100 was designed without a keep, and this principle was adhered to in the reconstruction of 1200. The emphasis was on a strong curtain wall, strengthened by regular towers, and this is evident also at Windsor and Dover, in spite of their keeps. Dover looks even further ahead than the others. Its twin-towered gatehouses, its barbicans and its (intended and ultimately completed) concentric plan mark it out as something unique, ahead of its time, and a worthy link between the old and the new styles of medieval castle.

Dover was one of the last great rectangular keeps to be built, but the story of the keep as a feature of medieval castles does not end there. In a new form it had a further lease of life during much of the following century, albeit alongside castles in which the keep had no place. Although the rectangular type looked immensely strong it had a serious design defect which made a new shape both desirable and necessary. Its salient angles could be attacked from two sides with a view to undermining, and if one corner of the building could be made to collapse then further resistance became extremely difficult, if not impossible. The angles also created blind spots for a sentry on the rampart walk above.

The answer, in the late twelfth and first half of the thirteenth century, was a keep with a circular ground plan. With such a shape there are no salient angles vulnerable to undermining. Any attempt to breach the foundations has to be made directly from the front, with very little chance of concealment. The circular plan also made the task of the sentry much easier. Although his view was still to some extent restricted by the curvature of the tower there was no absolute blind spot such as that formed by the right-angled corners of a square tower. In addition to circular keeps there were also polygonal ones which were another answer to the shortcomings of the rectangular plan. In principle, however, they were virtually the same as circular keeps and they were never very numerous.

Of the polygonal sites the two with the smallest number of faces are Chilham (Kent) and Odiham (Hants) which are octagonal in plan. Chilham (built between 1170 and 1180) is 48 ft across (measured between opposite angles), with walls 10 ft thick. There is a rectangular stair-turret against the north-east side, masking two of the angles, and a triangular annexe next to this, masking a third angle, so that only five angles are exposed and these are much shallower (135 degrees) than the 90-degree angles of a rectangular keep. Odiham was somewhat larger than Chilham, some 60 ft across, with buttresses at each of the eight angles and walls 10 ft thick. It was a royal castle, built for King John, between 1207 and 1212, at a cost of over £1,000. It was of three storeys, with entry at first-floor level although no trace of a stairway or forebuilding now remains. It stood within a trapeze-shaped bailey in a bend of the River Whitewater. Athlone (Co. Westmeath, Ireland) was ten-sided although only the base courses now remain. It was some 70 ft across with plain, unbuttressed angles and walls about 9 ft thick. It was built in 1210, apparently not very efficiently, for it collapsed the following year and was rebuilt in 1215. A keep at Tickhill (Yorks.), revealed only by excavation, was eleven-sided, with buttresses at the angles as at Odiham. It was some 56 ft across with walls 10 ft thick. Expenditure on the castle recorded in 1178–80 must refer to the building of the keep at that time. The keep stood on a motte, with an attached bailey, much of the stone curtain wall of which survives.

Orford (Suffolk), built around 1170, is the earliest of the polygonal sites, and the most unusual. It has, in theory at least, twenty faces, so that there are only the shallowest of angles, and internally it is entirely circular. Moreover, much of the exterior is masked by three great rectangular towers which rise above the top of the keep and are the dominant aspect of the external elevation. Only twelve of the twenty wall faces are thus visible and the lower halves of three of these are further masked by a forebuilding beside one of the towers. The keep originally stood within a stone-walled bailey with square towers, but little or nothing now remains of these outer works.

The angular shape of the rectangular keep had been echoed in the towers on the curtain wall. Likewise, when the keep assumed the circular form, so did the wall towers, for the same influences operated on both, even in those castles without keeps. There were also polygonal wall towers, but just as polygonal keeps were something of a rarity, so also were wall towers of the same shape. The outstanding use of polygonal towers is at Caernarvon Castle (below, p. 96), but as will emerge later this was a rather special site with very particular reasons for this form of tower. At Dover the additions made by King John, only a decade or so after Henry's rectangular work, included wall towers on the outer curtain wall which were D-shaped in plan, so that they presented a semi-circular face towards the exterior of the castle. Wall towers did not, in fact, need to be completely circular. Provided the portion projecting beyond the walls provided no salient angles the shape overall did not matter and the inner portion could be rectangular (which was more convenient), and wall towers were quite often D-shaped in plan rather than truly circular.

Circular keeps were never as numerous as the rectangular type, partly because they were built during a shorter period, about half a century, and partly because they were in competition for popularity with other types of castle without keeps, so that they represent only part of the total output of castle building. Castles with the circular keeps form a transitional group between the earlier castles, dominated by the rectangular type, and the later castles in which the keep has been dispensed with. But the difference between the early castles and the transitional ones did not reside simply in the shape of the keep. Many of the castles with circular keeps built in the first half of the thirteenth century also display, in more developed form, the new ideas on fortification noted earlier at Dover and its associated sites. Conisbrough (Yorks.) provides an excellent starting point, possibly as early as 1180, when Henry II's square keep at Dover was still under construction. Conisbrough consists of a great circular keep, which survives very nearly to its full height, standing in an oval bailey surrounded by a curtain wall. It was almost certainly the work of Hamelin Plantagenet who held it from 1163 to 1202. The keep, which is the earlier part, was probably built about 1180 and the curtain wall about ten years later. The keep, about 55 ft in diameter and still standing over 75 ft high, had four storeys above a stone-vaulted basement, although much of the top storey is now missing. The most striking features of Conisbrough are the six great buttresses which rise to the full height of the tower, almost masking its basically circular shape. These, added to the thickness of the walls (15 ft), and the height of the solid plinth (20 ft) made Conisbrough an immensely strong structure, and this is probably why the keep is so well-preserved today. Entry was at first-floor level and access to the upper floors was by means of a staircase rising concentrically with the keep in the thickness of the walls, rather than by the usual spiral staircase.

The bailey at Conisbrough is roughly oval in plan (c. 250 x 160 ft) and is defended by a curtain wall, approximately 8 ft thick, strengthened by a series of semi-circular towers. These are, in fact, solid and must have acted as substantial buttresses to the curtain wall. However, they must have had a more positive function as well. Even if they rose no higher than the curtain wall, by their projection they would still have allowed defenders to command the stretches of wall between. Raised above curtain-wall level they would have added extra range to projectiles fired from their summits. Although Conisbrough is one of the earliest of the new-style circular keeps, it still is, basically, an older type of castle, part of the long tradition of keep-and-bailey castles. The features which do look forward to the following century are the regularly spaced semi-circular curtain-wall towers, even if they are still solid and buttress-like.

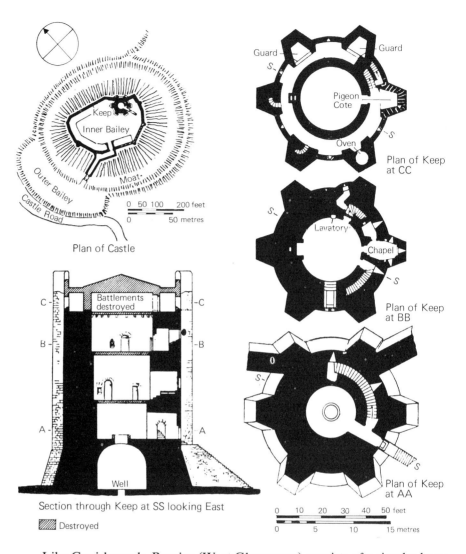

Plan of Keep at CC

Plan of Keep at BB

Plan of Keep at AA

Section through Keep at SS looking East

▨ Destroyed

Plan of Castle

Plan of Conisbrough (Yorks.), built *c.* 1190, a keep and bailey castle with solid, semi-circular towers, on the bailey wall.

Opposite:
The Conisbrough keep is dominated by the six great buttresses which rise to the full height of the tower.

Overleaf:
Pembroke Castle, built around 1180, stands on a promontory above the Pembroke River.

Like Conisbrough, Penrice (West Glamorgan) consists of a circular keep abutting the curtain wall of an irregular triangular bailey, although it is somewhat larger (*c.* 300 x 200 ft) and more elaborate than the Yorkshire site. However, its chief point of interest is that it too has solid round towers on the curtain wall. A date of 1190 has been suggested for the building of the castle and this would correspond very well with the date put forward (above) for Conisbrough. At Penrice the circular keep, the domestic buildings, and the gatehouse form a single block on the north-west side of the bailey. The gatehouse has two D-shaped towers attached to the front of a single rectangular tower which must have formed the original entrance. The D-shaped towers were probably added in the first decade or two of the following century.

It is instructive to compare Skenfrith (Gwent) with both Conisbrough and Penrice. Although built within a decade or two of them it displays very noticeable differences, both in its plan and its use of curtain-wall towers. The circular keep stands near the centre of the bailey and does not abut the curtain wall as at Conisburgh, Penrice, and many other sites. The bailey is

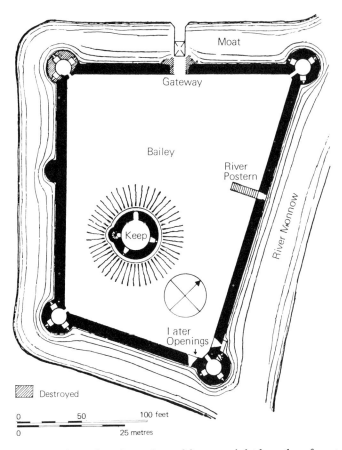

Skenfrith Castle (Gwent), built *c.* 1200, is an early example of rectilinear planning, with straight curtain walls linking four boldly projecting angle towers.

trapeze-shaped and consists of four straight lengths of curtain wall linked at the angles by four towers. These are circular, hollow, and business-like, each with three arrow loops below and two above. It is, however, their projection which marks them as part of the new thinking on fortification. Three-quarters of their circumference stands beyond the curtain giving the defenders great command over the adjacent stretches of wall. A fifth half-round tower on the west side was a later addition. There was a gatehouse, now destroyed, on the north side; it appears to have had twin towers, but details are lacking. The whole site was surrounded by a wet moat on three sides and the River Monnow on the fourth.

At Longtown Castle (Hereford and Worcs.) the circular keep stands on a high motte with two baileys in line to the south. The keep is of two storeys, with only two main rooms, the lower about 25 ft in diameter, the upper about 30 ft. Access was via a flight of steps from the Inner Bailey up the side of the motte and then up the side of the solid stone plinth (*c.* 10 ft high) on which the keep stood. The remains of the curtain walls and entrances are slight, but the Inner Bailey gateway consists of two small solid D-shaped towers projecting entirely beyond the wall which separated Inner and Outer Baileys.

Pembroke Castle (Dyfed), built about the same time as Conisbrough, has an equally impressive keep. Unlike Conisbrough, however, it is a simple, uncluttered cylindrical shape, about 53 ft in diameter and 80 ft high to the top of the dome which crowned the structure. It stood within, but very close to, the curtain wall of a triangular bailey in a promontory position, with slopes down to the river on the north-eastern and western sides. Some time during the first half of the following century (1200–50), a large outer bailey was added defended by a curtain wall in the same style as Skenfrith. There are boldly projecting circular angle towers and circular intermediate towers linking straight lengths of curtain wall. There is also a gatehouse consisting of two rectangular towers, originally with a barbican in front. The entrance passage between the two towers had a formidable array of defences including two portcullises and two double-leaved gates. Further protection was provided by two arrow loops on each side, firing into the space between the inner and outer portcullises. The two structural phases at Pembroke span most of the period under review. The first phase exemplifies the old keep-and-bailey tradition. The second is very much a structure of the thirteenth century, looking ahead to those castles which would be built from the beginning in the new style.

At Helmsley Castle (N. Yorks.) the keep is neither round nor square but D-shaped, and appears to be the result of a partial rebuilding. The keep straddles the north curtain wall and is rectangular towards the interior. Beyond the wall, however, it is semi-circular, thus providing a D-shaped plan. Presumably the keep was originally rectangular. For whatever reason, the outer portion was rebuilt, acknowledging the then current style of circular keeps. Features presumably associated with the square keep included a square, single-tower gatehouse at the north-east angle, and a square tower on the south curtain wall. The (presumably) later features, associated with the rebuilding of the keep, were all on a circular plan, including the towers at three angles which project for about three-quarters of their circumference. There is also a gatehouse on the west curtain wall with a D-shaped tower on either side. A date within the first two or three decades of the thirteenth century seems appropriate for such a range of features.

At Barnard Castle (Co. Durham), the circular keep appears to have been added (c. 1200) to earlier curtain walls of twelfth-century (possibly early twelfth-century) date with square towers and gatehouses. The castle consists of four baileys, the smallest of which contains the keep and the domestic buildings which form a single block, with access to the keep from the hall range at first-floor level. The keep, nearly 40 ft in diameter and originally about 60 ft high, was of three storeys, with communication via mural rather than spiral staircases. If the keep was an addition then it looks as if the original castle was of the curtain-wall type, i.e., a keepless castle of the early period.

Chartley Castle (Staffs.) displays regular planning in its bailey. The castle was built about 1220, possibly as a replacement for an earlier timber castle. The fact that the circular stone keep stands on a motte suggests that it could well have had an earlier (presumably timber) phase. The bailey is a regular rectangle with projecting circular corner towers and at least one interval tower, half-round in plan, mid-way along one of the curtain walls. The remains are mostly foundations, but the overall plan is clear.

The most notable feature of Dynevor Castle (Dyfed) is the fine range of fifteenth-century buildings on the north front, probably added in the time of Henry VII (1485–1509). However, the earliest portion of the castle is the

At Dirleton (Lothian), built between 1225 and 1250, the circular keep forms part of a cluster of towers at the south-west corner of the site, flanking the main entrance.

circular keep (*c.* 45 ft in diameter) in the north-east corner of the bailey, built about 1200. The bailey is pentagonal and, because of the rocky nature of the situation, is surrounded by a plain curtain wall with only one tower, at the north-west angle, which originally projected for three-quarters of its circumference, although this has been reduced by the later additions mentioned above. The curtain wall and tower have been attributed to the time of Edward I, but if boldly projecting corner towers could be built at Skenfrith around 1200 then there seems no reason why they could not have been built here, i.e., at the same time as the circular keep.

Dirleton Castle (Lothian), built about 1225–50, stands on a rocky promontory with steep falls on the north and west. On these sides only a plain curtain wall was called for. Approach was a little easier from the south and east, and there were boldly projecting angle towers, about 35 ft in diameter, on these sides. This part of the castle is heavily overlaid with later buildings, but the lower portions of the angle towers remain. The entrance was in the south curtain wall and did not form part of any gatehouse. However, the south-east angle tower was only 20 ft away in one direction and the keep and its accompanying features even less in the other, so that they in effect provided the same service as a gatehouse. The circular keep (*c*. 40 ft in diameter) forms part of a group of towers in the south-west corner of the site. As well as the keep there is another, smaller circular tower, and a small rectangular tower, forming a sort of composite keep. It is noticeable that the Dirleton keep occupies a forward position in the castle's defences. It stands out before everything else, advancing to meet any attack, in a position, in relation to the other defences, more akin to an Edwardian gatehouse than to a passively defensive keep.

Bothwell Castle (Strathclyde), built around the middle of the century, has both a circular keep and a double-towered gatehouse. In both this and Kildrummy Castle (below), the same overall pattern is evident. The keep is withdrawn from the forward position which is occupied by a twin-towered gatehouse. Moreover, in both cases, the adjacent curtain walls retreat, leaving the gatehouse standing forward of the rest of the castle. As originally built the Bothwell keep was 65 ft in diameter and contained four storeys; the surviving, inner portion still rises to very nearly its original height which must have been in the region of 80 ft. About three-quarters of its circumference projected beyond the curtain wall of the bailey. The smaller inner segment was cut off from the bailey by means of a substantial ditch. Access was via a drawbridge between the northern end of this ditch and the north-west curtain wall. There was also an external ditch around the projecting portion of the keep. The pentagonal bailey consisted of five lengths of straight curtain wall with circular towers at three of the angles, the gatehouse at the fourth, and the keep at the fifth. There was also a square tower midway along the eastern curtain wall. At the northern end of the site the curtain walls converged and at the apex was the twin-towered gatehouse. The plan makes it clear that both towers were extended towards the interior and they were almost certainly linked at first-floor level and above, forming the massive keep-like structure which, in many another site, would have been the dominant structure in the castle. Bothwell perpetuates the keep-and-bailey concept, but it also acknowledges the new ideas of fortification which, already in other areas, had ousted the keep as a feature of castle building.

Kildrummy (Grampian) bears a very close resemblance to Bothwell. It is D-shaped in plan with the circular keep occupying one of the angles and the gatehouse a central position on the curving part of the curtain wall. The keep is about 50 ft in diameter and there is another circular tower, only slightly smaller (40 ft in diameter) at the opposite angle. Midway between each of these towers and the centrally placed gatehouse are two more D-shaped towers, round towards the exterior, square internally. This is a more regular, symmetrical version of Bothwell. The gatehouse was probably inserted in the existing Kildrummy Castle (built *c*. 1250) in 1300 or thereabouts when Edward I was campaigning in Scotland. There must, however, have been an original gatehouse, possibly on a smaller scale. Kildrummy tells the same story as Bothwell. Around the middle of the century the tradition of the keep, in circular form, was still strong, but so now was the gatehouse, which looked forward to some of the greatest achievements of medieval military architecture.

Nenagh Castle (Tipperary, Ireland) consisted originally of a keep straddling a pentagonal curtain wall (*c*. 8 ft thick), with four D-shaped wall towers, two of which formed an entrance but not yet a gatehouse. Half of the circular keep projected beyond the curtain wall; it was 55 ft in diameter and originally rose over 80 ft high. The castle was built early in the thirteenth century. In the second half of the century a rectangular back portion was added to the entrance, turning it into a true gatehouse. The site is in many ways an earlier, simpler version of Bothwell and Kildrummy.

Two sites, Pontefract Castle (W. Yorks.) and Clifford's Tower (York) represent refinements of the circular-keep idea. Not much of Pontefract is preserved, but the plan is fairly clear from surviving foundations. The keep is basically circular, with four half-round lobes attached to it giving it a

The surviving portion of Bothwell Castle (Strathclyde), built around 1250, with the keep in the background, acting as one of the angle towers.

quatrefoil plan. This is, in effect, the semi-circular wall-tower idea applied to a keep instead of a curtain wall. The keep was large, over 100 ft in diameter, measured across the widest part, and over 50 ft in diameter across the interior, which was basically circular. The lobes were largely solid, with only small recesses internally reflecting their external shape. Eventually there were three baileys at Pontefract, although probably only the oval inner bailey belongs to the first phase. This closely resembles the oval bailey at Conisbrough (above), particularly in the regularly-spaced half-round towers, and must be of about the same date, about 1190 or 1200. The keep is later

Kildrummy Castle (Grampian) is almost symmetrical in layout and illustrates the more regular planning of the thirteenth century. The gatehouse is a later insertion, probably added around 1300.

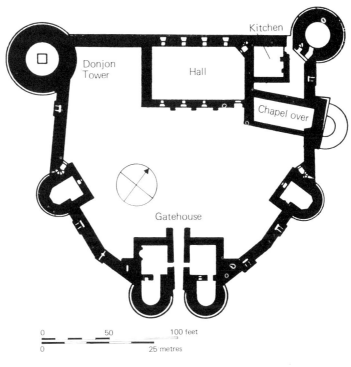

Donjon Tower

Hall

Kitchen

Chapel over

Gatehouse

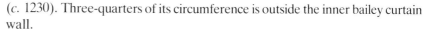

0   50   100 feet

0   25 metres

(*c.* 1230). Three-quarters of its circumference is outside the inner bailey curtain wall.

Clifford's Tower follows the general pattern of the Pontefract keep but on a less massive scale. The tower is smaller (*c.* 80 ft wide overall), the walls are thinner (9 ft), and it was only two storeys in height. Its internal space is also quatrefoil. The keep stands on top of a massive motte within the city of York. Clifford's Tower was built between 1245 and 1272. Like Pontefract, the quatrefoil plan represents the application of the circular wall-tower principle to a circular keep.

The result of applying the same principle to a rectangular keep can be seen in a small group of sites in Ireland which need to be considered here. They can be regarded in a sense as a compromise between the rectangular and circular plan. They consist of a rectangular tower in which the four angles are occupied by prominent circular towers, projecting for three-quarters of their circumference. The resultant shape is quite distinctive and probably the best-known example is the much later Nunney Castle (Somerset, built *c.* 1373), although Dudley Castle (Staffs. built *c.* 1320) shows the same tendencies in a less marked form (below, p. 183). In Ireland, there are remains of about half

The surviving portion of Clifford's Tower (York) consists of the large motte, surmounted by a stone keep which is quatrefoil in plan, built around the middle of the thirteenth century.

a dozen such towered keeps. Of these there are substantial remains at Carlow (Co. Carlow), Ferns (Co. Wexford), and Lea (Co. Leix). Carlow was probably built by William Marshall, Earl of Pembroke, early in the thirteenth century during the reign of King John. The nucleus of the structure, the rectangular tower, was 70 x 46 ft with walls 9 ft thick. The original height is not known for certain but from a print of about 1791 it would appear to have been in the region of 75 ft forming three storeys. At that time the structure was still largely intact but early in the nineteenth century the eastern half fell down and the remains have since been removed, leaving the north-west and south-west towers, the long west wall and about half each of the shorter north and south walls. The surviving towers are 25 ft in diameter, and presumably the other two were the same. They project for more than three-quarters of their circumference giving great command along the adjacent walls. Access was at first-floor level, with access to the upper and lower floors by means of straight staircases in the thickness of the long western wall, the same type of staircase as at Nunney, although there the entrance was at ground-floor level. All traces of associated buildings and of the surrounding curtain wall within which the Carlow tower-keep once stood have now gone.

The towered keep at Ferns (Co. Wexford) was built a little later than Carlow, probably around the middle of the century (c. 1250), and was a much larger affair, its main rectangular block measuring roughly 100 x 80 ft. Three of the four angle towers survive and these too were larger, about 30 ft in diameter. The interior space on all three storeys was approximately 80 x 60 ft and this must have been subdivided into smaller units by partition walls which have not survived. There is now no trace of the entrance which was presumably at first-floor level. The most striking feature of the surviving remains is the beautiful chapel on the first floor of the south-eastern tower. Ferns was quite clearly a large, imposing, and important towered keep, originally standing, like Carlow, within a curtain wall, with other associated buildings.

The towered keep at Lea (Co. Leix) is very similar to Carlow, although slightly larger, and appears to be about the same date as Ferns (c. 1250). It stands at the centre of an oval bailey, attached to which is a larger outer bailey or courtyard with a gatehouse. The towers of the keep, of which one is more or less complete, were 30 ft in diameter. The entrance doorway was in the same position as Carlow and the stairways were similarly arranged on either side.

The remaining Irish towered keeps can be dealt with quite briefly. There appears to have been a keep of this type at Terryglass (Co. Tipperary), although only the lower storey survives and it is not possible to say how high the building was originally. There are records of a possible towered keep at Wexford (Co. Wexford) and actual remains of another at Enniscorthy (Co. Wexford), although this appears to be a rebuilding (c. 1586) of an earlier structure, presumably also a towered keep, of the same general date as those considered already.

This completes a survey of castles built in the years 1180 to about 1250 which display 'new features' such as regularly spaced, round wall towers, angle towers, twin-towered gatehouses, and barbicans. In fact, these features, in square form, had already appeared at the end of what may be termed the rectangular-keep period (i.e. 1066–1190), as demonstrated at Carisbrooke, Windsor, Framlingham and, most particularly, Dover. They appeared at a time when the round keep was just beginning to take the place of the rectangular type, and it is thus in the company of round keeps that we encounter these examples of 'new features'. The solid, round towers of Conisbrough, Penrice, and Pontefract, all built around 1190, quickly give way to hollow, round, and D-shaped towers which, apart from their defensive function, also provide, on their different floor levels, an appreciable part of the castle's domestic accommodation. Rectilinear planning soon follows and with it the emphasis on corner towers which project to give command along the face of the two adjacent curtain walls. By the end of this transitional period (1180–1250), the double-towered entrance was well-established at Penrice (probably in addition to an original, single-towered square gatehouse), Pembroke, Helmsley, Bothwell, Kildrummy, and Nenagh. Such entrances were still only steps on the way to the great gatehouses of the second half of the century, and in every case the castles of which they formed a part still boasted a formidable and separate keep. In a very real sense the existence of the keep hindered the full development of the gatehouse. So long as the functions remained split between the two, the older type (the keep) would survive and the newer type (the gatehouse) would not fully develop. When the same functions were concentrated in one at the entrance, then the gatehouse came into its own as the centrepiece of the later medieval castle.

2
Castles Without Keeps

The castles with circular keeps described in the last chapter are only part of the story of castle development in the first half of the thirteenth century. Alongside them was a range of castles built without keeps, consisting of curtain walls, regular round or D-shaped towers and, in many cases, twin-towered gatehouses. The existence of castles without keeps was noted in the earliest period of castle building (Chapter 1), and of course, of the four castles quoted there, Framlingham was of the keepless type. In that sense it can be regarded as the forerunner of the castles to be considered here.

Beeston Castle (Cheshire) was built by Randulph de Blundeville, Earl of Chester, on his return from a Crusade in 1220. Randulph was also (from 1217) Earl of Lincoln, and his undertaking at Beeston was only part of a larger castle-building programme which included also Chartley Castle (Staffs), dealt with in Chapter 1 (p. 29), and also (probably) Bolingbroke Castle (Lincs. below p. 40). It is an interesting commentary on early thirteenth-century fortification that a single programme of castle building could embrace one site with a circular keep and two in which the keep had no place. Beeston is renowned in particular for its siting, at the head of a great, rocky promontory which on the north and west rises sheer from the Cheshire plain several hundred feet below. A great rock-cut ditch on the southern and eastern sides cuts off the inner bailey from the rest of the castle. The inner bailey is defended by a curtain wall, a double-towered gatehouse, and three wall towers. Because of the precipitous nature of the site the northern and western sides were defended by a plain curtain wall, following the contour of the promontory. In such a situation the provision of towers to provide flanking fire along the walls would have been superfluous. The entrance, midway along the south curtain wall, consists of two D-shaped towers, linked at first-floor level above the vaulted entrance passage: thus it was a true gatehouse and not simply an entrance between two towers. East and west of the gatehouse there are two more D-shaped towers and there is a third, rectangular tower on the short, eastern section of curtain wall. It is noticeable that there are no towers at the angles (which are all clearly defined), even though in three cases, at the south-west, south-east, and north-east, there are towers close-by. The answer may be that in such a compact site the angles are well covered from the immediately adjacent towers. In any case, the main weakness of salient angles, that of undermining, may not have been considered much of a problem in a castle founded on solid rock. The large outer bailey (c. 800 x 500 ft) stretches down the slope of the promontory to the east, south-east, and south. It was protected by a curtain wall with regularly-spaced, open-backed, D-shaped towers, although more than half of the total length (originally c. 2,200 ft) has now gone. About

750 ft of outer curtain wall on the east and south-east is preserved, at least in its lower part, including the lower courses of the outer gatehouse which enable its plan, but not much else, to be established.

In the absence of a keep, with its three, four and sometimes five storeys of available living space, where was accommodation provided at Beeston? The answer must be first of all in the gatehouse and secondly in the wall towers. Although in the form of two towers at ground level, the gatehouse was a single structure above, some 70 ft wide and 50 ft deep (from back to front), and was therefore bigger than most contemporary keeps, although it probably did not have the same number of floors. In addition to the gatehouse, however, there were also three separate wall towers, one of which, at least, was of keep-like proportions. All the towers were bigger than they needed to be for purely defensive purposes. Their external projection was necessary to cover the adjacent walls. Their internal projection must have been to enlarge them so that they could have a dual function, military and domestic. They must have provided accommodation on at least two floors and this, added to what the gatehouse could offer, must have provided more than adequate compensation for any shortage of living space occasioned by the lack of a keep.

Like Beeston, Cilgerran Castle (Dyfed) occupies a position which dictates much of its layout. It is situated on a high, rocky promontory in the angle formed by the River Teifi and the tributary Plysgog stream in the old county of Pembrokeshire. The castle is triangular in plan with steep natural slopes on the north-east and west and a wide ditch on the south. Within the main triangle a smaller triangle at the end of the promontory forms the Inner Ward and it is here that the principal remains are located. Although there are fragmentary remains of a twelfth-century castle, all the remaining structures are thirteenth-century or later. The main defences of the Inner Ward were the work of William Marshall, Earl of Pembroke, in the years following 1223. They consisted of two great drum-like towers which dominate the site, a third and smaller rectangular tower, forming a gatehouse, and three straight lengths of curtain wall. These features were linked to form an arc of defences facing south-west, south, and south-east. In both round towers the walls towards the exterior are noticeably thicker than elsewhere, up to 15 ft thick in the case of the larger, West Tower. This is 45 ft in overall diameter with internal rooms, on four floors, some 23 ft in diameter. As originally built it was entered only at first-floor level, like a keep, probably by means of a wooden stairway. Later, in the fourteenth century, a ground-floor door was inserted, together with a spiral staircase to give access to the rooms above. The West Tower occupied the central position in the defences, with the East Tower on one side, linked by 25 ft of curtain wall, and the Gatehouse Tower on the other, linked by another 20 ft.

The East Tower was built on the same lines but was somewhat smaller (40 ft in diameter externally, 22 ft internally, with walls up to 11 ft thick). Like the West Tower two-thirds of its circumference projects beyond the curtain wall. It too was of four storeys with access to the ground floor by means of a doorway directly from the courtyard. There was, however, no direct access from here to the upper floors which were reached via another door from the courtyard leading to a spiral staircase. In the curtain wall immediately below the tower to the west is a gate, originally protected by a portcullis, giving

Previous page:
The south-west angle tower of Carew Castle (Dyfed), built around 1270.

access to the rock-cut ditch in front of the Inner Ward defences of the castle.

These features (the three towers and the three lengths of curtain wall) provide the defences on the approach side of the promontory. The defences, mainly a curtain wall, on the two remaining sides, above the steep natural slopes, are of slightly later date, but still within the thirteenth century. A rectangular tower at the point of the promontory was added in the fourteenth century. The Outer Ward was protected by a 10-ft-thick curtain wall, the only surviving portion of which runs across the end of the inner ditch. In it there was a sally-port through which defenders, having emerged from the gate below the East Tower (above), could make their way round the curtain wall and take would-be attackers by surprise. The outermost defence of the castle was a ditch, some 60 ft wide, which ran right across the promontory, confining access to the causeway between its western end and the head of the natural slope.

Llanstephan Castle (Dyfed) standing high above the estuary of the Tywi in what used to be Carmarthen, is first mentioned for certain in 1146, but the greater part of the existing remains, although not all of one period, are the work of the de Camville family who held the castle from around 1200 until 1338 when the male line ended. The present stone-built castle was preceded by a timber-built ringwork and bailey castle, on the same lines as the later structure, and it was this earlier work which was the subject of the reference in 1146. The earliest part of the stone castle, the wall around the Upper Ward, replacing the timber structure, was built about 1200, thus probably being early in the de Camvilles' tenure of the castle. This was followed within a generation or so by a square gatehouse, the Inner Gate, between the Lower and Upper Wards. The major building, however, transforming the castle to its present shape, took place in the second half of the century and was the work of either William de Camville II or Geoffrey de Camville II, or both, since more than one structural phase was involved. The new work consisted of a curtain wall around the Lower Ward, a bastion (so-called), two D-shaped towers, and a gatehouse. Of these the gatehouse appears to be slightly later, but probably only by a matter of a couple of years.

The whole castle is roughly D-shaped in plan, with the straight side to the south. On this side there are very steep natural slopes and in acknowledgement of this there is only a plain curtain wall, without towers, in this sector. At the south-east angle there was the East Bastion which was simply a short section of a curtain wall slightly higher and thicker than the rest. From here, round the north-east, north, and north-west sides there was a series of straight sections of curtain wall interrupted by the two D-shaped towers and the gatehouse. Although the latter is of slightly later date it must have been preceded by an earlier entrance, probably in the form of a single tower. Without some feature such as this there would have been too long a gap between the two other towers positioned on the circumference at that time.

The gatehouse, the dominant feature of the site, is almost certainly copied from the east gatehouse at Caerphilly Castle (p. 63), which was under construction from around 1268 onwards, so that a date about 1275–80 seems likely for the Llanstephan gate. It consists of two D-shaped towers joined above the entrance passage to form a single structure. At the inner angles there were small circular turrets. Around 1500 the entrance passage was blocked up and the gatehouse became a tower-residence; the same sort of process took place at Dunstanburgh Castle (Northumberland, p. 147). A new entrance was contrived alongside the old, but this was a much simpler affair, indicating clearly that Llanstephen's role as a medieval stronghold was long since over.

Old Bolingbroke Castle (Lincs.) was the third of the trio of castles built by Randulph de Blundeville, and although different in siting from Beeston, followed its style rather than that of Chartley with its circular keep. The castle was built in the years 1220 to 1230, although it is chiefly famous as the birthplace of Henry Bolingbroke (hence the name), later King Henry IV (1399—1413). The site is hexagonal in plan with D- or U-shaped towers at five of the angles and twin towers forming an entrance. The walls, both of the curtain and the towers, are 13 ft thick. The towers are flat on the inside and are flush with the inner face of the curtain wall. There is no inward projection. The courtyard enclosed by the curtain wall is about 200 ft from east to west and about 175 ft from north to south. Externally there was a substantial moat approximately 100 ft wide.

This is the same formula as Beeston, basically curtain wall and towers (two of which form an entrance), enclosing what is, in fact, a courtyard in which can be placed the ordinary domestic buildings, such as the hall, the central feature of all medieval domestic accommodation, and the kitchens. There was, in fact, a hall built against the curtain wall at Old Bolingbroke, between the entrance and the east tower, and other domestic buildings against the curtain wall between the south and south-east towers. The formula thus exemplified by Beeston and Old Bolingbroke, and by other castles to be described, forms the basis of all later medieval castle building. The features involved develop in three main ways in those castles where greater strength is aimed at: first, an additional line of curtain wall and towers is thrown around the castle, forming a concentric arrangement;

At Old Bolingbroke Castle (Lincs.), built 1220–30, the defences consist of a curtain wall linking a series of towers and a double-towered gatehouse.

Opposite:
View across the moat at Framlingham Castle (Suffolk), built around 1200. The defences consist of a stone curtain wall and regularly spaced rectangular towers, but no keep.

Overleaf:
Aerial view of Windsor Castle showing the central shell-keep and the great east and west baileys.

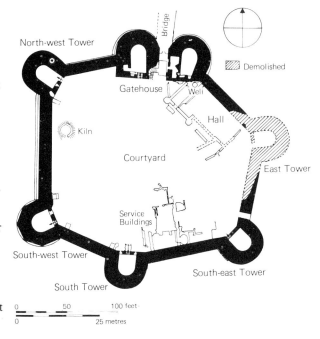

North-west Tower

Bridge

Demolished

Gatehouse
Well

Hall

Kiln

East Tower

Courtyard

Service Buildings

South-west Tower

South-east Tower

South Tower

0   50   100 feet
0   25 metres

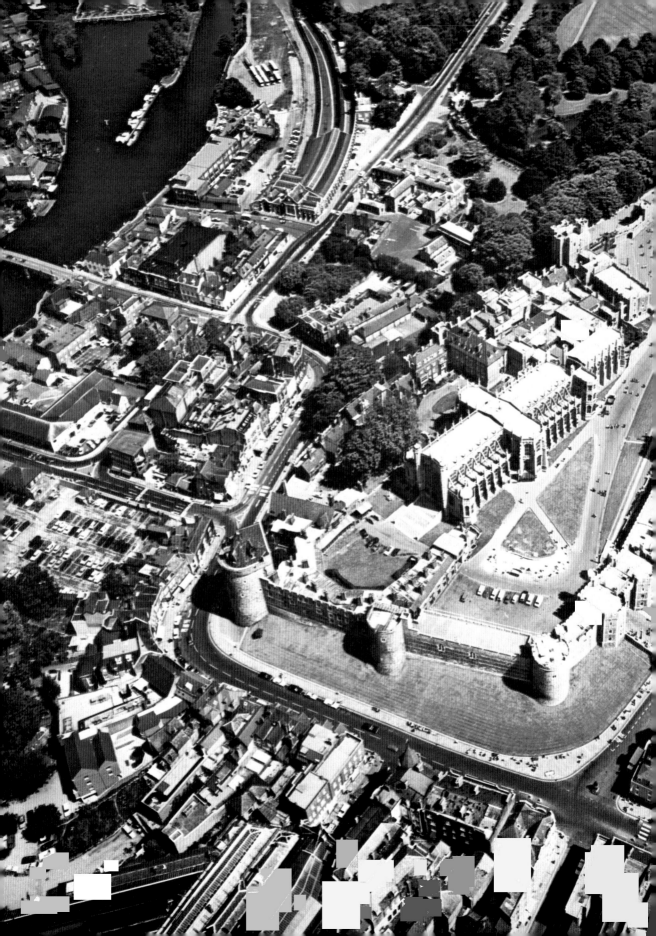

Opposite top:
General view of the remains
of Kildrummy Castle.

Opposite bottom:
View of Skenfrith (Gwent),
showing the circular keep
and the north curtain wall
with the remains of the
double-towered gatehouse.

Above:
The most prominent feature
at Llanstephen Castle
(Dyfed) is the double-
towered gatehouse added
during the major
reconstruction of the
fourteenth century.

secondly, an additional enclosure is placed alongside the main courtyard, forming an outer ward, defended in the same way as the rest of the castle, which had to be traversed to reach the main, inner ward or courtyard; and thirdly, the gatehouse is enlarged and made independent of the rest of the castle—a virtual return to the keep principle. In some cases two of these developments are incorporated in one castle.

Clifford Castle (Hereford and Worcester), built early in the thirteenth century, follows the same lines as Old Bolingbroke, although it is rather more compact in plan. The courtyard is only about 70 x 60 ft and the hall within, against the north curtain wall, is correspondingly small (36 x 17 ft). The defences consist of a polygonal curtain wall, three D-shaped wall towers and two similar towers forming a gatehouse on the eastern side. The whole castle stands on a low motte, surrounded by a ditch, and without the towers it would virtually be a shell-keep of an earlier period. Beyond the ditch are two baileys, one to the north-east and one to the south-west.

Castell Coch (meaning Red Castle) in South Glamorgan is unusual in that its present appearance, complete with conical roofs to its towers, is the result of Victorian rebuilding. Nevertheless, in spite of minor details, it appears to have captured externally, as far as one can judge, much of the appearance of the original thirteenth-century castle which once stood on the site. Internally, however, the castle is almost entirely Victorian, and although it can be enjoyed for its own sake, it has little or nothing to do with the original internal appearance of this or any other medieval castle. The rebuilding was the work of the third Marquis of Bute (John Patrick Crichton-Stuart, 1848-1900), and his architect William Burges. The same two men

The external elevation of Castell Coch probably gives a fairly accurate impression of what a small medieval castle would have looked like in its original state.

were also responsible for the even larger-scale rebuilding of Cardiff Castle which was in progress about the same time.

Although the external elevations are the work of Burges, and to that extent conjectural, they are based on genuine medieval foundations which preserve the basic plan of the original castle. When he surveyed and planned the ruins in 1872, Burges found portions of the towers still standing up to 25 ft high, so that there was very solid evidence of what the original layout had been. The plan appears to have been generally similar to Clifford Castle just described, although without the double-towered gatehouse. It consists of three round towers each about 40 ft in diameter and only about 30 ft apart in an L-shaped arrangement, linked by a curtain wall, which also surrounds an oval courtyard in the angle thus formed. The entrance on the east side is through a single square tower abutting the south-east angle tower, and the hall is on the south side of the courtyard between the latter and the south-west tower. The whole site is very compact and the courtyard measures only 60 x 45 ft, smaller again than Clifford Castle. In fact, Burges's survey in 1872 uncovered evidence of an earlier and simpler stage when the castle consisted simply of the south-west tower, the hall, and a curtain wall on the west, north, and east. The addition of the south-east and north-east towers and the gate tower appears to have taken place around 1260–70, so that presumably the simpler first phase belongs to the first half of the century.

In many ways the most striking features of Castell Coch are the conical roofs on the three round towers. These give the castle a very French appearance, mainly because such roofs are preserved on many French castles while there are no original examples in Britain. Since Burges was working from foundations alone there was absolutely no evidence as to how the towers were originally roofed and his choice of the conical form was purely speculative. However, some sort of effective roofing would have been required and the conical form is very suitable for a round tower. If such roofs were being used in France at this time then there is absolutely no reason why they should not have been in use here. Again, there is no proof, and this has been the main basis for objections to the restoration, but in the circumstances the conical form seems to be not only one of a number of reasonable suggestions but, in the writer's view, the most reasonable. Its appearance certainly fits very comfortably with the rest of the castle, as visitors will be able to judge for themselves.

Morgraig Castle (Mid Glamorgan), known from excavation, was on the same general lines as Old Bolingbroke and Clifford Castles. It was pentagonal in plan with four boldly projecting U-shaped towers at four of the angles and a rectangular tower at the fifth which was of keep-like proportions (70 x 50 ft). The projection of the U-shaped towers was remarkable, two of them extending far over 40 ft in front of the curtain wall, and the other two only marginally less. The square, keep-like tower also stood entirely beyond the wall, projecting up to 60 ft beyond its line. Unlike Old Bolingbroke and Clifford Castle there was no gatehouse. The entrance was a simple break in the curtain wall between two of the angle towers. The absence of a gatehouse is not necessarily an early feature. The same pattern appears in some of the Edwardian castles in North Wales (pp. 80 and 91). On the other hand, the presence of a keep-like tower, and particularly its situation at the 'back' of the castle, well away from the entrance, may be indicative of an old-fashioned or conservative approach to castle design in which the idea of a gatehouse instead of, or even in addition to, a keep had as yet no place.

It was suggested earlier for Clifford Castle that without the wall towers it would look like an old-fashioned shell-keep. White Castle (Gwent) was, in fact, originally built without wall towers which are a thirteenth-century addition (c. 1220) and qualify it for inclusion here. As built in the twelfth century it consisted of a generally oval (actually many-sided polygonal) curtain wall about 150 ft long and about 100 ft wide. At the southern end, straddling the curtain wall, are the foundations of a small rectangular tower (c. 33 x 30 ft). Curtain wall and tower stand on a low motte with a wide surrounding ditch and outworks to the north and south. Whether this is regarded as a keep-and-bailey castle (although the keep is very small), or a shell-keep with a wall tower makes little difference. What is certain is that before or when the wall towers were added the rectangular tower was dispensed with and the curtain wall was built across its remains. In effect, the new towers were added to a plain, curtain-walled enclosure, whether it is

Inverlochy Castle (Highland) showing two of the circular angle towers, and one of the simple entrances through the curtain wall.

called (or was) a shell-keep or a bailey, and the transformation was such that it was virtually a new castle. There were six such new towers, more or less regularly spaced, with a marked projection beyond the face of the curtain wall. Two formed a twin-towered gatehouse at the tapering northern end of the site. Beyond this to the north was a large outer bailey with a similar curtain wall and towers. A postern gate at the southern end of the site was situated close to the south-west angle tower and had a crescent-shaped outwork in front of it.

Apart from Beeston, Cilgerran, and Llanstephan which were irregular in plan because of their siting, the other sites considered so far in this chapter have all been irregularly polygonal in shape: that is, they consist of straight lengths of walling linked at the angles by towers, unlike earlier enclosures in which the curtain wall was curved. To this extent they acknowledge rectilinear planning, although not to any marked degree. However, much more strikingly rectilinear planning has already been seen in many of the castles with circular keeps considered in the last chapter, such as Skenfrith, Helmsley, Dirleton, Bothwell, and Kildrummy. None of these is yet truly rectangular, but they all display clear signs of a regard for regular layout in the period from about 1200 to around 1250.

In the group of castles to be considered next, built from about 1210 to 1270, there is a much clearer indication of the desire for a regular, rectangular plan. One of the earliest such buildings appears to be Limerick in Ireland, which was built within the first decade or two of the thirteenth century. The castle was made up of four circular angle towers and a double-towered gatehouse linked by a curtain wall, and was fairly close to a rectangular plan, although the northern front has a pronounced angle just east of the gatehouse. This consists of two D-shaped towers, their flat portions now flush with the inner face of the curtain wall, although originally they projected inwards in rectangular fashion. The gatehouse is still 75 ft wide and must have been some 40 ft deep when originally constructed. The angle towers were also substantial, some 45 ft in overall diameter and around 20 ft internally. The south-east angle tower is now missing, having been removed in 1611 to make way for an artillery bastion, and the other three have also been lowered in height to accommodate heavy guns. The east and west curtain walls have also been destroyed. The surviving portions of the castle consist of the gatehouse, the north curtain wall and the towers at either end, and the south curtain wall and the south-west tower. The north-west angle tower, although similar in plan, was originally higher than the other three and was presumably considered the most important. In this differentiation of one tower can be seen a still surviving acknowledgement of the idea of a keep, even in a castle which is nominally keepless. Nor should such an acknowledgement be surprising at this date; castles with circular keeps were still being built, and went on being built for another thirty or forty years.

Inverlochy Castle (Highland) exemplified the principle of rectangular planning in its simplest form. It is almost square in plan (*c.* 100 x 90 ft internally) and consists of four circular angle towers linked by four straight lengths of curtain wall, and little else. There are two entrances, but no gate-house, the entrances consisting simply of doorways in the curtain wall closed by two-leaved doors and additionally protected by portcullises. Additional defences consisted of a wide ditch on three sides, fed by the River Ness which formed the fourth, on the west. The material excavated from the ditch was placed in a bank on its outer edge as an additional obstacle. A thin, outer curtain wall (*c.* 3 ft wide), with four small corner towers, was added to the castle in the fifteenth century, forming a concentric plan, but not a concentric plan in anything like the manner of the great concentric castles of the Edwardian period. The main part of the castle was built in the third quarter of the thirteenth century. The main curtain wall was about 9 ft thick and 30 ft high. Apart from that the chief interest in the castle are the four angle towers. These are not, in fact, all of the same size. Three of them were around 30 ft in diameter while the fourth, at the south-west angle, was nearer 40 ft and once again must be seen as an acknowledgement of the keep principle, even though it is here acting fully as an angle tower like the other three. All four towers, of three storeys each, were served by mural rather than spiral staircases, a type noted much earlier at Conisbrough (p. 23) which rises concentrically with the tower in the thickness of its wall. The towers rose some 10 or 15 ft above the height of the curtain wall, the sentry walks of which ran behind each tower at the angles, allowing for rapid circulation and also allowing each tower to be isolated from the curtain in time of danger.

Barnwell Castle (Northants.) built about 1266 and therefore of very much the same age as Inverlochy, exemplifies the same rectilinear planning although in rather more elaborate form. The virtually rectangular courtyard (135 x 95 ft), in which all the internal buildings have been destroyed, is surrounded by a massive curtain wall, 12 ft thick and 30 ft high, most of which is still preserved. At three of the angles (north-west, north-east, and south-west) there are three-quarter-projecting round towers about 30 ft in

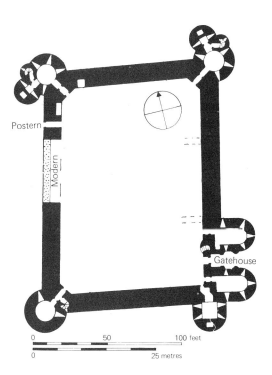

Postern

Modern

Gatehouse

0   50   100 feet

0   25 metres

Barnwell Castle is an early example of the rectangular planning which became a feature of Edwardian and post-Edwardian castles. Unlike Inverlochy it had a formidable gatehouse.

diameter. The one on the south-west is a simple tower, but the other two are trefoil in plan, with two lobes attached to the main tower. The smaller lobes housed the spiral staircases, the larger the latrines, while also providing much greater covering fire along the adjacent curtain walls. Adjacent to the north-west tower, in the west curtain wall, was a postern gate, for which the main projecting lobe acted virtually as a gate tower.

The main entrance to the castle was in the south-east corner and consisted of a substantial, twin-towered gatehouse (*c.* 55 x 35 ft) with two long D-shaped towers, projecting some 25 ft in front of the east curtain wall; the south wall of the south tower was in line with the south curtain wall. This meant that there was no projection on that side from the gatehouse, and to provide flanking fire along the south curtain wall a third tower, D-shaped in plan, was added at the south-east corner. This was, in effect, the fourth angle tower, but D-shaped rather than circular, because the angle had been masked by the building of the gatehouse in this position. The whole castle was originally surrounded by a ditch but there is little or no trace of this on the ground now.

A great deal of later building has been done at Carew Castle (Dyfed), but there is no doubt that the original plan consisted of four angle towers linked by curtain walls, forming a trapeze-shaped rather than a truly rectangular plan, probably not dissimilar in shape to Inverlochy. The two castles were built about the same time (Carew, *c.* 1270), and further resemble each other in the absence of any twin-towered gatehouses. Although the bulk of the existing remains are thirteenth-century or later there is some evidence of an earlier, twelfth-century castle. This consists of the remains of a square gatehouse tower on the east curtain of the later castle. Presumably there were additional features, but if so these cannot now be identified in the existing remains.

Around 1270 a new castle on the same site was begun by Sir Nicholas de Carew, a distinguished soldier. Only three of the four main angle towers are preserved but presumably the missing one on the north-east would have been fairly similar to the surviving south-east tower. If so these two were less substantial than the two massive western towers which rise from square bases some 35 x 35 ft. Between them was the west curtain wall, 70 ft long and 9 ft thick, behind which was the Great Hall (80 ft x 25 ft internally) at first-floor level, with an undercroft beneath, forming the west side of the internal courtyard. This western portion of the castle of 1270 is separated from the other surviving portions by later building. Of these the south-east tower has been mentioned already. The other substantial portion includes the Lesser Hall, on an undercroft, with other private apartments above, and the large polygonal Chapel Tower, which projected nearly 30 ft in front of the east curtain wall and must have provided flanking fire to cover the entrance, supported no doubt by corresponding fire from the south-east tower on the other side. In the angle between the Lesser Hall and the Chapel Tower is the Great Turret which may simply be the north-east angle of the castle carried up to form a square tower and this may have taken the place of the conventional projecting angle tower.

A great deal of building work was carried out by Sir Rhys ap Thomas in the reign of Henry VII (1485–1509), but the additional building for which

The Elizabethan range at Carew Castle.

Kenilworth Castle (Warwicks.) had a great rectangular stone keep, an impressive range of domestic buildings, and elaborate water defences, now unfortunately gone.

Carew Castle is best known is that by Sir John Perrot, who also remodelled Laugharne Castle (p. 125) during the reign of Queen Elizabeth I (1558-1603). Across the north side of the castle Sir John built a high and imposing suite of rooms, with two tiers of windows along a 150-ft front, including two large, two-tier semi-circular windows.

The castles considered so far in this chapter have all been new, or virtually new, works reflecting in their whole structure current ideas on fortification. Inevitably, however, older castles, which probably far out-numbered newly-

built ones, were affected by the same changes of style and fashion. Few castles remained structurally static. The desire for greater military strength, for greater domestic comfort, or for increased architectural splendour, or sometimes all three, led almost inevitably to additional building works in many castles, and the period under review, the thirteenth century up to the accession of Edward I, was no different from earlier or later periods in this respect. It was, in fact, a time when there were many new ideas on fortification and these are reflected not only in newly-built castles but also in castles added to or altered about this time.

Kenilworth (Warwicks.) started life as a timber-built motte-and-bailey castle in the time of Henry I. As in many other cases the timber works were eventually replaced by stone buildings, in the case of Kenilworth probably in the second half of the twelfth century. The stub of the original motte lies beneath the great red sandstone keep, and the bailey probably occupied the area now taken up by the Inner Bailey and its stone curtain wall, now itself partly obscured by later buildings. Around this first stone castle was a wide moat, probably an enlarged version of the one surrounding the original timber-built castle. Thus at the beginning of the thirteenth century, Kenilworth was already a strong castle, but no different in type from the many other stone keep-and-bailey castles built during the twelfth century.

During the next seventy years or so, however, in the reigns of John and Henry III, a great deal of time, money, and effort were spent on the castle, transforming it into what we recognise today as Kenilworth Castle. The principal addition, probably in John's reign, was the Outer Bailey, irregularly oval in plan, some 500 ft from north to south and about 800 ft from east to west, surrounded by a stone curtain wall, some 2,200 ft long, with regular buttresses, three angle towers, and two gatehouses. In all of these features can be recognised the new ideas on fortification current at the time. The addition of the Outer Bailey transformed the site into a sort of concentric castle, at about the same time as the more positive trans-formation of Dover Castle. The Inner Bailey and its buildings were completely embraced by the new outer curtain wall, although only on the south and west were the two lines close enough to constitute a true concentric arrangement. On the north and east the lines were several hundred feet apart and were no more concentric than, say, the inner and outer lines at Beeston (above, p. 37). Nevertheless, Kenilworth exemplified the principle of multiple lines of defence, with one enclosure embracing another, even if the concentric ideal was not fully pursued.

The two gatehouses also display thirteenth-century ideas. The north gate has been destroyed but it appears to have consisted of twin D-shaped towers, the curved ends projecting beyond the curtain wall, the squared ends projecting inwards. The main entrance, Mortimer's Gate, was on the south-eastern side and although destroyed down to its foundations, the main lines of the plan are reasonably clear. There appear to have been two structural phases. In the first phase, presumably of the same period as the outer curtain wall, the south-eastern entrance consisted of a single rectangular gate tower of a type common in many twelfth-century castles. Later, the entrance was strengthened by the addition of twin D-shaped towers in front of the original square tower, the old and new structures between them defining an entrance passage some 80 ft long. In front of the entrance was a long causeway which also acted as a dam, retaining the waters of a stream and thus forming a great lake (now drained again) to the south and west of the Outer Bailey and providing the waters for a double moat to the north and east. There was a second gatehouse at the outer end of the dam and a third on the barbican, a small artificial island with an outwork (another small island) between it and the main bank. Altogether Kenilworth boasted a formidable array of defences and in its heyday it must have been as powerful and impressive a work as Dover.

The southern and western sides of the outer curtain wall, protected by the lake, had no wall towers. These were confined to the north and east and were only three in number: Swan Tower, at the north-west angle, Lunn's Tower at the north-east angle, and the Water Tower at the south-east angle. Swan Tower, now a ruin, although rectangular at its base, was actually octagonal above, a shape which is in a sense a compromise between the old rectangular towers and the newer circular types. Lunn's Tower was indeed circular, with flat buttresses around its circuit. The Water Tower, like Swan Tower, was rectangular at base level but semi-octagonal above on the external face. Thus all three towers, in their shape and in their bold projection beyond the curtain wall, are typical of the fortification works of the first half of the thirteenth century.

There was much later work done on the castle which can only be mentioned here. The principal additions were the Great Hall across the western end of the Inner Bailey, built by John of Gaunt in the late fourteenth century, and the north gatehouse (Leicester's Gatehouse), added by Robert Dudley, Earl of Leicester, in 1570, together with another building at the south-east corner of the Inner Bailey. In its wide range of structures covering five centuries Kenilworth Castle embraces much of the history of medieval fortification.

Like Kenilworth, Scarborough Castle (North Yorkshire) has a history before the period under review, the thirteenth century. Indeed its history as a fortification goes back even beyond its square keep, for on the cliff edge, within the Outer Ward, are the remains of a late Roman signal station, built *c.* AD 370. The central feature of this was a stone tower, some 45 ft square, which must have risen to something like twice its width, that is to roughly 90 ft. As such it was not very much different from the medieval keep, which was 55 ft square and probably around 100 ft high. Although there was an earlier medieval tower on the site (built *c.* 1140), the existing keep (the western half of which was destroyed in 1645 by the Roundheads) was the work of Henry II in the years 1157–69. The keep stands on a triangular promontory on the North Sea coast, the steep cliffs on the east and north-west and a moat, at the foot of a natural slope, on the south-west, cutting off about 19 acres. Within this area was a triangular, walled bailey, associated with the keep. This is for the most part the castle built by Henry II in the second half of the twelfth century.

Important additions were made to the castle in the thirteenth century, under John, and Henry III. The curtain wall of the Outer Ward may be part of the original castle built by Henry II, or it could be a new or rebuilt feature of John's time. What is certain is that the series of semi-circular towers attached to it are the work of John, built in the same style as the towers he added to the curtain wall of the Middle Bailey at Dover. A more striking addition was the barbican built in front of the isthmus which provided the main means of access. This was probably the work of Henry III, although part of it may have been built in John's time. As finally completed, by about 1250, it consisted of a high-walled causeway across the isthmus, interrupted by two drawbridges (now replaced by permanent stone bridges), with an irregularly-shaped barbican, with a double-towered entrance, at the outer end, through which an attacker would have to fight his way before even gaining access to the causeway. This follows the same principles as the causeway and barbican at Kenilworth, although without the aid of water defences. At some stage a wall was added around the edge of the promontory above the sea. Certainly by 1278 it was reported as being very much in need of repair, so that a date for its construction in the first half of the century seems likely. It could well have been built at the same time as (although on a smaller scale than) the main curtain wall across the promontory, or when it was strengthened by the addition of semi-circular towers, if the two were not built together.

Preoccupation with entrance defences, seen already at Kenilworth and Scarborough, is evident also at Newcastle-upon-Tyne where the Blackgate, the entrance to the bailey, was added between 1247 and 1250. There was a castle at Newcastle as early as 1080, almost certainly of timber (motte-and-bailey) construction. The existing stone keep was built by Henry II between 1172 and 1177 and stood within a triangular bailey with the River Tyne to the south, a ravine to the east, and a moat to the west. It was across this moat, at the north-west corner of the castle, that the new gatehouse was built by Henry III. It bore some resemblance to the Constable's gate at Dover completed some twenty years earlier (1227), although, in spite of the formidable appearance of the latter, the Newcastle entrance was more advanced in its planning. At Dover there is an impressive array of towers on either side of the entrance, giving the structure great width (c. 120 ft), but not much depth; beyond the drawbridge, for example, there is only a single passage (with a portcullis and double doors) some 55 ft in length. At Newcastle, on the other hand, the gatehouse structure is only about 50 ft wide, but the distance to be traversed from the drawbridge to the interior is nearly twice that—roughly 100 ft.

The Newcastle gatehouse is, in fact, a double gatehouse, with inner and outer sections, not in line but at an angle of 45 degrees to each other, and separated by a small triangular courtyard, with linking walls on either side. Although not much remains of the inner gatehouse most of the outer one is preserved, the upper portions having been rebuilt in 1619. The outer gatehouse is an oval structure, consisting of a central passageway, flanked by two D-shaped towers which acted as guard chambers. The passage contained a portcullis at the outer end and a double-leaved door about half-way along. Beyond the outer gatehouse is the linking courtyard, with high walls on either side, beyond which is the second gatehouse, the axis of which is at an angle of 45 degrees to the outer entrance. At the back of the courtyard is a deep pit, from wall to wall, across the front of the inner gatehouse, which was crossed by a drawbridge. The inner gatehouse was a rectangular structure (c. 50 x 40 ft), with a central passageway, presumably protected by a portcullis and a two-leaved gate, although because of the

Bamburgh occupies a magnificent position on a high, rocky ridge on the Northumberland coast.

ruinous state of the structure few details are available. The whole gatehouse complex projects some 90 ft beyond the curtain wall, giving great command over the western side of the bailey and also command of its outer ditch.

Bamburgh Castle (Northumberland) seems to have reached its present extent by about 1250 under Henry III, after about a century of intermittent building which began with the great square keep which still dominates the whole complex. The site occupies a long narrow plateau of rock, running more or less east and west, which stands directly above the sea shore. The site has a long history stretching back to prehistoric times but, as far as medieval castles are concerned, the story begins with the keep, the precise date of which is not yet firmly established. It is certainly of the twelfth century, and is usually attributed to Henry II, but there is no record in his reign of expenditure on Bamburgh sufficient for the building of a keep. This is not conclusive, but it is possible that Henry's expenditure was for the repair and maintenance of an already existing keep, which could have been built in the reign of Stephen (1135–54). Presumably, like other keeps of the period, it was accompanied by a bailey and it is difficult to see anything other than the present Upper Ward as the original bailey, although, like the rest of the castle, it has been heavily restored in recent times. Presumably there was a plain curtain wall following the edge of the rock (possibly now incorporated in the later and more elaborate curtain wall), with an entrance at the western end between the curtain and the keep, not dissimilar to the arrangement at Scarborough. One probably had to reach the entrance, as now, around the eastern end of the bailey and along its north side, turning through 180 degrees to enter between the end of the curtain wall and the north face of the keep. The outer entrance arrangements are almost certainly later than the original keep-and-bailey castle.

If the keep and bailey are attributed to Henry II (or his predecessor), then the remainder of the castle is the work of John and Henry III, both of whom are known to have spent a considerable amount of money on Bamburgh. The keep-and-bailey castle occupied less than half of the rock plateau and it must have seemed an obvious precautionary move to take in the whole summit, probably around the turn of the century (i.e. 1200). As extended, the castle included three enclosures: the original Inner Bailey, an Outer Bailey, and a West Bailey. The latter appears to be more in the nature of a defended outwork and the main walls of the castle appear to have embraced only the Inner and Outer Baileys. The north wall of the Outer Bailey overlapped that of the Inner Bailey providing an outer line of defence flanking the approach to the inner entrance described earlier.

The curtain walls of the Inner and Outer Baileys incorporate a series of towers, some rectangular, some semi-circular. The rectangular towers, attached to the inner curtain wall, may be part of the original keep-and-bailey scheme (whether built by Henry II or Stephen), or they may be later additions, in which case they are most probably the work of Henry II. The newer-style semi-circular towers must date to the turn of the century (1200) or later, in which case they are the work of John or Henry III. This leaves the gatehouse at the eastern end of the site to be described. Since this could only have been built when the works already described were complete, it must have been one of the last works to be undertaken before the general terminal date of 1250. It must, therefore, be the work of Henry III. In chronological terms, therefore, the building of the castle can provisionally be divided as follows: the keep and Inner Bailey, with square towers, by Henry II (or partly by Stephen and Henry II); the Outer Bailey and the western outwork, and possibly the semi-circular towers by John; and the eastern gatehouse, and the semi-circular towers (if not by John) by Henry III. This scheme accounts for only the major features. The recorded expenditure indicates many other lesser works which it would be difficult to attribute to any particular king.

Although the entrance itself is substantially intact some of its associated features are no longer visible. It is now approached over a stone bridge, but originally there was a gap in the causeway, spanned by a drawbridge. In front of that again (although now entirely gone) was a barbican or outer defence which had to be passed before the drawbridge could be reached. If the plan in the Official Guide-Book is to be believed this outer gate was oval in plan, with a central passage and two D-shaped towers, back to back, very much on the lines of the outer gatehouse at Newcastle, built in

1247. The scheme is also on the same lines as the barbican at Scarborough, the completion of which was attributed to Henry III, around 1250. The other barbican scheme described earlier, at Kenilworth, was also of this period and everything points to the direction of a similar date for the eastern entrance at Bamburgh and completion by Henry III. The surviving gatehouse consists of two D-shaped towers with an arched entrance between, again suggestive of a date in the first half of the thirteenth century.

As well as military considerations a great deal of attention was paid to domestic comfort. Internally, apart from the keep, the main accommodation was in a range of buildings against the south curtain wall of the Inner Bailey. These appear to have been mainly the work of Henry III and his son Edward I, although the original buildings have been so altered and restored as to be almost unrecognisable for what they were.

Chepstow Castle (Gwent) may well be one of the earliest stone castles (if not the earliest) in the British Isles, and its construction may have been started by Earl William fitz Osbern, a relative of William the Conqueror, within a few years of the Conquest, between 1067 and 1071. Apart from its (probable) early date, Chepstow is unusual (although not unique) in having no keep. The restricted nature of the site and the underlying geology make both a normal motte-and-bailey plan and timber construction unlikely, and the buildings were probably of stone from the beginning. Their plan was dictated by the situation, a narrow east/west ridge bounded on the north by the cliffs above the River Wye and on the south by a steep ravine. The castle was centred on the narrowest part of this ridge, with baileys to east and west widening in hour-glass fashion. Instead of a keep, the central feature was a stone-built hall, a standard Norman type of domestic building, oblong in plan (in this case 110 ft x 40 ft) with a vaulted lower storey and the main hall at first-floor level. The castle at Richmond (North Yorkshire) as first built (c. 1090) also consisted of a stone-built two-storey hall and a curtain wall (the square keep was a later addition), and there are other examples: Saltwood Castle (Kent), Framlingham Castle (Suffolk), and Grosmont Castle (Gwent).

The castle remained more or less in this form until the thirteenth century when a series of major additions brought Chepstow to its present shape and extent. Between 1200 and 1250 the castle was extended to both east and west, creating a third (lower) bailey and a barbican. To the west a small barbican was built beyond the rock-cut ditch which had been the original western limit of the site. This consisted of a curving curtain wall enclosing a small area (c. 60 x 90 ft) beyond the ditch, with two wall towers and, towards the end of the century, a single-tower gatehouse. The most considerable addition, however, was on the east side of the castle where a third bailey was added (Lower Bailey), with a twin-towered gatehouse on its eastern side. At the same time the two-storey stone hall which formed the nucleus of the castle was transformed into a virtual keep by the addition of a third storey, almost doubling its height.

These changes established the main lines of the castle as it stands today, although there were considerable additions in the latter part of the century (c. 1270–1300). Most of these were, however, internal and domestic and consisted of the great range of buildings on the north side of the (new)

Lower Bailey which are still a prominent feature of the site and which include two complete suites of rooms, each with its own hall. There was, however, one addition which affected the external appearance of the castle, Marten's Tower, at the south-east corner of the Lower Bailey. This was a D-shaped tower of keep-like proportions on a rectangular base some 55 ft x 42 ft. By means of portcullises it could be isolated from the courtyard and from the curtain walls on either side, and was clearly intended to be used as a self-contained residence. It had a basement and three large rooms on each of three floors above, together with garderobes and a chapel. With its large rooms (*c.* 25 x 18 ft), and its massive walls (12–15 ft thick), it must have provided very commodious and very safe accommodation in times of trouble.

Like Chepstow, Grosmont Castle in the same county was built in a hall-and-bailey arrangement, about 1150. The hall occupies the east side of the site with a roughly circular bailey to the west, the whole structure being surrounded by a deep ditch. The original bailey wall was plain, but in the first half of the thirteenth century it was rebuilt and wall towers and a

Chepstow (Gwent) was one of the earliest stone castles in the British Isles. This view shows part of the extensive additions of the thirteenth century.

gatehouse were added, bringing the site more or less to its existing shape. There was also an outer bailey on the south-west side.

Saltwood (Kent) likewise had a hall and bailey rather than a keep and bailey, although the remains of the existing hall are of thirteenth-century date. Presumably, however, there was an earlier hall built at the same time as the curtain wall (*c.* 1160), which enclosed an oval bailey measuring about 325 x 225 ft. The south side of this was replaced by a straight length of walling in the thirteenth century and it was against this that the hall mentioned above was built, together with kitchens, chapel, and other apartments. The curtain wall had three internal rectangular towers, one of which formed a gatehouse. There were two smaller projecting towers on the original curtain and two additional projecting rectangular towers on the straight south curtain. The thirteenth-century military additions to the castle consisted of the building of an outer bailey on the eastern side, defended by a curtain wall with round towers, built about 1240. There were three angle towers, projecting for three-quarters of their circumference, one half-round intermediate tower and a gatehouse. It is noticeable that the new, outer gatehouse was not built in the contemporary twin-towered style, as one might have expected around 1240, but follows the plan of the earlier, inner gateway, built nearly a century earlier, with its single rectangular tower. In the following (fourteenth) century it was this inner entrance which received one of the final embellishments of the castle, a double-towered gatehouse built on to the front of the existing structure, between 1381 and 1396.

Pevensey Castle (Sussex) was sited within the walls of an 8-acre Roman fort, built about AD 300. Around 1100 a rectangular keep some 80 x 50 ft was built in the south-east corner with a bailey extending to the west and north-west within the Roman fort area. In the thirteenth century the bailey defences were rebuilt in the current fashion with wall towers and a double-towered gatehouse. The bailey is sub-rectangular in plan (*c.* 200 ft square) with medieval defences on the north, west, and south, and the old Roman wall on the east. There were three boldly projecting D-shaped towers, and a double-towered gatehouse, with long D-shaped towers, on the west. Noticeable features of the three wall towers were the postern gates or sally-ports (two per tower) which opened on each side from the bailey to the wide space or berm between the curtain wall and the ditch. Also unusual were the five massive bastions of the keep. These may have been added at this time, but equally may have been part of the original keep structure.

Lewes Castle (Sussex) is unusual in having two mottes at the north-eastern and south-western ends of an oval bailey. Both were originally crowned with shell-keeps although only the south-western motte now has any visible stone remains. The castle was built about 1080–1100. In 1264 two semi-octagonal towers were added to the south-western shell on the southern and western sides, i.e. the exposed sides away from the bailey. At a later date, early in the fourteenth century, a very well-preserved barbican was built in front of the existing entrance. The early gate was a rectangular tower with its front flush with the curtain wall. The new double-towered gatehouse was placed some 25 ft in front of this and linked to it by flanking walls on either side, exemplifying again the principle seen already in the Blackgate at Newcastle.

An aerial view of Pevensey showing the Roman fort and the medieval keep and bailey in the south-east corner.

Rothesay Castle (Bute) is generally described as a shell-keep although it is somewhat larger than most (*c.* 170 x 150 ft) and does not stand on a motte but simply on the sub-rectangular plateau formed by the excavation of the very broad moat. It is perhaps more correctly described as a curtain-wall castle, without a keep, and is virtually circular in plan. The curtain wall, originally plain, is 9 ft thick and stood 20 ft high. The castle was probably built around 1150. After a siege in 1230, when considerable damage was done, the castle was strengthened by the addition of four round towers, each roughly 35 ft in diameter, projecting boldly beyond the

One of the four large round towers added to the defences of Rothesay in the thirteenth century.

curtain wall. Later again, towards the end of the fifteenth century, the curtain wall was raised by 10 ft all round and a large rectangular gatehouse, with residential accommodation above, was built in front of the entrance, projecting some 70 ft in front of the curtain wall and into the moat.

A curtain wall with regularly-spaced D-shaped towers was built at Trim Castle (Co. Meath, Ireland), about 1220. The nucleus of the castle is an unusual square keep with four smaller square towers projecting from the middle of each side, started around 1190–1200 when the square keep was being replaced by the circular form, to reduce the threat of undermining presented by the salient angles. At Trim, however, the additional towers meant that there were no less than twelve vulnerable salient angles, instead of four. This may have been the reason for the building of outer defences in the curtain wall-and-tower style, and of a barbican entrance of unusual type. These form the south side of the bailey. The north side, with a square gatehouse and rectangular towers, is of slightly earlier date and probably contemporary with the keep. The more up-to-date southern defences probably represent a change of plan while building operations were still in progress for the keep was not actually finished until approximately 1220.

The southern defences consisted of five D-shaped towers (20–30 ft wide) and the South or Dublin Gate, linked by a curtain wall. The towers are open at the back: thus they are simply defensive devices and do not provide any additional accommodation as was the case elsewhere. The Dublin Gate was of somewhat unusual form, with a barbican, although it bears some resemblance to the Black Gate at Newcastle. The entrance consists basically of a circular tower (c. 40 ft in diameter) with the entrance passage running through the middle, leaving D-shaped guard chambers on either side. From the outer end of the passage parallel walls project forward, carried across the ditch on a bridge, to an outer entrance some 30 ft in front of the tower. The net result is that an attacker, having breached the outer entrance, would then be faced with a passage 70 ft long, interrupted by a drawbridge, with the guard chambers and innermost entrance beyond.

It is appropriate to conclude this survey of the pre-Edwardian period (i.e. pre-1272) with Caerphilly Castle. Although it was probably not completed until Edward's reign was well under way it was certainly started before he ascended the throne, probably between 1267 and 1272. However, the original scheme was probably less ambitious than the present remains indicate and the final plan was probably the result of several decades of building and of several changes of design. Its later stages must have been contemporary with the works of Edward I in North Wales and it would be difficult to maintain that Caerphilly was not to some degree influenced by developments there. The essential feature of Caerphilly is its concentric plan, and the key question is whether it was conceived from the beginning on concentric lines or whether it was made concentric later. It certainly bears a close resemblance to Harlech Castle and it is tempting to suggest that it developed, under the influence of the very ambitious castle-building programme then proceeding in the north, into the elaborate castle which Caerphilly finally became. However, there is not a great deal of evidence on the structural development of the castle and the question of its original plan must be left open. Whatever its structural history may eventually prove to be, Caerphilly Castle is a most impressive piece of military architecture and a worthy introduction to the great period of Edwardian castle building.

The Inner Bailey is very much what one would expect to find in a newly-built castle of about 1270: a rectangular curtain wall (c. 200 x 160 ft overall), with four three-quarter projecting round towers at the angles and a double-towered gatehouse. In fact, there are two gatehouses, east and west, and of the two the smaller west gatehouse appears to belong to the castle as first built; the more elaborate east gatehouse is a slightly later addition closely resembling the gatehouse at Harlech (below, p. 103), and presumably represents the influence exercised by the North Wales castle-building programme mentioned earlier. Leaving this addition to one side, the remaining structures described could well represent Caerphilly as first planned, a simple, rectangular curtain-wall castle with four angle-towers and a twin-towered gatehouse: in fact, a straightforward castle of the period.

Surrounding the Inner Bailey, and forming a fully concentric plan, is the Outer Bailey, defined by a plain curtain wall, without towers, except at the outer gatehouses, east and west. Its curtain wall is only 6 or 7 ft high above the interior which thus forms a sort of terrace, some 40 ft wide, around the main structure, the Inner Bailey. Externally, the outer curtain wall falls some 30 ft to the level of the surrounding water. The outer gatehouses are directly in line with those on the inner curtain and are approached by drawbridges across the waters of the lake, in the case of the west entrance from the outwork (below), and in the case of the east entrance from the huge barbican or screen wall which covers the whole eastern approach of the castle. This barbican is, in effect, a dam and provides Caerphilly with one of its principal defences, water, and this raises the whole question of water defences in thirteenth-century military architecture. Caerphilly is an outstanding example, but it is by no means the only castle where water played an important part in the scheme of things.

Although the use of water, in wet moats, was not new, water defences did not figure largely in earlier castles, very often for topographical reasons. Where, for reasons of greater safety, elevation was sought after, the surrounding moats were necessarily dry. Even in low-lying situations, unless there was water close-by, it was not possible either to feed in or retain water in sufficient quantity to constitute an effective outer defence. In the earlier period of castle building the dry moat was very much the norm, and even in many later castles the topographical situation, precluded any idea of water defences. Beeston, for example (above, p. 37), could never have had water defences, nor could Harlech (below, p. 100), in both cases because elevation was the overriding factor in their siting; and the same was true of many other castles, even during the later period of building.

Two castles built around the beginning of the later period provide examples of the fairly simple use of water defences. Pembroke Castle (c. 1200, above p. 28) stands in a U-shaped bend of the Pembroke River which thus acts as a very substantial wet moat on two of its three sides. The water is an important part of the defensive system, but no water engineering was involved. The castle simply exploits the advantages of the situation, just as Beeston does in a different way. Both castles are situated on

Kenilworth Castle once relied heavily on water for its defence, although most of the water has now drained away.

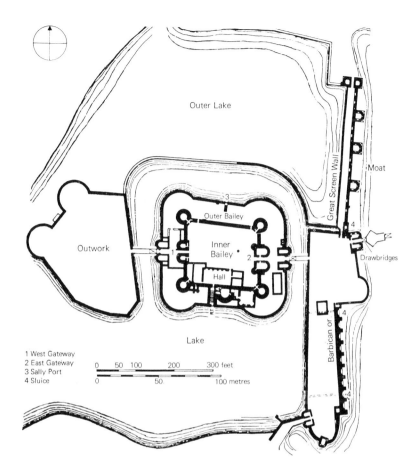

Plan of Caerphilly Castle (Glamorgan), a concentric castle with elaborate water defences, retained by the great barbican which is, in effect, a dam, on the eastern side.

promontories, with natural defences on two sides. In the case of Beeston the natural defences are steep cliffs, in the case of Pembroke they are the waters of the Pembroke River.

The second castle is Skenfrith (above, p. 24), also built about 1200 and, in fact, some fairly simple water engineering was involved. The castle was built on level ground immediately alongside the River Monnow which thus acted as a wet moat outside the east curtain wall. When a ditch some 30 ft wide (now largely filled in) was dug on the three remaining sides, water from the river was led in at the north-east angle, flowed round the castle and rejoined the river at the south-east corner. As compared with some of the sites to be considered below the engineering was of the simplest kind and a fairly obvious solution to the problem of providing water defences, given that there was a river in the general area where the castle was to be built. Nevertheless, in spite of its simplicity, Skenfrith shows a positive approach to the use of water as an element in military architecture.

A much more positive approach is demonstrated at Kenilworth Castle, described earlier, which falls in time between Skenfrith (*c.* 1200) and Caerphilly (*c.* 1270). The enlargement of Kenilworth was carried out during the reigns of King John and Henry III, the provision of the extensive water defences probably, and necessarily, coming late in the scheme, around the middle of the century; the whole project appears to

A view of Caerphilly Castle from the barbican showing the Inner and Outer Baileys and the surrounding waters of the lake.

have been completed by about 1260. The castle stands at the lower (eastern) end of a small valley with a stream flowing through it, from west to east. The building of the large Outer Bailey (above, p. 53), and of the causeway from the main (south-east) entrance, effectively blocked the valley, in the manner of a dam, and allowed the water from the stream to build up to form the Great Lake (now gone again), three-quarters of a mile long and about a quarter of a mile wide. This ran up to the Outer Bailey wall on the south and west, while the same waters filled a double moat on the northern and north-eastern sides. On the south-east the main causeway was flanked by the Great Lake on one side and a large pool on the other. The waters of the Great Lake also surrounded the island which formed a

barbican in front of the entrance at the outer end of the causeway. There is no doubt that water formed a very important part of the defensive scheme at Kenilworth, which was put to the test shortly after completion when the castle was besieged for six months in 1266, during the Barons' War (1258–67). All the assaults of the royal forces failed and it would be difficult not to attribute some of that failure to the elaborate water defences added only a decade or so earlier. The garrison of Kenilworth did in the end surrender, but only through starvation and disease; the castle was not taken by force.

A similar solution, the creation of an artificial lake, was adopted at Caerphilly although there the dam was a very much larger and more elaborate affair, over 1,000 ft long, built across the east end of a small valley and retaining the waters of two streams. Unlike Kenilworth, the lake is still there and shows the whole scheme very much as it was executed in the thirteenth century. In spite of its great length, however, the dam, or barbican, was much more than a simple retaining wall. It was a complete fortification in itself, with three double-towered entrances, four large wall-towers and a series of particularly massive buttresses at the southern end of the structure. These features and the linking curtain wall define not so much a simple dam or barrier as a great platform flanking the concentric castle to the east and linked to it by a drawbridge. The northern section of the platform (c. 400 ft long) consists of inner and outer walls forming a barrier some 30 ft thick. At the northern end there is a twin-towered gatehouse giving access to the barbican from the north edge of the valley, and along the east (outer) face, three very substantial semi-octagonal towers on square bases, about 30 ft square.

The central section of the barbican is very much more of a platform, some 175 ft long and over 100 ft deep from back to front. At its north-east corner there is another double-towered gatehouse, reached by two draw-bridges, with an intermediate island, across the wide moat which runs in front of the barbican for the whole of its length. At the south-east angle there is a great semi-circular projection or bastion, providing great cover in both directions, north and south. On the west (inner) side of the platform was a bridge and drawbridge across the moat to the east entrance of the Outer Bailey.

The southern section of the barbican is a longer, but narrower, platform, some 350 ft long and 80 ft wide. On its east, outer face, it is reinforced by a series of massive rectangular buttresses while at the southern end there is a projecting D-shaped tower and a double-towered gatehouse giving access from the south side of the valley, corresponding to the entrance at the north end of the barbican.

This massive structure provides a complete, self-contained outer defence to the east of the main castle and also retains the waters of the artificial lake which surround it. Incorporated in the barbican are three sluices controlling the level of the water in the lake; one of the sluices powered the wheel of a water mill. The overall area of the complex thus created (the castle proper, the barbican, the outwork to the west, and all the surrounding waters) was some thirty acres, leaving an attacker with 300–400 ft of water to cross on those sides (the north and south) not covered by outer defences (i.e. the barbican to the east and the outwork to the west). The outwork referred to

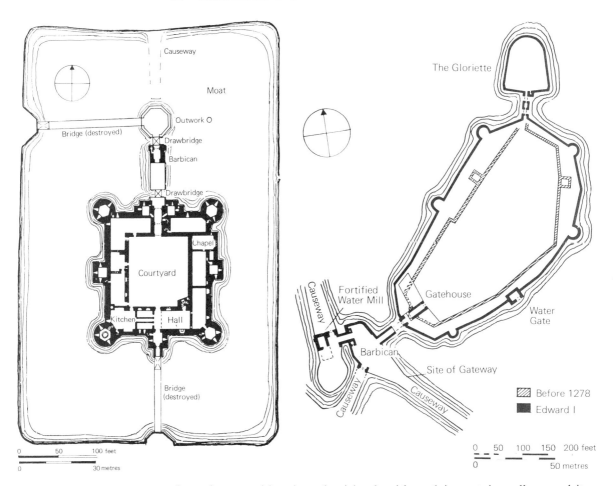

above is a roughly triangular island, with a plain curtain wall around its edge, protecting the whole west side of the main castle and linked to the outer west entrance (at a distance of some 60 ft) by a bridge and drawbridge. On its north-west side are two large rounded bastions between which was the entrance, via bridge and drawbridge, from the facing north-west shore of the lake.

Like both Kenilworth and Caerphilly, Leeds Castle (Kent) owes much of its strength and appearance to the damming of a river, in this case the Len, thus forming three islands in line, one of which, nearest the shore of the lake, constituted a barbican, the next a bailey and the third, outermost island, a keep. The castle owes this keep-and-bailey arrangement to its Norman origins, although nothing of this early work now remains above ground. As it stands the castle is substantially the work of Edward I (although heavily restored in modern times), and was built about 1280, and this is almost certainly the time when the elaborate water defences were contrived. The whole concept is very much in keeping with thirteenth-century work elsewhere in the country involving water as a means of defending castles.

The barbican, the smallest of the three islands, near the south-west corner of the lake, is approached by three causeways, each originally barred by a gate, from the south-east, from the south-west, and from the north, the latter linked by a bridge. From the barbican a bridge and drawbridge led across a stretch of water some 60 ft wide to the largest island, the bailey, oval in plan, nearly 500 ft long and 250 ft wide. The Edwardian defences standing immediately above the water consisted of a curtain wall with regularly-spaced half-round towers, a rectangular water gate and two entrances, one facing the barbican at the southern end and one facing the keep at the northern. Within these defences are remains of an earlier curtain wall with square towers, belonging to the Norman castle, probably of the twelfth century. At this stage, before the water defences were contrived, the castle must have occupied a knoll in the valley which later formed the basin for the lake. The Edwardian defences, 20–40 ft in front of the earlier walls, were presumably built in conjunction with the new water defences so that the curtain wall and towers rose sheer from the lake.

About 50 ft beyond the northern end of the bailey is the keep, known as the Gloriette, reached originally by a bridge with two lifting sections. The Gloriette is shaped in plan like a round-ended spade, about 120 ft long and 100 ft wide. Although it rises sheer from the water and looks keep-like (i.e., like a single block) from the outside, it has, in fact, a small internal courtyard around which the buildings (hall, chapel etc.) are ranged so that technically it is more in the nature of a shell-keep, although any close resemblance to either type of keep has been masked by the extensive modern restoration. A postern gate provided a final means of escape should the keep be about to fall, or a means of supply across the water, independent of the rest of the castle should this be in enemy hands.

Kenilworth, Caerphilly, and Leeds Castles are outstanding examples of the use of water defences in the medieval castle. Other examples are less elaborate and can be dealt with more briefly. Whittington Castle (Shropshire) is, as far as its main structure is concerned, a fairly typical mid-thirteenth-century castle, rectangular in plan with boldly projecting circular angle towers, one of which (the south-western) also acts as the southern gatehouse tower, a fifth tower being provided immediately to the north of it to complete the entrance. This rectangular structure now stands as a platform some 15 ft above its immediate surroundings. Just showing through the platform surface in the centre of the courtyard are the remains of a rectangular keep (c. 50 x 40 ft) with a forebuilding on the north side. The only other stone structures on the site are a twin-towered outer gatehouse and linked section of curtain wall with a round tower; these are in the Outer Bailey to the west of the main structure (Inner Bailey), separated from it by a ditch.

Although the site has not been planned in detail it is quite clear from the extensive earthworks which surround it that water played a considerable part in the castle's defences. Most of the water has now gone but it is clear that some engineering work must have been undertaken to dam up the waters of a nearby stream and to retain the waters so accumulated. In particular, the rectangular Inner Bailey must have been completely surrounded by water. The immediate dry surroundings above which it stands as a 15-ft-high platform were originally below water, possibly to a depth of 4 or 5 ft, and water at this depth would have extended over a much wider area giving an entirely new dimension to the castle's appearance. A large mound on the south side of the Inner Bailey forms a protective outwork in

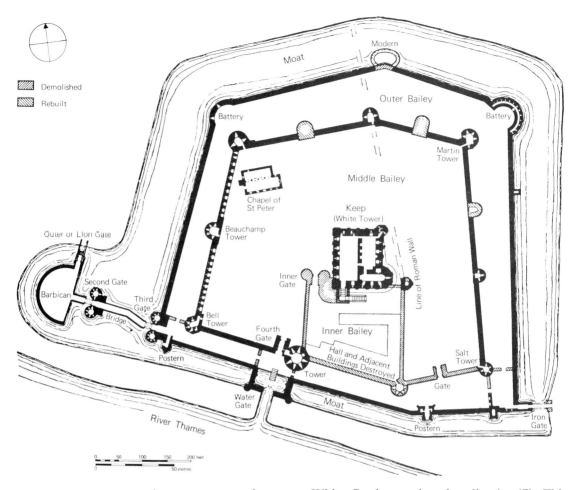

The concentric plan of the Tower of London was the work of Edward I. Included in his extensive rebuilding of the castle was the wharf along the river frontage which enabled the castle to have a continuous wet moat on all four sides.

the same way as the one at White Castle mentioned earlier (p. 47). This may have been the bailey, or part of it, of an earlier motte-and-bailey or keep-and-bailey castle. There is a small surviving stretch of water to the north and north-west of the Outer Bailey, but the extensive earthworks to the south of the castle indicate some fairly extensive water engineering, and a detailed plan of the whole complex would probably be very informative.

Water played an important part in the defences of the Tower of London as redesigned by Edward I between 1275 and 1285. These will be dealt with in Chapter 5, but some details of the water defences can be noted here. Around his greatly enlarged castle Edward provided a new moat, between 75 ft and 125 ft wide. At the south-west corner, however, there was a D-shaped extension of the moat some 200 ft long and over 200 ft wide (now filled in), and the waters thus enclosed provided the setting for the D-shaped barbican and other structures which formed part of the elaborate main entrance to be described later (p. 117). By building a wharf along the Thames frontage Edward was also able to provide a moat on this side as well, continuous with the moat on the three other sides and separate from the waters of the river. The same arrangements also allowed the provision of an elaborate water gate, through the wharf and into a section of the moat enclosed by a box-like extension of the outer curtain wall, and then by a flight of steps to the Outer Bailey proper. Under Henry III the water arrangements of the Tower had been similar to those at Skenfrith: the river on one side and a moat open to the river on the three remaining sides. Under Edward the new arrangements achieved the status of true water engineering, with the waters so managed as to achieve precisely what he wished to achieve in terms of defence.

Caerlaverock Castle (Dumfries and Galloway) will be dealt with in Chapter 5 (p. 129), but its water defences can be noted here. The castle is unusual in plan and its triangular main structure is surrounded by two moats. The castle walls rise sheer from the wide Inner Moat which still retains much of its water. The moat is 50–60 ft wide, although somewhat narrower at the angles where the towers have a considerable projection. Beyond the moat, and retaining its contents, is a broad bank, 30–40 ft wide, which probably also supported a timber palisade. Outside this bank was a second moat (now dry), with a low bank on its outer edge, the purpose of which was to maintain the water level. The water defences and their associated banks provide a strong cordon, 100–150 ft wide, all round the castle, adding many times to its overall area. Although far less sophisticated than Caerphilly, Kenilworth, or Leeds, it is an advance on sites such as Skenfrith in that it was not simply a question of letting water flow in from an adjacent river. At Caerlaverock it was necessary to take deliberate measures to retain the waters, and that those measures were successful, at least as far as the inner moat is concerned, is demonstrated by the still surviving stretch of water there.

The water defences at Bodiam Castle (Sussex) make it one of the most picturesque castles in England. The castle proper (built *c.* 1390), will be described later in Chapter 7, but its water defences are more appropriately dealt with here. The moat (so-called) is so wide and so regular in overall plan that it is, in effect, an artificial lake, *c.* 500 ft long and 350 ft wide. The dimensions of the castle buildings within are 180 x 170 ft so that there was clearly a great expanse of water surrounding it. The lake was fed from the nearby River Rother. The approach to the main gatehouse on the north front was quite elaborate and involved a right-angled change of direction. From the west bank near its northern end there was originally a drawbridge leading to a long, fixed bridge (now destroyed) which led in turn to an outwork in the form of a small octagonal island, some 150 ft out into the lake. On the south side of the octagon (*c.* 40 ft wide) was another drawbridge which led across to a barbican, with a stone-built gatehouse at its outer end, in front of the main entrance. From the south end of the barbican a third drawbridge led across to the double-towered main gatehouse. The approach to the postern gate was more direct. Another wooden bridge (also gone), with drawbridges at either end, led across a 100-ft stretch of water to the south front and its centrally-placed single-tower rectangular gatehouse.

The examples quoted above do not represent the sum total of existing water defences, but they illustrate adequately enough for present purposes the way in which water was and could be used to protect medieval castles. Apart from surviving examples, there may originally have been water defences at many sites which are now dry, although evidence for the existence of these still has to be found.

3
Early Edwardian Castles

The reign of Edward I (1272–1307) witnessed a programme of castle building on an unprecedented scale which marked the climax of medieval military architecture not only in Britain but in Europe as a whole. Nothing built subsequently matched the achievements of Edward's master builder, James of St George, in North Wales, and few other regions in Europe can boast such a range of impressive and well-preserved medieval castles. More than a dozen entirely new castles were involved, together with another half-dozen or so existing castles on which substantial additional work was done. Even in an age when castle building and repair were a continuous process it was a formidable achievement and deservedly forms the centrepiece of this survey of the later medieval castle.

Edward I, one of the greatest English kings, was born at Westminster on 17 June 1239, the first child of Henry III and Eleanor of Provence. His father had a special regard for the pious King Edward the Confessor (1042–1066), and named his son Edward in his memory. Edward did not succeed to the throne until 1272, when he was thirty-three, but his involvement with, and responsibility for, North Wales began long before. In 1254, while he was still in his teens, Edward received from his father the gift of all the king's lands in Wales. The idea was not only to provide him with a source of income, but also with experience as a ruler, anticipating his succession to the full responsibilites of kingship. In fact, both as prince and later as king, Wales brought Edward more expense than income, the major expense being the colossal outlay on the castle-building programme which was intended to be the final solution to the North Wales problem.

Edward was widely travelled, even as a young man. His part in the Crusades, his interest in jousting tournaments, and his continental possessions had taken him to the Near East, North Africa and many parts of Europe long before he became king. He must have become familiar at first hand with a wide range of castles, either from within as a guest or from without as an attacker, and what he learned he put to good use in North Wales and elsewhere. He was, in fact, in Sicily, as a guest at the court of King Charles, when news of his father's death reached him late in 1272, having just returned from Palestine where he had been wounded. It might have been expected that he would return to England as quickly as possible to claim his inheritance, but not so. The succession was not in doubt and Edward did not finally return to England until August 1274, more than eighteen months after his father's death. The return was, in effect, a leisurely, triumphal procession through western Europe by a young, widely-known, and popular king who was received with great acclamation wherever he appeared on his journey home.

One of Edward's stopping places was Savoy where he stayed as the guest of Count Philip of Savoy at his castle of St Georges-d'Espéranche. It was presumably there that he became familiar with the work of Master James of St George who was to become his master builder in North Wales a few years later. Among other works Master James was responsible for the construction of the castle of St Georges and from it he took the name by which he is generally known, James of St George. He was probably responsible for several other castles in Savoy as well and there is no doubt that he was a very experienced castle builder. He was still working in Savoy in 1275, but by early 1278 he was in North Wales, directing Edward's vast castle-building programme. It was the combination of Edward's great financial resources and Master James' building talents which produced the magnificent group of castles which are still a striking feature of the North Wales landscape.

The chief cause of Edward's troubles in Wales was Llywelyn ap Gruffydd (1246–82), the last native Prince of Wales, and the focal point of Welsh resistance to English sovereignty. His territory, the lordship of Gwynedd, included the old counties of Anglesey, Caernarvon, and Merioneth, now conveniently renamed Gwynedd by the recent reorganisation of local government. Welsh resistance to English rule had reached its climax under Llywelyn ap Iorwerth, Llywelyn ap Gruffydd's grandfather, in the first half of the thirteenth century when he extended his territory eastwards as far as Chester and southwards as far as Carmarthen Bay, eventually declaring himself Prince of all Wales. After his death in 1240 he was succeeded briefly by his son David (1240–46), under whom Welsh territory shrank again. In turn, David was succeeded by Llywelyn ap Gruffydd who strove to continue his grandfather's policy and who first came up against Edward in 1256, long before the final struggle which was to take place when Edward became king.

The immediate cause of this early contest was Edward's attempt to impose English law on his Welsh possessions. The Welsh refused to give up their traditional laws and they turned to Llywelyn ap Gruffydd for help. Glad of the opportunity to exercise his leadership Llywelyn quickly occupied Denbighshire and Flintshire, only two royal castles holding out, Dyserth and Deganway. Edward's attempts to regain his territory ended in failure and Llywelyn remained in possession. Eventually, after the Barons' War (1258–67), Edward and Llywelyn agreed to the Treaty of Shrewsbury in 1267, arranged by the papal legate. This was something of a victory for the Welsh, for it left them in possession of Flintshire and Denbighshire and recognised Llywelyn as Prince of all Wales. However, it also brought about peace which Edward wanted and which endured until the end of his father's reign.

However, within a few years of ascending the throne in 1272 Edward was again in conflict with Llywelyn ap Gruffydd, and it was this conflict which led directly to the construction of the outstanding range of castles in North Wales. Before dealing with these, something needs to be said about the existing castles in the area, because some of these early castles were reused by Edward as part of his control of the North Wales region.

The earliest castles in the area were at Chester and Shrewsbury which were established within five years of the Conquest, between 1066 and 1071,

Previous page:
General view of Rhuddlan Castle, looking across the River Clwyd. Rhuddlan, started in 1277, was one of Edward I's earliest castles in North Wales.

Opposite:
Edward I seated with bishops and monks before him.

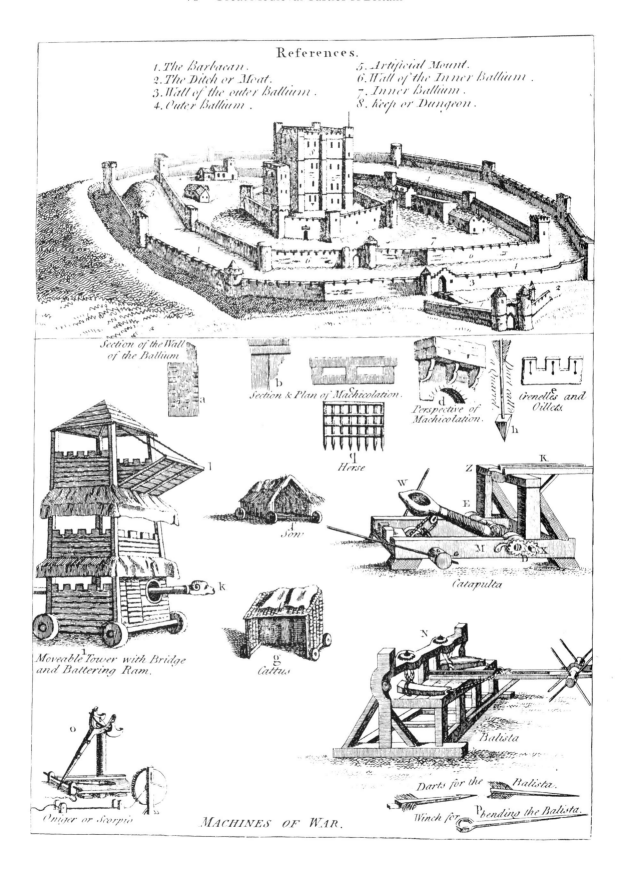

References.
1. The Barbacan.   5. Artificial Mount.
2. The Ditch or Moat.   6. Wall of the Inner Ballium.
3. Wall of the outer Ballium. 7. Inner Ballium.
4. Outer Ballium.   8. Keep or Dungeon.

Section of the Wall of the Ballium.
Section & Plan of Machicolation.
Perspective of Machicolation.
Crenelles and Oillets.
Dart called a Quarrel.
Herse.
Moveable Tower with Bridge and Battering Ram.
Sow.
Cattus.
Catapulta.
Balista.
Oniger or Scorpio.
Darts for the Balista.
Winch for bending the Balista.
MACHINES OF WAR.

forming the seats of two of the great Marcher lords, the Earls of Chester and Shrewsbury. At this stage the castles were almost certainly of earth and timber, in a motte-and-bailey arrangement, although the timber was later replaced by stone. Within another fifteen years (by 1086, when William died) there were further castles at Rhuddlan, Oswestry, and Montgomery, again of the earth-and-timber motte-and-bailey type. These were followed by several dozen more to judge from the existing earthwork remains, many of them in the Flintshire/Denbighshire area, probably reflecting the increasing control exercised by the Earls of Chester over the North Wales region. Most of them have little or no recorded history and have no relevance to the later medieval castle. Only Rhuddlan, mentioned already, and an original motte-and-bailey castle at Caernarvon, will be mentioned again.

The remaining early stone-built castles can be divided into two groups. The smaller group, of three, consists of the castles of Deganway, Dyserth, and Montgomery, all built by Henry III. In fact, these are the only three entirely new castles he ever built. In spite of his long reign and the large resources he expended, most of his efforts were directed to the repair, maintenance, and improvement of existing castles rather than the building of new ones. Not much remains of either Deganway or Dyserth which were effectively superseded by Edward's castles at Conway and Rhuddlan respectively, but Montgomery survives as an example of Henry's work. It is perhaps an indication of the long-standing nature of the North Wales problem that Henry's only new castles were in that area.

The second group consists of native Welsh castles, concentrated mostly in Gwynedd (formerly Anglesey, Caernarvon, and Merioneth). These were castles erected by the Welsh for their own protection against the encroaching Marcher lords. The area must have been plagued for long periods by almost continuous petty warfare, with castles and towns changing hands at frequent intervals. There were about a dozen such castles although only seven have surviving visible remains: Criccieth, Dolwyddelan, Castell y Bere, Dolbadarn, Dinas Bran, Ewloe, and Dolforwyn. The first three are important because they were reused by Edward I, Criccieth in particular being heavily rebuilt in Edwardian style. Criccieth, Dolwyddelan, Castell y Bere, and Dinas Bran all had rectangular keeps, while those at Dolbadarn and Dolforwyn were circular. The keep at Ewloe was apsidal, that is, rounded at one end, square at the other. Criccieth, Dolwyddelan, and Castell y Bere will be described later as part of Edward's building programme.

Edward's castle-building activities in North Wales included ten new or virtually new castles: Builth, Flint, Rhuddlan, Aberystwyth, Ruthin, Hope, Conway, Caernarvon, Beaumaris, and Harlech. Of these not much remains of Aberystwyth, Hope, and Builth, and the latter is not, strictly speaking, in North Wales anyway, although it was certainly involved in events there. However, some details of their structure are known and will be dealt with later. In fact, at both Builth and Hope there had been earlier castles but Edward's rebuilding appears to have been on a scale sufficiently large to justify their treatment as new castles. The remaining castles were entirely new and are splendidly preserved. With the exception of Ruthin, which is within the grounds of an hotel, all of them are in the care of the

As castles became more sophisticated, so too did the weapons designed to attack them. Seen here is some of the equipment used in siege warfare.

Department of the Environment and are therefore readily accessible. They form by far the most impressive and informative group of late medieval castles in the British Isles, or anywhere else for that matter, and are an eloquent testimony to Edward I's endeavours in North Wales.

The new royal castles and the three restored Welsh castles were by no means the total of castle-building activity in North Wales at this time. There were also four new, or virtually new, buildings which although not strictly 'royal' castles were nevertheless very much a part of Edward's policy and were probably built in conjunction with the other castle-building activities going on in the area. These 'lordship' castles were built by men to whom Edward granted great tracts of land, the revenues from which financed the building of the castle (which was an integral part of the arrangement). Although not paid for by the crown, there is little doubt that at the four sites involved (Hawarden, Denbigh, Holt, and Chirk) there was considerable co-operation and consultation with the king's builders, and the advice of the master builder, James of St George, was almost certainly sought and just as certainly heeded.

In summary, then, castle-building work was proceeding on seventeen sites in and around North Wales during the last few decades of the thirteenth century. Fourteen new or virtually new castles were being built and three Welsh ones were being adapted to English use; in addition, four border fortresses (Chester, Shrewsbury, Oswestry, and Montgomery) were being strengthened. North Wales at this time must have been a hive of building activity, not only because of work on the separate sites but also because of the necessary movement of men and materials on the scale required for such a vast undertaking.

The events which led Edward to commit himself to this huge expenditure of money, time, and effort can be described briefly. In Edward's absence abroad (1272–4), the Archbishop of York, Roger Mortimer, and Robert Burnel, all three appointed by Edward as his representatives while he was away, acted as regents. Through them all the great earls and barons, with the exception of Llywelyn, declared their allegiance to the new king. Llywelyn saw himself as the sovereign of an independent Wales, owing homage to no man. Even after Edward's return in 1274 he failed to declare his allegiance and eventually it became clear that, despite all his excuses, he had no intention of doing so. In 1276, his defiance was translated into open warfare along the Welsh border, most particularly in Cheshire and Shropshire, so frequently the battleground in the see-saw contest between the English and the Welsh.

Late in 1276 Edward decided that the time had come for decisive action against Llywelyn and preparations were made for a campaign in North Wales in the following year. The details of the campaign can be summarised quite briefly. Starting from Chester, Edward advanced along the North Wales coast via Flint and Rhuddlan where new castles were begun almost immediately. Llywelyn offered very little resistance and simply retreated into the mountain mass of Snowdonia, probably feeling that he could remain there in safety until he was ready to resume his marauding along the English border. But he reckoned without Edward's determination. Llywelyn was left where he was, but all the exits from Snowdonia were blocked and communication with Anglesey, the source of his food supply, were cut off.

Before the year was out Llywelyn's forces were starving and in November he emerged to accept the terms of the Treaty of Conway. The terms were nominally severe, but Edward was magnanimous and did not enforce them. At Christmas Llywelyn attended court at Westminster and made his long delayed homage to the king. There was peace again in North Wales, at least for the moment.

The Treaty of Conway represented the achievement of Edward's short-term objective, the defeat of Llywelyn ap Gruffydd. But simultaneously with the campaign which produced this result he also made the first moves in a longer-term policy, the containment of the Welsh within more or less fixed boundaries. This involved the construction of six new or virtually new castles, at Builth and Aberystwyth in mid-Wales, and at Flint, Rhuddlan, Hawarden, and Ruthin in North Wales. They were begun in 1277 or shortly thereafter and in themselves represent a very considerable castle-building programme, although the major works, occasioned by the war of 1282–3, were still to come. It should be emphasised that in 1277 Edward's objectives, even the long-term ones, were limited. He had, at that time, no intention of taking over direct control of North Wales. That decision was reached only as a result of the second outbreak of trouble in the area some five years later.

The first of the six castles to be started was at Builth, in the former county of Brecon, now Powys. There had been a motte-and-bailey castle there since about 1100, and this had been refortified by John about a century later. This castle had been completely destroyed by Llywelyn in 1260, in the course of the Barons' War, so that when Edward came to build in 1277 he was virtually starting from new. He did not, however, have a completely free hand. What Llywelyn did not destroy were, of course, the earthworks of the motte-and-bailey arrangement, and unless Edward was prepared to find a new site he had to take these into account in planning his new castle. Nothing now remains of Edward's castle either, although a summary (in Latin) of the work completed by 1280 indicates most of its salient features. The motte appears to have been surmounted by a shell-keep, that is, a circular curtain wall, with buildings against its inner face. Below this was an inner bailey with a stone curtain wall, six wall towers, and a double-towered gatehouse, surrounded by a ditch, beyond which was a stone-walled outer bailey. For 1277 the plan is old-fashioned, but as already indicated, this was dictated by the existing earthwork remains. It was probably simpler to accept the limitations imposed by these than to try to put a different type of castle on to a foundation which had not been designed for it. It would be difficult to believe that the towers mentioned above were other than circular, so to that extent the curtain wall, the towers, and the gatehouse were up-to-date for 1277. The castle was seriously damaged by Welsh rebels early in the fifteenth century, during Owen Glendower's uprising, and although repaired shortly afterwards, it was probably destroyed during Elizabeth's reign (1558–1603). As its function as a castle was at an end, it is likely that the rubble was used for building materials.

At Aberystwyth, as at Builth, virtually nothing remains above ground. Again, however, there is some evidence of its former appearance, as well as a well-preserved site at Rhuddlan which it appears to have resembled closely, so that any further comment on Aberystwyth will be deferred until Rhuddlan has been dealt with.

The two sites most closely associated with the 1277 campaign, and with Edward's policy of making his major North Wales castles independent of land supplies, were Flint and Rhuddlan. Like Conway, Caernarvon, Harlech, Beaumaris, Criccieth, and indeed Aberystwyth, they could be supplied by sea so that they could not be starved out by any Welsh siege. The ring of such castles around the North Wales coast was Edward's answer to the incessant warfare of the previous century or so. Work at Flint began in 1277. By the end of July nearly two thousand men were involved and some three thousand by the end of August. However, not all of these were necessarily engaged on Flint Castle. Flint appears to have been an assembly point for workers who had been recruited for castle building, and many of them probably moved on from there quite quickly to sites such as Rhuddlan and Ruthin where work was going on at the same time. The eventual cost of Flint Castle was around £7,000, representing the equivalent of a modern outlay of about £1½ million pounds.

Perhaps the most unusual aspect of Flint Castle is the fact that it boasts a circular keep, the internal plan of which has never been satisfactorily explained. In other respects the castle is what one would expect in the second half of the thirteenth century: a rectangular enclosure (185 x 165 ft overall) with boldly projecting corner towers. The tower at the south-east angle (the keep), is, however, much larger than the others (c. 70 ft in diameter), and is separated from the main enclosure (the Inner Ward) by its own surrounding ditch. The Inner Ward had a moat only on its southern and western sides; on the two remaining sides the waters of the River Dee originally came virtually up to its walls. On the southern, landward side, there was a large Outer Ward surrounded by a plain curtain wall with a wide moat beyond.

The feature at Flint that has given rise to most discussion is the great circular tower at the south-east corner. Its position, at one corner of the Inner Ward, is not new. At a number of other sites there is a ditch between a circular keep and a courtyard; Bothwell (p. 31); Kildrummy (p. 31); and Caldicot (p. 183). At all of these, however, the main curtain wall runs across the intervening ditch and up to the walls of the keep. At Flint, on the other hand, the keep is absolutely separate from the rest of the castle and is approachable only by a drawbridge. To that extent it is an improvement on the castles mentioned above, and this complete isolation is perhaps one justification for James of St George's design. Further justification may be found in the position of the keep in relation to the other parts of the castle. By its position it dominates the Inner Ward to the north-west and the Outer Ward to the south. It also dominates the harbour to the east, a vital point in a castle intended to be supplied by sea.

The most controversial aspect of the keep at Flint is the plan of the lower storey. This consists of inner and outer walls with a circular gallery or passage between, running the whole circuit of the tower. The gallery is at a slightly higher level than the central room or basement (c. 25 ft in diameter) and communication between the two is by means of three doorways and three short flights of steps. The only access to this lower storey is via the entrance passage of the tower and a flight of steps, which,

Opposite top:
View of the great keep-like tower at the south-east angle of Flint Castle.

Opposite bottom:
Aerial view of Flint showing the ditch separating the keep from the rest of the castle.

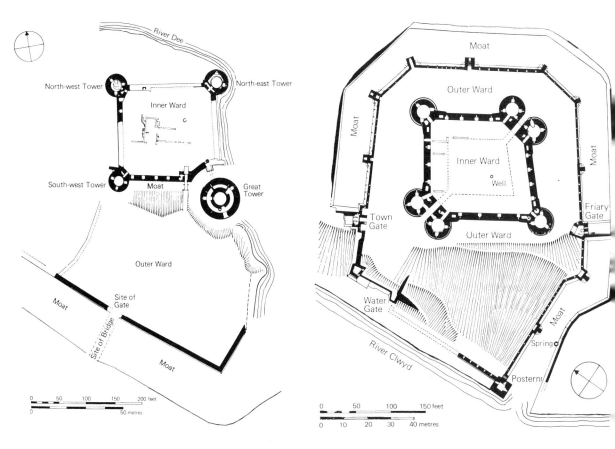

Left:
Plan of Flint showing the
rectangular Inner Wall and
the Outer Wall to the south.

Right:
Rhuddlan was the first
concentric castle built by
James of St George in North
Wales.

passing over the top of the gallery, lead directly into the central basement
room. These are the main structural details of the Flint basement. The
controversy centres on what they mean in practical terms. Perhaps the
most likely explanation is the one put forward by W. D. Simpson. He
suggests that attackers who had succeeded in crossing the moat and
breaking through the doorway of the keep would then probably rush on
along the entrance passage and down the flight of steps into the basement,
presuming that this was the main means of access to the keep as a whole.
Instead, they would end up in a dimly-lit, circular basement which led
nowhere. Moreover, defenders concealed in the surrounding gallery could
then emerge from the three doorways (Simpson's internal sally-ports), and
assail them from three sides at once, in a confined space. In the present
state of our knowledge this appears to be the best solution available,
although arrow loops from the gallery to the central room might have been
more effective (and safer for defenders), than three 'internal sally-ports'.

Like a number of other North Wales castles Flint was accompanied by a
walled town, containing a settlement of English people whom Edward
induced to settle there as part of his policy of promoting peace and security.

Of the six castles planned in 1277 there seems little doubt that Rhuddlan,
near the mouth of the River Clwyd, was regarded as the most important.
Certainly during the first full year of its construction (1278) more money
was spent on it than on Flint, Aberystwyth, and Builth combined, nearly
£3,000—the equivalent in modern terms of about £600,000. The site owes

much of its importance to its position at a river crossing which was also part of the coastal route into the heart of North Wales. As mentioned earlier, a motte-and-bailey castle was built at Rhuddlan within a few years of the Conquest, the earthworks of which are still visible a little to the south of the present castle. The motte was originally surmounted by a wooden tower but there is some evidence that it was replaced by a stone keep, probably in the twelfth century. The other buildings, however, were still of timber, for there are records that they were being repaired, with timber, as late as 1242. Like Edward's later castle, this Norman structure was accompanied by a walled town, with earthwork and timber defences, of which parts of the ditch are still visible to the south and east of the motte. In the centuries following the Conquest castle and town changed hands many times in the see-saw struggle between the Marcher lords and the Welsh. It was in English hands in 1242 when the repairs mentioned above were carried out, but by 1256 it was in Llywelyn ap Gruffydd's hands where it remained until Edward's campaign in 1277.

Edward's new castle at Rhuddlan was not only a replacement for the existing castle on the site, but also for the castle at Dyserth, built by his father, Henry III, in 1246, and destroyed by Llywelyn ap Gruffydd in 1263, during the Barons' War. The works at Rhuddlan included not only a building operation (the castle itself), but also a very considerable engineering job (the re-channelling of the River Clwyd), and of the two the engineering work was probably the greater achievement. Rhuddlan is about 2½ miles from the sea and in order to ensure the delivery of sea-borne supplies and reinforcements, Edward immediately put in hand work which would allow ships to sail right up to the castle. The lower reaches of the river at that time were probably badly silted and followed a meandering course through marshy land. Edward straightened the channel, probably by cutting across the numerous bends, and made it of uniform depth throughout, deep enough to accommodate vessels of up to forty tons fully laden. The present course of the Clwyd from Rhuddlan to the sea is one of the lasting results of Edward's work in 1277 and the years immediately following.

Rhuddlan, planned if not actually begun in the same year as Flint (1277), was a very different type of castle, built on concentric lines, the first of four such to be built by James of St George in North Wales. The most substantial remnant of the castle is the Inner Ward which is diamond-shaped rather than rectangular in plan. It is surrounded by a high curtain wall and six drum towers, four of which form two twin-towered gatehouses at diagonally opposite corners, east and west. There are single towers at the north and south angles. The curtain wall is 9 ft thick, increasing to 11 ft at the towers, which are 40 ft in diameter, similar to the dimensions at Flint, Conway, and Beaumaris, as if there was something of a standard size. The towers still stand 65 ft high and the curtain wall, in places, 40 ft, both close to their original heights of (probably) about 70 ft and 45 ft. Each stretch of curtain wall is pierced by four arrow slits, except on the north-west where there are only three, a doorway between the Inner and Outer Wards occupying the position of the fourth. There are similar arrow slits in each tower, three each in the two angle towers and four each in the four gate towers, making thirty-seven firing positions in all. All four towers were four storeys in height and the south tower additionally had a basement. This range of circular rooms, each about 20 ft in diameter, would have provided quite a lot of the castle's accommodation, but the larger apartments such as the hall and kitchen would have been built against the inner face of the curtain wall, probably in timber-framed style, leaving the centre of the Inner Ward as an open courtyard.

The Inner Ward (c. 150 x 130 ft internally) stood within an Outer Ward which surrounded it closely on three sides but less closely on the fourth side, towards the river. To that extent it is not strictly concentric but quite clearly the riverside situation and the need for a dock made it desirable, and indeed necessary, to extend the Outer Ward so that the western wall was washed by the river and its southern wall formed one side of the dock. The concentric principle was only marginally infringed and the gain in ensuring sea-borne supplies considerable. In keeping with this three-sided arrangement there is a moat on only three sides as well, although the river and the dock between them fill the same function on the remainder of the circuit. The moat (c. 50 ft wide and 15 ft deep) was dry (because of its height above river level), and was stone-lined on both inner and outer faces. The inner face, carried upwards, formed the outer curtain wall which probably stood 6 or 7 ft high above the level of the Outer Ward. It was pierced by arrow slits, a series low in the wall directed downwards to cover the moat and an alternating series at a higher level suitable for a standing archer to direct fire across the ditch. This outer curtain wall was only 2–3 ft thick and not wide enough to carry a rampart walk. It was, therefore, probably not crenellated, but probably had a plain horizontal top. In effect, the Outer Ward was the rampart walk, with fire directed through the curtain wall, via the arrow slits, rather than over it. The external face of the curtain was strengthened by a series of buttresses and turrets. The turrets concealed flights of steps down into the moat, forming sally-ports from which an attacker might be taken by surprise. On the outer edge of the moat a timber palisade formed an additional outer obstacle to the castle's enemies.

On the southern side of the site the inner and outer retaining walls of the moat were continued down the slope to the river to form a small dock. The river level was higher then and at high tide there would have been sufficient water to flood the outer part of the dock, allowing a ship to berth and unload under the cover of the castle defences. At one side of the dock entrance there was a strong square tower (Gillot's Tower, still substantially preserved), which could not only protect the dock and ships therein, but also act as a watch tower, commanding the river in both directions. Immediately alongside the tower was an entrance (Dock Gate) to the lowest part of the Outer Ward.

Accompanying the castle was a new walled town, in furtherance of Edward's policy of settling groups of loyal English traders among the Welsh to form secure centres in times of trouble. Like Flint, the town was surrounded by timber-and-earthwork defences rather than a stone wall, and remains of the earthworks can still be seen on the north-west side. The existing streets reflect the original Edwardian plan, with the High Street dividing the town into two parts and two streets at right angles further subdividing each side into blocks which still form the basis of the present layout.

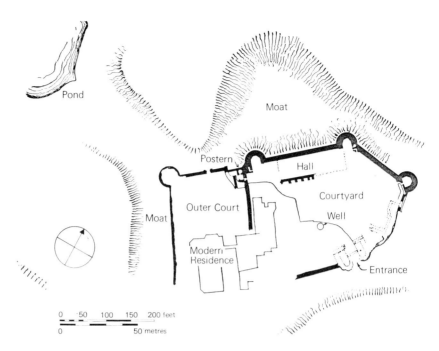

Plan of Ruthin Castle
(Clwyd).

Aberystwyth, of which now very little remains, followed the same
general lines as Rhuddlan. Both inner and outer curtain walls were
diamond-shaped in plan, with the longer axis running north and south.
There was a double-towered gatehouse at the east angle of the inner
curtain and single towers at the other three angles. There was a postern
gate in the north-west curtain, and there were two entrances in the outer
curtain, in line with those inside. In many ways the most interesting aspect
of both Rhuddlan and Aberystwyth is the adoption of a diamond-shaped
plan. In the absence of any concrete evidence this can probably best be put
down to an interest in experimenting with plans other than the purely
rectangular. Further variations, around the same period, are the triangular
plan of Caerlaverock Castle (p. 129), and the pentagonal plan of Holt
Castle (p. 113).

Ruthin Castle, at the upper end of the Clwyd valley, was the complement
of Rhuddlan, about 15 miles away to the north, near the mouth of the
river. Between them these two formed a front line with Flint and
Hawarden to the rear and behind these the old base of Chester, the five sites
involved forming a great fortified triangle which might effectively contain
any renewed aggression by the Welsh. Ruthin Castle stands within the
grounds of an hotel, called (inevitably) The Ruthin Castle Hotel, in the town
of Ruthin. The hotel buildings, formerly a private house, occupy the south-
western portion of the castle (open only to hotel guests), but enough
remains elsewhere to enable the main lines of the plan to be established.
The inner ward was pentagonal in plan, with round towers at four of the
angles (one of them now gone), and a twin-towered gatehouse. Three sides
of the ward (north, west, and south) were at right angles to each other; the
fourth side projected in triangular fashion to the east, with a round tower
at the apex. The space enclosed by the inner ward was about 350 x 250 ft
with the hall (at least 100 ft long by 40 ft wide) built against the north

Much of the site of Ruthin Castle is now occupied by the Ruthin Castle Hotel. The castle remains are beyond and to the right of the hotel.

curtain wall. There was a rectangular outer ward, at a lower level, on the west side, with angle towers at its north-west and south-west angles, the latter now gone.

Hawarden Castle (Clwyd) is the last of the six castles connected with the war of 1277. The lordship was granted to Roger de Clifford in 1281, almost certainly on condition that he rebuild the castle there, thus completing

Edward's first castle-building programme in Wales. There had been a motte-and-bailey castle on the site probably since Norman times and, as at Builth, the remains dictated to a large degree any additions in the latter part of the thirteenth century. Fortunately, the motte was formed by a natural hillock of rock and this enabled it to support the substantial stone tower which formed the nucleus of the new castle. The earlier motte-and-bailey castle, in which the timberwork had later been replaced by stone, was destroyed by Llywelyn ap Gruffydd in 1265. Subsequently the lordship changed hands a number of times in quick succession until eventually it came to Roger de Clifford. Hawarden was one of the castles attacked at the opening of the 1282–3 war, probably because, like a number of others in the North Wales area, it was still under construction and was to the Welsh a visible symbol of increasing English domination. Roger de Clifford had been in possession for only about fifteen months when the castle was attacked so that it is unlikely that building work was then very far advanced. A substantial part of the castle must have been built after 1283 when the Welsh had been defeated for the second time.

It consists of a great round tower, over 60 ft in diameter, standing on the motte, with a polygonal bailey, enclosed by a curtain wall to the east. The plan is an old-fashioned one, but it was almost certainly dictated by what was there already. Without moving to an entirely new site it would have been difficult to build anything radically different. A concentric castle, for example, would have been out of the question. The tower is described (in the Welsh Commission Inventory, p. 37) as being 40 ft high. This is certainly the height of the present remains, but this seems very low for a tower over 60 ft in diameter; it seems likely that the height was nearer 60 or 70 ft with three instead of the postulated two storeys. At ground-floor level the walls are 15 ft thick with three arrow slits pointing north, west, and south; the entrance was on the east, facing into the bailey, some 30 ft below and reached by a flight of stone steps up the side of the mound. At first-floor level the main central room is octagonal (the room below is circular), and there is a passage or gallery in the thickness of the wall from which a series of arrow slits opened. There is also a small chapel in the thickness of the wall, some 14 ft long and 7 ft wide. If there was a third storey then it too presumably consisted of a large central room supplemented by mural chambers in the thickness of the wall, unless there was another gallery similar to the one below, as in the two-tier system at Caernarvon. There are many other features in the tower which suggest the hand of James of St George, and although Hawarden was a lordship castle rather than a royal castle there seems little doubt that Master James was involved in its design and construction. Roger de Clifford's second marriage took place at St Georges d'Espéranche in 1273, during his stay there with Edward, so he was probably already well acquainted with the king's master of works and would be likely to seek his advice and assistance in any castle-building project of his own.

Much of the curtain wall of the polygonal bailey has now gone but there was at least one circular, projecting tower at the south-east angle. The Hall, of which only a fragment remains, was built against the inner face of the east curtain wall. The entrance was on the north-eastern side, although not much of it survives above ground.

4
The Later Welsh Campaigns

Hawarden Castle was still under construction when the Welsh rose again in 1282. The five years since the treaty of 1277 had been uneasy ones, marked by growing resentment of Edward's policy on the part of the Welsh, not only in the north but in the south also. They saw Edward's castle-building programme as a sign of growing oppression, but what most excited their wrath was his attempt to impose English law on the territories under his direct control (broadly Flint, Denbigh, Cardigan, and Carmarthen). The supression of Welsh traditions and institutions added further fuel to the flames. Even David, Llywelyn ap Gruffydd's brother and Edward's ally against him in 1277, joined in the protests, but to no avail. The result was a reconciliation with his brother and an alliance which burst into open warfare in March 1282.

The war opened with attacks on the castles of Hawarden, Flint, Rhuddlan, Aberystwyth, Carreg Cennen, and Llandovery. David himself attacked Hawarden and captured Roger de Clifford, although on the approach of the king's forces a few months later he withdrew to the west, slighting his own castle (Caergwrle) as he went. As soon as hostilities began Llywelyn crossed the Conway from his own territory in support of his brother, and devastated the country as far to the east as Chester. Further south, insurgents in Cardigan and Carmarthen captured Aberystwyth. The castles at Flint, Hawarden, and Aberystwyth, still under construction, probably represented a particularly bitter provocation to the Welsh who saw the English grip becoming tighter and tighter.

Having treated the Welsh very magnanimously in 1277 Edward was enraged by the new outbreak and resolved to settle the Welsh problem once and for all. He summoned his forces from all quarters and soon encircled Snowdonia as he had done in 1277. On this occasion, however, Llywelyn escaped, to reappear on the upper reaches of the Wye where, before the year was out, he was killed in a minor skirmish near Builth. His brother David, Edward's former ally, then took on the leadership of the insurgents but was captured in Snowdonia the following summer (1283), as a result of treachery. With his capture the war was over and Edward could turn his full attention to the new castle-building programme which was to provide the solution to the Welsh problem. David ap Gruffydd was brought to trial in Shrewsbury and was hung, drawn, and quartered on 3 October 1283.

One of the results of the war of 1282–3 was the construction or reconstruction of no less than eleven castles, in addition to the six already described. They include what are undoubtedly the four outstanding sites in North Wales, the royal castles of Conway, Caernarvon, Harlech, and

Beaumaris, all of which are outstandingly preserved and an impressive tribute to the quality of their building. They also include three new 'lordship' castles, Holt, Chirk, and Denbigh, the last two still with substantial remains. The four remaining sites, Criccieth, Dolwyddelan, Castell y Bere, and Hope (Caergwrle) all had earlier castles on them but were rebuilt at royal expense as part of Edward's network of North Wales fortifications. Of the eight royal castles, only Hope is in too poor a state of preservation to be adequately described or discussed, but since it was in the forefront of the uprising in 1282, and was probably rebuilt before any of the other castles were begun, it will be dealt with first.

The lordship of Hope was David ap Gruffydd's reward for his support of Edward in 1277. However, five years later he used his castle there, above the present-day village of Caergwrle, as the base for his attack on Hawaiden which, with other simultaneous attacks, opened the war of 1282–3. When, in June, Edward's forces arrived at Caergwrle Castle (a more convenient name since the castle is in Caergwrle and not Hope which is about one mile to the north), they found that David had withdrawn, slighting the castle (rendering it useless) before he went. Work on rebuilding began within a week. Unfortunately, such is the present state of the remains that it is difficult to discern the full plan of the castle and impossible to distinguish between the rebuilding of 1282 and earlier work. The accounts show that building work on the castle, completed in October 1282, amounted to £300. This is a considerable outlay, but not enough for the building of a new castle or even the alteration (other than minor alteration) of an existing one. From the level of the expenditure it would appear that the building work of 1282 was limited to the rebuilding of the castle on the same lines as before, following the existing plan. Although whatever is now visible of the castle dates from 1282 (or later, allowing for subsequent additions), it is essentially the earlier castle repaired. Even so, it still probably belongs to the second half of the thirteenth century and such facts as are known of its structure tend to confirm this.

The main structure is described (in the Welsh Commission Inventory) as an irregular parallelogram, that is, an asymmetrical four-sided figure, the irregularity almost certainly being due to the shape of the hill on which it stands. There are remains of a double-towered gatehouse at the north-east angle and of a single octagonal tower at the south-west angle. It seems a reasonable assumption that there were corresponding towers at the two remaining angles, although there are no surviving remains to confirm this. If such towers did exist then Caergwrle Castle would fall into place as a typical, but fairly ordinary, castle of the second half of the thirteenth century. The lengths of the four curtain walls linking the towers give some indication of the size and possible shape of the area enclosed: north, 33 ft; south, 45 ft; east, 115 ft; west, 120 ft. The castle was thus a little on the small side but still in keeping with the general run of castles of the period. There was an outer bailey to the north-west but its defences are so ruinous that it is difficult to say anything about their original structure.

The following year, 1283, saw the beginning of three of the four major royal castles mentioned earlier: Conway, Caernarvon, and Harlech. Beaumaris did not follow until 1295, as a result of events to be described later. Of the four, only Beaumaris and Harlech are of the concentric type.

Previous page:
Aerial view of Harlech
Castle from the east.

Conway and Caernarvon follow the same broad plan, conditioned in each case by the nature of their situation, and both are accompanied by virtually complete town walls, among the best-preserved of their type in Europe.

Work on Conway Castle and town walls, which were a single project, began in March 1283. Within five years, by the end of 1287, work on both castle and town defences was virtually complete, at a cost of just over £14,000. Using a multiplication factor of about 200 this represents an outlay in modern terms of something like £3,000,000, expended on only one site in a very large building programme.

Conway Castle is situated on the North Wales coast, on a rocky knoll in the angle formed by the River Conway and its tributary the Gyffin. The site is an ideal one for a castle, but not for one of the concentric type. At Conway the plan is dictated by the situation and the shape of the castle follows the shape of the rock on which it stands. Also missing at Conway, and probably again because of the situation, are the double-towered gatehouses found in so many Edwardian castles. The site dictated a long, narrow plan; safety required two entrances, which almost inevitably meant that they had to be at the opposite, narrow ends of the castle. At these ends, however, the corner towers are only 40–50 ft apart, so that there is little or no room for gatehouses. On the other hand, the corner towers are so close anyway that they virtually form gatehouses themselves, and are further strengthened by the barbicans in front.

The essential features of Conway Castle are the eight more or less evenly spaced round towers, linked by a high curtain wall, forming a slightly irregular oblong lying east and west. The towers are 40 ft in diameter, about 70 ft high above the interior level of the castle, and about 120 ft high above the level of the town. The tower walls are 10 ft thick so that the series of superimposed rooms within each of them, which provided much of the accommodation within the castle, were some 20 ft in diameter. The curtain wall linking the towers is also about 10 ft thick and rises some 40 ft above the interior and 80 ft above the level of the town. A cross wall of similar dimensions divided the interior into two sections, the Inner Ward to the east and the Outer Ward to the west, and this division is fundamental to the understanding of the castle's design. In other circumstances the Inner Ward might well have been contained within the Outer Ward, forming a concentric arrangement. However, the severe restrictions imposed by the knoll of rock meant that the two enclosures had to be side by side. This being so, it was essential that they could be isolated from each other, should the need ever arise, which is why the dividing wall is of the same size and strength as the main, outer curtain wall, and why it was equipped with a narrow entrance with a drawbridge in front.

The main eastern and western entrances have been mentioned already. In front of each was a barbican providing additional protection. The west barbican consisted of a narrow terrace in front of the entrance with an outer curtain wall and three half-round towers on its western side. Access to the terrace was via the narrow gap (c. 8 ft wide) between the northernmost of these and the north-west tower of the castle proper, with a flight of stone steps beyond, leading up from an outer entrance between two small towers. Beyond this again was a gap, crossed originally by a drawbridge, approached by a long sloping ramp from within the walled

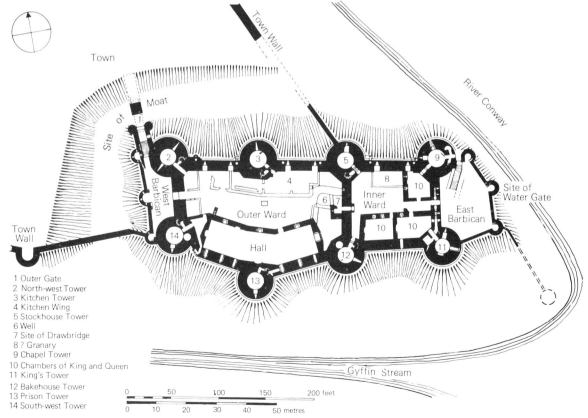

1 Outer Gate
2 North-west Tower
3 Kitchen Tower
4 Kitchen Wing
5 Stockhouse Tower
6 Well
7 Site of Drawbridge
8 ? Granary
9 Chapel Tower
10 Chambers of King and Queen
11 King's Tower
12 Bakehouse Tower
13 Prison Tower
14 South-west Tower

town area. Virtually the whole of the ramp has now disappeared, but the highest portion immediately in front of the entrance is still preserved. The town wall abuts the southernmost barbican tower on one side and the Stockhouse Tower on the other. This means, in effect, that the Outer (western) Ward of the castle stood within the town walls, although still capable of separate defence should the town fall. The western entrance was probably the normal means of access to the castle.

The east barbican protected a gateway which was probably intended more as an emergency escape route than a regular means of access. It had a wider terrace than the western entrance but was likewise defended by an outer curtain wall with three projecting towers. Between the northernmost of these and the Chapel Tower a flight of steps led down to a Water Gate, now gone, on the Conway shore. The division of the castle, by means of a cross-wall and its relationship to the town's defences, meant that the Inner (eastern) Ward and its barbican were effectively beyond the town walls. This meant that even if the town and the Outer Ward fell to an enemy, the Inner Ward could survive, with a way of escape should that prove necessary, and a means of supply should prolonged resistance be resolved upon.

The four towers at the angles of the Inner Ward, which is more or less square in plan (*c.* 80 x 70 ft), are surmounted by circular turrets some 20 ft high. Within the ward there is an L-shaped, two-storey range of buildings along the southern and eastern curtain walls, leaving a small courtyard in the north-west quarter (*c.* 50 x 40 ft). The upper storey of the L-shaped range, together with the corresponding floors of the two adjacent towers, formed a suite of private apartments for the king when he was in residence, including the King's Hall, the King's Chamber, and the Presence Chamber. The Hall was a dining-cum-living room for the royal family and their immediate followers, smaller and more private than the Great Hall in the Outer Ward (below). The King's Chamber was a more private apartment to which the royal family could withdraw from the Hall, while the Presence Chamber was a more formal apartment where affairs of state could be conducted. There was a chapel in the Chapel Tower to the north-east and royal bed-chambers in the King's Tower to the south-east.

The main building in the much larger Outer Ward was the Great Hall, somewhat irregular in plan as a result of being built against the angled, south curtain wall. This was a very large apartment, some 120 ft long and 32 ft wide internally, and must have been a most imposing structure when complete. Although it probably was used for great banquets and other social occasions, no doubt it was also used very much as the administrative and judicial centre of the town and the surrounding area, for trials, hearings, and other necessary business of the community. The kitchens and stables were placed against the north curtain wall although little of them now remains. A considerable amount of accommodation was provided by the towers, most of which had three storeys. These must have provided rooms and suites of rooms for the senior officers and officials housed in the castle. The two western towers, flanking the west entrance, formed a suite of rooms for the Constable (or Commandant) of the castle, placed in charge of it by the king.

Integral with the castle, and built at the same time, was the new walled town of Conway, the best surviving example of Edward's policy of planting

Opposite top:
Conway looks the epitome of the stern, uncompromising medieval castle, but its dark and forbidding exterior was, in fact, originally limewashed and the white walls and towers must have stood out vividly against the landscape.

Opposite bottom:
The plan of Conway Castle was largely dictated by the natural knoll of rock on which it stood, making a concentric arrangement impossible, and the two principal enclosures were therefore placed side by side.

The town wall of Conway was planned and built with the castle as a single undertaking. The triangular circuit contains twenty-one wall towers, a series of which are shown here.

colonies of loyal English settlers among the rebellious Welsh to provide a series of secure centres in time of trouble, centres which would provide support for the castle rather than the means of overthrowing it. The relationship of the castle to the town wall has already been indicated. From the Stockhouse Tower the town wall ran off in a straight line to the north-west, parallel to the shore, for some 400 yds; it then turned and ran south-west for about 420 yds, the greater part again in a straight line. At the west angle it turned again and ran on an irregular but generally eastward course, rejoining the castle at the south tower of the west barbican, completing a triangular circuit with the castle in the eastern corner. On this circuit there are three double-towered gates (Upper Gate, Lower Gate, and Mill Gate), and twenty-one wall towers at intervals of 130 ft on the north-west and south and 150 ft on the north-east, the side towards the river. There was an additional tower, now gone, at the end of a wing wall extending from the north angle, restricting access to the beach below the town walls. There was also a postern gate near the first tower to the north-west of the castle, from which anyone attacking the Inner Ward could be taken by surprise from the rear. As at Rhuddlan, the present street plan of Conway is the street plan of the medieval town as laid out in Edward's time. The present church (St Mary's) is the original monastic church of the abbey which was moved to make way for the building of the castle and town, after being bought out by Edward.

In terms of plan Conway and Caernarvon are very much the same type of castle, but they differ noticeably in their external appearance. Conway was plain, practical, and down-to-earth. Its eight (virtually identical) towers and linking curtain wall were unredeemed by any decorative features, and the whole castle was, in any case, completely limewashed when finished, further emphasising its utilitarian role. Caernarvon, on the other hand, was a castle of 'unparalleled architectural magnificence' (to quote Douglas Simpson's words), with thirteen towers, no two of which were exactly alike, and colour-patterned stonework which was quite clearly meant to be seen and admired and not covered with anything so mundane as whitewash. Why this marked difference in treatment of two castles which formed part of the same overall plan, which had the same basic function, and which were started in the same year under the direction of the same master-builder, James of St George? The simple answer is that Edward intended Caernarvon Castle to be a centre of royal government and a palace for the Prince of Wales; but the reasons why he chose Caernarvon in preference to anywhere else calls for some more detailed comment.

Before the Edwardian castle was built there was an earlier motte-and-bailey castle on the site, built in the early days of the Conquest, and this comes into the story. But before both medieval castles there was an even earlier fortification, a Roman auxiliary fort (Segontium), the remains of which can still be seen some 700 yards from the present stone castle. Whether justified or not, this castle had become associated in Welsh legend with the Emperor (for a time) Magnus Maximus, who ruled Britain, France, Spain, and Morocco from AD 383–88. He had been declared Emperor by the British garrison, possibly at Segontium, just as Constantine the Great had been declared Emperor (and survived as such) by the troops in York in AD 306. Many emperors had been made by the army and to that extent the election of Magnus Maximus was part of a long and well-established tradition. However, he never finally succeeded in being recognised in Rome. When he invaded Italy in 387 the Emperor of the eastern Roman Empire, Theodosius, took action and Maximus was defeated and executed six years after his election by the army. He was never fully Emperor of the western Empire, even though he ruled much of it for six years. None the less he had the aura of imperial power and that aura, in Welsh legend and in the Welsh imagination, became associated with the site of Segontium and, inevitably, Caernarvon. There seems little doubt that Edward was aware of this legendary association and that it influenced his choice of Caernarvon Castle as the seat of government. As such, and as the residence of the Prince of Wales, it needed to be something more than a utilitarian castle. It had to be a fitting symbol of kingship, something with a striking external appearance and this goes a long way to explaining the very different architecture of Caernarvon Castle as compared with the other great castles of North Wales, Conway, Harlech, and Beaumaris.

Impressive as Caernarvon still is, it may not yet tell the full story of Edward's intentions. The motte-and-bailey castle which preceded the present stone castle has been mentioned already. With the huge resources at his disposal it would have been perfectly easy for Edward to remove the motte entirely in building his new castle, and indeed it would have seemed a sensible thing to do. A motte could have had very little military use in such a castle. But this mound was retained, explaining the shape of the east bailey which surrounded it; the last portion of it survived until 1870. (The terms east and west bailey are used since there appears to be some disagreement as to which of the two enclosures is the Inner and which is the Outer Bailey). Since the motte was quite deliberately retained in such circumstances, there must have been a very good reason for doing so, and Douglas Simpson has suggested that it was to add even more to the

The interior of Caernarvon Castle now forms a single space, but originally it was intended to divide it into east and west wards by means of a building across the middle of the castle.

architectural impressiveness of the castle: 'Evidently it was intended to rear upon the motte a lofty tower, dominating the entire castle, like Edward III's remodelling of the round tower that crowns the motte at Windsor. Plantagenet imperialism was to have a second capital in the new Principality of Wales'. The plan was never carried out, probably because the castle as a whole was never quite finished and such a non-military feature would almost certainly have come last in the sequence of building.

The two most striking architectural features of Caernarvon Castle are the polygonal towers, instead of the more usual round form, and the

colour-banded masonry. Although these features occur separately elsewhere they are found significantly together in one place, the city walls of
Constantinople, the eastern capital of the Roman Empire founded by
Constantine the Great (AD 306–37), although the walls were actually built
by a later emperor Theodosius (AD 379–95), the man who defeated
Magnus Maximus. Caernarvon was the reputed birthplace of Constantine
and the idea of imitating the walls of his capital in the new castle there must
have been an appealing one, both to Edward and to his Welsh subjects. As
a result of the crusades there must have been many men in Edward's
service who had seen Constantinople, possibly including James of St
George himself. There was also a description of the city in 1203 by G. de
Villehardouin which must have been familiar to many who had not been
there. The resemblance between the two sites, however, is so close that it
suggests an actual eye-witness and there was at least one such person in
Edward's following: Sir William de Cicon, a branch of whose family held
territory in Euboca, part of the Latin Empire of Constantinople, who was
almost certainly familiar at first hand with Constantinople and its defences.

Work on the castle began in June 1283 and on the associated town wall
the following year. After about ten years some £12,000 had been spent
(£2,500,000 in modern terms), but the work was by no means complete,
and there was to follow an event which was to add considerably to the
expense. In 1294 the Welsh rose in revolt and Caernarvon was captured
and held for six months, during which time a great deal of damage was
done to both castle and town walls. This damage had to be made good,
greatly adding to the ultimate cost. Between 1295 and 1301 another £5,600
was added to the bill and by 1330, when work was still going on, the total
cost of Caernarvon Castle and town walls was in the region of £27,000
(£5,500,000 in modern terms). The sheer size of this bill is a reflection of
the architectural elaboration of Caernarvon Castle. The same plan carried
out in the style of Conway Castle would certainly have cost considerably
less.

The castle and accompanying town are situated near the south-west end
of the Menai straits on an expanding tongue of land between the mouths of
the Rivers Seiont and Cadnant. The castle forms the southern flank of the
town defences which are roughly D-shaped in plan. The castle, lying east
and west, is considerably larger than Conway, nearly 600 ft long as
compared with under 400 ft, and is correspondingly wider. The curtain wall
linking the towers is both thicker and higher on the exposed southern flank
of the castle than on the side towards the town, within the town walls. The
most notable feature of this thickened section are the two superimposed
galleries in the thickness of the wall which, together with the positions at
the wall head, provided three tiers of firing positions for the defenders. In
plan the curtain bulges out towards the east to accommodate the motte of
the earlier castle, mentioned above. The interior now forms a single space,
end to end, but the original plan, never completed, envisaged a substantial
dividing block mid-way in the castle's length, behind the King's Gate.

The curtain wall at Caernarvon is splendidly preserved, and so too are its
thirteen towers, no two of which are exactly alike. They vary in size from
the Watch Tower, less than 20 ft across, to the great Eagle Tower, with its
triple turrets, some 70 ft in diameter. They vary also in shape; although

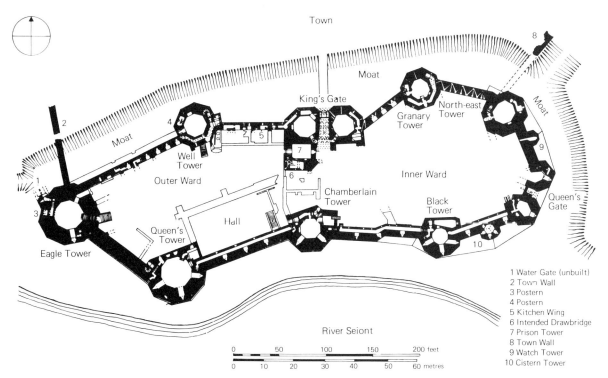

Town

Moat

King's Gate

North-east
Tower

Granary
Tower

Moat

Moat

2

Well
Tower

4

5

7

Inner Ward

9

Outer Ward

6

1

Chamberlain
Tower

Black
Tower

Queen's
Gate

3

Queen's
Tower

Hall

10

Eagle Tower

River Seiont

1 Water Gate (unbuilt)
2 Town Wall
3 Postern
4 Postern
5 Kitchen Wing
6 Intended Drawbridge
7 Prison Tower
8 Town Wall
9 Watch Tower
10 Cistern Tower

0	50	100	150	200 feet
0	10 20 30 40 50			60 metres

Caernarvon followed the same general lines as Conway but was larger. The shape of the Inner Ward was dictated by the motte of the earlier motte-and-bailey castle which survived until 1870.

they are often described as octagonal, which some of them are, there are some which have more and some which have less than eight sides, and as a group they are best described as polygonal. Four of the towers form two gatehouses (King's Gate and Queen's Gate, below). Of the remaining nine two are quite small (Watch Tower and Cistern Tower), and two very large (Eagle Tower and Queen's Tower). The other five are each about 45 ft across, although again no two are exactly alike. The Eagle Tower and the Queen's Tower are both of keep-sized proportions, but it is the Eagle Tower which is most keep-like in its position. Two-thirds of its perimeter projects beyond the castle walls and more than half beyond the town walls, very much in the manner of keeps described earlier. In the projecting section there is an additional means of entry and exit so that the Eagle Tower could be supplied separately if it was isolated from the rest of the castle, and so that, as a last resort, the defenders could make their escape if the Eagle Tower was in danger of being finally captured.

The principal gateway of the castle was the King's Gate, facing north into the town. Unfortunately the whole gatehouse block behind it was never completed but the original idea was that it should provide access from the main entrance passage to both eastern and western baileys. The main entrance passage, some 60 ft long leading in between the twin towers, was equipped with no less than six portcullises and five sets of double doors. Much of this passage survives. It was intended to lead into an octagonal hall or vestibule (a fragment of which survives), from which two passages, also equipped with doors and portcullises, led off at right angles, one to the east into the east bailey and one to the west into the west bailey. A comparable arrangement exists in Denbigh Castle (below), and there are other similarities between the two sites which suggest the hand, or at

The rampart walk and north-west angle tower at Harlech (Gwynedd), James of St George's second concentric castle in North Wales.

least the influence and advice, of one man, James of St George. The Queen's Gate, opening beyond the town walls, is of simpler, more conventional twin-towered plan. Its outer approaches have now gone and its threshold stands high above the present external ground level, which is, in fact, the bottom of the original ditch. Its outer edge, from which the bridge approaching the Queen's Gate must have sprung, has been removed to make way for later building, hence the present rather odd position of the entrance between the twin towers of the Queen's Gate, high on the castle walls.

Not much remains of the internal building and the castle was unfinished anyway. However, the foundations of the Hall survive, in the west bailey, which if the Conway plan were being followed, would indicate that this was the Outer Bailey. Similarly, the position of the Queen's Gate, corresponding to the east gate at Conway, would appear to indicate that the east bailey was the Inner Bailey, and the fact that it embraced the original motte tends to support this. However, the position of the Eagle Tower raises doubts about these attributions. If the Eagle Tower was conceived as a keep, as a final redoubt when the rest of the castle had fallen, in a position to be supplied by water, then one would have expected it to be part of the Inner Bailey, and this is presumably why both Sidney Toy and Douglas Simpson have so designated the west bailey. However, in a more recent publication (*History of the King's Works*, Vol. I, 376), Arnold Taylor follows the pattern of Conway and names the eastern end of the castle as the Inner Bailey or Ward. Much depends on the interpretation of the Eagle Tower. If it was not so much an operational keep as simply a splendid keep-like residence for the constable of Caernarvon, as has been suggested, then the other parts of the castle fall into place on the lines of Conway, although the correspondence between the two sites is not exact.

The walled town of Caernarvon, of which the walls are still substantially complete, is situated to the north of the castle and once again the present street layout follows the original Edwardian plan. The High Street running between the East and West Gates divided the area roughly into two and each half is further sub-divided by three streets at right angles, forming a series of blocks as at Rhuddlan. In spite of being conceived as the capital of North Wales the town is noticeably smaller than Conway (c. 480,000 sq ft as compared with 720,000 sq ft). Apart from the two twin-towered gates just mentioned (compared with three at Conway), there are eight other angle and interval towers (compared with twenty-one at Conway). This difference is accounted for partly by the shorter circuit and partly by the greater intervals between towers from 150 to 200 ft in the case of Caernarvon Castle.

With Harlech and Beaumaris, James of St George returned to the concentric theme which he had used at Rhuddlan, but which, because of their particular situations, was not suitable at either Conway or Caernarvon. Harlech was begun in 1283, virtually at the same time as Conway and Caernarvon, the simultaneous construction of three such formidable fortresses being an indication of Edward's determination to subdue Wales once and for all. Beaumaris was not to follow for another twelve years as a

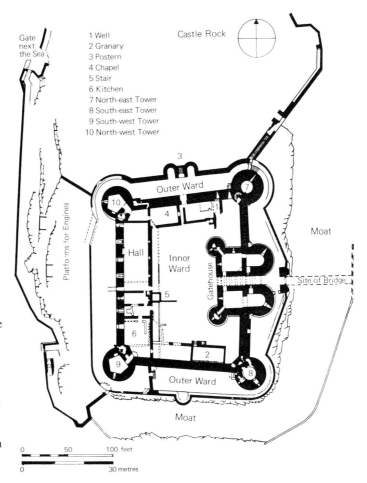

Right:
The plan of Harlech Castle (started in 1283), embraces three enclosures, two of which, the Inner and Middle Baileys, form a concentric arrangement.

Opposite:
Originally built in Norman times, Leeds Castle owes its present shape, and its extensive water defences, to Edward I who rebuilt it in the early decades of his reign.

result of events to be described later. Harlech took about seven years to build, being substantially complete by the end of 1290, although some minor works remained to be done. The cost was in the region of £9,500 (c. £2,000,000), less than Conway (£14,000) which included also the cost of the town walls, and very much less than Caernarvon Castle and town walls (£27,000) although much of the increased cost there must be attributed to the elegant architecture. Like Conway, Harlech is a fairly plain, straightforward and businesslike castle, although of a different plan.

Harlech stands at the head of a cliff overlooking the coastal plain and has natural defences on the north and west. Only on the south and east where approach was easier is there a rock-cut ditch which must have provided much of the stone for the castle's construction. The castle consists of Inner, Middle and Outer Baileys, of which, in this case, the Inner and Middle form the concentric arrangement. The Inner Bailey is rectangular (actually slightly trapeze-shaped) in plan, about 175 x 130 ft internally, with four boldly projecting angle towers, each approximately 35 ft in diameter and a massive, double-towered gatehouse midway in the east curtain wall. The curtain wall on this, the most vulnerable side of the castle, is thicker than elsewhere, up to 12 ft between the gatehouse and the south-east angle tower. The gatehouse is a massive structure, 75 ft wide and 65 ft deep, not counting the projecting angle towers at its south-west and north-west angles within the courtyard. At ground-floor level there was an entrance passage some 50 ft long with three portcullises, two double-leaved doors and eight machicolations (lines of openings in the roof of the passage through which the enemy could be attacked from above). Above ground-floor level the towers are linked to form a single structure which, on several floors, must have provided the prime accommodation in the castle, including, no doubt, that for the constable and his family.

The internal buildings are ranged around three sides of the courtyard, north, west, and south. The principal range was along the west wall and included the hall, the kitchen, and no doubt other domestic offices such as the buttery and pantry. The buildings along the other walls included a chapel and a granary. Apart from the main entrance, through the gatehouse, there were two postern gates, one on the west and one on the north. The external staircase against the back of the gatehouse is not part of the original structure.

Completely embracing the Inner Bailey and its defences is the Middle Bailey, which, in fact, takes the form of a relatively narrow terrace between the inner curtain wall and the ditch, very much in the manner of Caerphilly, although at the angles the space between the two lines at Harlech is very narrow, virtually a curving passage about 10 ft wide. Elsewhere the gap is 20–25 ft wide. In either case the defenders at the head of the inner curtain would have had enormous command over anyone attacking the outer curtain wall. This was quite plain except for an open-backed semi-circular turret in the middle of the south face. There were two small towers flanking the east gate, immediately in front of the main gatehouse, and two larger open-backed towers flanking the north entrance, in front of the north postern, providing for communication between the Middle and Outer Baileys. The latter is a much more irregular enclosure taking in the rocky slope to the north, north-west, and west of the castle

Grosmont (Gwent) was strengthened in the thirteenth century by the addition of circular wall towers.

and covering a long stepped approach up the west side of the site from the Water Gate below.

James of St George was the architect of Harlech. He was also one of its early constables. He was appointed to the post in August 1290 and held it for just over three years, until December 1293. It is quite possible, therefore, that Master James actually lived in the gatehouse which he himself had been responsible for designing and which is so characteristic of his work. In Beaumaris Castle he was to repeat this hallmark of his style not once but twice, and this is one of a number of features that make Beaumaris unique among a group of castles which were already unusual.

As mentioned earlier, the Welsh rose in revolt in September 1294, and held Caernarvon for six months, doing a great deal of damage to both castle and town walls. One of the results of this further example of Welsh

One of the showpieces of Beaumaris Castle is the chapel, housed in the D-shaped tower on the east curtain of the inner Bailey.

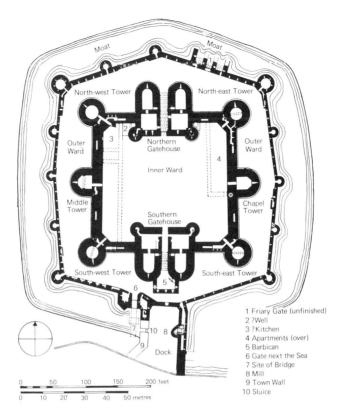

1 Friary Gate (unfinished)
2 ?Well
3 ?Kitchen
4 Apartments (over)
5 Barbican
6 Gate next the Sea
7 Site of Bridge
8 Mill
9 Town Wall
10 Sluice

In terms of its plan Beaumaris was the most complete and most elaborate concentric castle built by Edward's master builder, James of St George.

intransigence was that Edward decided he needed another castle to further strengthen the ring of defences around North Wales. Accordingly, when the revolt had been suppressed, an entirely new castle was begun at Beaumaris in Anglesey, in April 1295. Building work went on for thirty-five years, until 1330, when the cost amounted to £14,400 (c. £3,000,000 in modern terms), although the castle was never finally completed, most of the towers being roofed in at a lower level than originally planned. Nevertheless, the castle was, and still is, an impressive example of medieval fortification.

Although Caernarvon was undoubtedly the greater architectural achievement, Beaumaris was James of St George's masterpiece in terms of fortification technique. In it the medieval castle reached its fullest development and the concentric castle its most eloquent expression. One of the great advantages of the chosen site was that it was quite level, unlike either Conway, Caernarvon, or Harlech, and this allowed the architect a free hand in planning the layout of the castle, unhampered by natural features. The Inner Ward was quite symmetrical about a north/south centre line and was a large and powerful structure, with a massive curtain wall (15 ft thick), six large towers (each of c. 40 ft in diameter), and two enormous gatehouses, each nearly 100 ft square, which provided much of the castle's accommodation. The almost square curtain wall was 220 x 210 ft and the boldly projecting towers and gatehouses gave overall dimensions of about 300 x 300 ft. There was a three-quarter projecting round tower at each angle, a D-shaped tower projecting over 30 ft beyond the wall in the middle of the east and west curtains, and the huge gatehouses in the middle of the north and south curtains. The internal arrangements of the gatehouses will be considered later. The D-shaped tower on the east curtain housed the chapel, one of the show-pieces of the castle, with accommodation above—almost certainly for a priest.

Completely surrounding this inner structure, which in other circumstances would have been considered a more than adequate, not to say powerful, castle on its own, was an Outer Ward, defended by an eight-sided curtain wall, with two gatehouses (one never completed), twelve towers, a dock (capable of accommodating vessels up to forty tons), and a moat (60 ft wide) now filled in on the east and south-east, but still water-filled on the north, west, and south-west. The space between the inner and outer lines of defence varied from around 20 ft (between the projecting inner towers and the outer curtain), to c. 60 ft (from inner to outer curtain). Both outer gatehouses are offset from the line of those on the inner curtain, imposing on an attacker several changes of direction. Although it was described as eight-sided the outer curtain wall is basically rectangular (c. 340 ft square), with the centre of each side projecting in a shallow V to accommodate the gatehouses in the north and south sides and the D-shaped towers on the east and west.

In a castle full of interesting features there is no question that the most outstanding are the two great gatehouses, north and south, although the rear section of the latter, projecting within the curtain wall, was never completed. However, there is no doubt that both were intended to be gatehouse-keeps, i.e. capable of being isolated from, and surviving independently of, the rest of the castle. The North Gatehouse had a portcullis and doorway at either end of, and another portcullis and doorway halfway along, the entrance passage, and there is no doubt that the Southern Gatehouse would have been completed in the same way. The question which immediately arises is why two keep-gatehouses in one castle? The answer may simply be double protection. If one gatehouse fell the defenders, retreating to the upper floors, could make their way along the top of the inner curtain wall to the other and continue the resistance from there. Conway, Caernarvon, and Harlech all had two entrances, on opposite sides or at opposite ends of the castles concerned, and it may be that Master James, having concluded that he must provide two gatehouses at Beaumaris, then decided that he might as well make both, rather than just one, of them into a keep-gatehouse. It has to be remembered that James of St George had been building and experimenting with castles for the whole of his working life. The North Wales building programme gave him an unparalleled opportunity and Beaumaris may be simply another example of his original and inventive approach to the problems of fortification.

Between them North and South Gatehouses provided a great deal of accommodation and this may provide a clue to an alternative explanation of the twin gatehouses, or at least throw an interesting side-light on possible royal occupation of the castle. The castle provides no less than five complete suites of rooms, each suite having its own hall and chamber together with ancillary rooms. Each gatehouse contains two suites and the fifth was intended to be in the courtyard against the east curtain although it was never actually built. This may have been intended for the constable of the castle, leaving the other four suites to be accounted for. It has been suggested that these were in anticipation of the time when the castle might need to accommodate not only the king's and queen's households (needing a suite each), but also the households of the Prince of Wales, heir to the throne, and his wife, the future queen. Although the provision of so many suites need not necessarily be connected with the double gatehouse arrangement, it would have been difficult to provide so much accommodation around the courtyard; given that two entrances were to be provided, the two gatehouses may have presented themselves as a practical and compact answer to the problem.

The great technical interest of Beaumaris is not matched by its architectural appearance. It is much more striking in plan than in elevation in which it is a poor second to Caernarvon. Much of this is due to the fact that the upper parts of the towers were never completed. With towers of the originally-planned height, almost certainly surmounted by turrets, the castle would have presented a much more striking profile than it does now, with its range of somewhat stunted towers.

In addition to newly-built castles Edward made use of a number of existing Welsh castles, including (in the order in which they were captured), Dolwyddelan, Criccieth, and Castell y Bere. Dolwyddelan was symbolically important as the birthplace of Llywelyn the Great (1200–40), and was probably built at the end of the twelfth century. It was captured by Edward in January 1283 and work began almost immediately on making good any damage caused in its capture. The castle was of a fairly simple type, not unlike Criccieth (below), consisting of an irregular polygonal wall with two rectangular towers, one of them a keep, which still dominates the site, although the upper portions are late medieval and modern. The keep was originally two storeys high, entered at first-floor level by a flight of stone steps. In the late fifteenth century a third storey was added, while the present roof and battlemented parapet are nineteenth-century restorations which, nevertheless, add greatly to the impressive appearance of the tower. The second tower, on the north-west, was rebuilt almost as soon as the castle was recaptured. The roofs of both towers may have supported catapults for throwing missiles; an inventory of the castle made in 1284 mentions two wooden catapults for a tower and the assumption is that they were mounted on the only two towers in the castle.

Two months later, in March 1283, Criccieth was captured and likewise converted to English use, although on a more elaborate scale than Dolwyddelan. Criccieth occupies the summit of a rocky knoll which stands on a promontory projecting southwards above Cardigan Bay. There are two fairly distinct parts of the castle: the original Welsh castle and the addition made by Edward. The original Welsh castle was certainly in existence in the reign of Llywelyn the Great, grandfather of Llywelyn ap Gruffydd who gave Edward so much trouble, and was probably built around the end of the twelfth century or the beginning of the thirteenth. It consisted of a roughly triangular curtain wall, about 300 ft from the apex at the north to the base, and roughly 150 ft wide, at the south. There was a gateway at the south-east corner, a tower at the north angle (the Engine Tower) and a much larger tower (c. 65 x 40 ft) at the south-west angle which probably acted as a keep, and resembled the keep at Dolwyddelan.

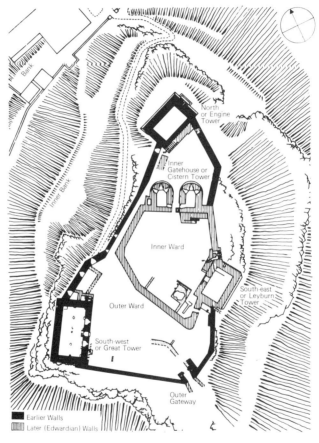

Plan labels: North or Engine Tower; Inner Gatehouse or Cistern Tower; Inner Ward; Outer Ward; South-east or Leyburn Tower; South-west or Great Tower; Outer Gateway; Inner Bank; Bank

Top:
Criccieth was originally a Welsh castle, built around 1200, which was converted to English use by Edward I after its capture in 1283.

Bottom:
In the plan of Criccieth the earlier Welsh portion with the keep-like tower, and the later English portion with the double-towered gate-house, are clearly distinguishable.

It was probably of three storeys, the lowest one originally accessible only from the floor above and used for stores. The doorway in the middle of the east wall is a later feature, probably added in Edward I or II's time, at the same time as the flight of steps against the north wall which gave access to the upper floors and the rampart walk.

This Welsh castle was used by Edward I as the Outer Ward of his newly-built Inner Ward. Construction work seems to have started almost immediately after the occupation, although whether on the existing defences or on new building is not certain. However, there is not much doubt that within a couple of years work was under way on the new Inner Ward of the castle and probably occupied the years 1285–88. The new enclosure was built across the middle of the existing castle, leaving a small area to the north and a much larger area to the south, across the base of the triangle, which became the Outer Ward. It consisted of a 7-ft-thick curtain wall surrounding an irregular six-sided area, approximately 100 ft from north to south and about 80 ft from east to west. At the north end there was a double-towered gatehouse, and on the south-east side a rectangular tower (*c.* 48 x 32 ft) known as the Leyburn Tower, after the second constable of Criccieth, Sir William de Leyburn, appointed by Edward on 23 December 1284, after a short tenure in the same office by Henry of Greenford who had assumed duty as soon as the castle was first occupied.

The completed structure consisted of both the Welsh and English portions, forming a castle with a double curtain wall on the north, west, and south and a single one on the east. The original approach to the outer gateway at the south-east corner ran below this east wall and it was presumably to exercise greater command over the roadway that the Leyburn Tower was built, projecting diagonally through the curtain wall. Further protection for the castle was provided by the Engine Tower at the north angle from which missiles, probably large stones, could be hurled at anyone approaching from the landward side.

Castell y Bere was founded by Llywelyn the Great in 1221. It was captured by Edward's forces in April 1283, but remained a royal castle for only about twelve years. Whatever work was done in the intervening years appears to have become a wasted effort in 1294 when the Welsh rose again. Castell y Bere was besieged by the rebels. The exact outcome is not known but the castle does not appear again in the exchequer accounts, and there is excavation evidence of burning and destruction in the late thirteenth century. The implication is that the castle was destroyed or badly damaged in 1294–5 and subsequently never repaired.

The castle stands on a high narrow ridge of rock running north/south and makes great use of natural features. The southernmost part of the original Welsh castle appears to have been an apsidal or D-shaped tower on the highest part of the ridge. To the south of it was a rock-cut ditch cutting off the castle from the southern tip of the ridge. The main Edwardian addition, probably in the years 1286–7, appears to be the substantial curtain wall around the southern end of the ridge, leaving the rock-cut ditch within the extended castle.

The new royal castles and the adapted Welsh ones were not, however, the end of the story of castle-building in North Wales at the close of the thirteenth century. There were, in addition, three new 'lordship' castles (together with Hawarden which had been built at the end of the 1277 campaign); these were castles built by trusted barons granted land in North Wales on the understanding that they would add in this fashion to the network of fortifications in the area. Two of these castles (Denbigh and Chirk) have substantial surviving remains, the former accompanied by contemporary town walls. Holt had only fragmentary remains but the main features of the castle are known from early accounts and sketches. All three castles were started in 1282 and will therefore be described in the order listed above.

There may well have been a Welsh castle at Denbigh before 1282, but if so there is no visible trace of it now. The existing remains date from 1282 or later and embrace both a castle and town walls, built simultaneously, the castle occupying the south-west angle of the enclosing walls. Edward

A general view of the court-yard of Denbigh Castle from the west.

granted the lordship to Henry de Lacy, Earl of Lincoln, on 16 October 1282, and work on the castle and town walls seems to have begun almost immediately. The structure is oval in plan and consists of two clearly distinguishable parts. The south and west sides are formed by the town wall and both the wall and wall towers differ from the other part of the castle which was formed by building a curtain wall on the north and east sides. On these sides the curtain was much thicker (10 ft as compared with 6 ft) and the towers both larger and different in shape (semi-octagonal as compared with semi-circular). There were two large semi-octagonal towers on the east curtain (45 x 50 ft wide) and an octagonal one (50 ft across) at the north-west corner at the junction of the thicker north curtain wall with the town wall. The most notable feature on the thicker curtain wall, however, was the gatehouse which was of unusual design, recalling Caernarvon Castle, as indeed do the octagonal towers.

The gatehouse consists of three towers linked by walls to form a triangle 120 ft long and 100 ft wide. Two of the towers are semi-octagonal in plan and flank the entrance in normal gatehouse fashion. The third, octagonal tower—50 ft across—is set well within the courtyard and linked to the other two by massive walls. Between them the three towers and linking walls define a central, octagonal hall at the heart of the gatehouse. The outer entrance passage comes into this hall, opposite the third tower from which an arrow slit points back down the passage, which was further protected by an outer portcullis and gate and a similar defence at the inner end. Access to the interior of the castle was via a passage on the west side of the octagonal hall, likewise protected by a portcullis and two-leaved door.

The Postern Gate at the southern end of the castle consists principally of a long passage with abrupt changes in direction, ascending the steep slope which protects the south and west sides of the castle. On these sides there is a mantlet or terrace with its own low protective wall in front of and below the main defences. The mantlet is about 50 ft wide and it is this which stands directly above the steep slope, rather than the main defences which form the back of the terrace. These defences consist of a 6-ft-thick curtain wall and four semi-circular or D-shaped towers about 30 ft in diameter.

As with Edward's own foundations, Denbigh consisted of both castle and linked town wall. The medieval town, standing high above present-day Denbigh, was triangular in plan, with overall dimensions approximately 1,000 x 1,000 ft. Apart from the walls themselves, which are largely preserved, the principal remains are the Burgess Gate, a stern twin-towered entrance at the north-west angle, and the Countess and Goblin Towers on the east. The latter is a semi-octagonal tower at the apex of a salient of rock which stands in front of and below the main town wall; the tower embraces a well, which was probably the reason for its existence.

Like Denbigh, Chirk was the result of a new lordship created by Edward I in 1282. In June that year he granted the territory to Roger Mortimer the Younger and, as elsewhere, work may have begun immediately. However, it has been suggested, because of the resemblance between Chirk and Beaumaris (not started till 1295), that work at Chirk likewise did not begin until nearer the end of the century. Whenever it started, progress seems to

The plan of medieval Denbigh with the town walls which formed the south and west sides of the castle.

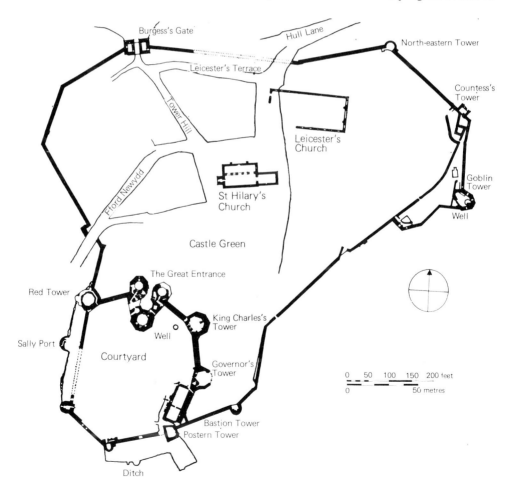

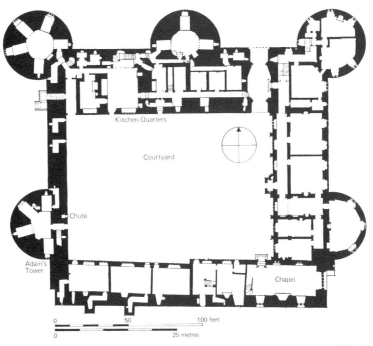

Kitchen Quarters

Courtyard

Chute

Adain's
Tower

Chapel

0   50   100 feet

0   25 metres

Chirk Castle was never
completed, the existing
layout shown here being a
little more than half of what
was originally planned.

have been slow and the castle was far from complete in 1322 when Roger
Mortimer fell from grace. In fact, the stronghold as originally conceived
was never completed, the existing structure representing just over half of
the intended plan. Instead of the projected southern portion a simpler
southern range, without towers, was eventually added just south of the east
and west interval towers. Chirk has been continuously occupied since the
fourteenth century and this also has had its effect on the present external
appearance of the castle.

Chirk was planned on the basis of a rectangular curtain wall (13 ft thick)
measuring 240 x 190 ft overall (Beaumaris was 225 x 210 ft). At the north-
east and north-west angles are circular towers, 47 ft in diameter, projecting
for three-quarters of their circumference. Midway along the north front is
a semi-circular interval tower of the same diameter. The present entrance
is between this interval tower and the north-east angle tower. There is no
gatehouse, but the towers just mentioned are less than 20 ft away in either
direction. There are two more interval towers along the eastern and
western sides, 75 ft south of the angle towers. Presumably the projected
south-eastern and south-western towers were a further 75 ft away to the
south, leaving only the south range to be dealt with.

The resemblance to the Inner Bailey at Beaumaris is close, although
clearly there was no intention of repeating the double gatehouse formula.
On the other hand, it would be hard to believe that there was not intended
to be at least one impressive gatehouse of the Beaumaris type, and this
would almost certainly have been on the south front, midway between the
angle towers, preserving the symmetry of the plan. A gatehouse similar in
size to Beaumaris would have produced a rather crowded effect, but a
smaller version (say 70–75 ft wide instead of 90 ft) would have fitted in
quite comfortably, with 40-ft stretches of curtain wall on either side,
between it and the angle towers.

The main structure of the northern half of the castle is well preserved, although most of the original arrow slits have been enlarged into later windows, which detracts to some extent from its military appearance. However, the chief shortcoming in this respect is the fact that the towers were not completed to their full height. They rise no higher than the curtain walls, giving the whole mass a somewhat squat effect. Nevertheless, Chirk was quite clearly planned on impressive lines and this is apparent in the surviving remains, in spite of the shortcomings mentioned above.

The remains of the last castle to be dealt with in this chapter are far less impressive and extensive than the castles considered thus far. Holt Castle was built between 1282 and 1311, the date of the first reference to it, by John de Warenne, Earl of Surrey, who had been rewarded with territory in the area in return for his services to Edward I in North Wales. Although little or nothing of the original plan can be made out on the ground there are early surveys and drawings which indicate the main lines of the castle's structure. The castle was built around a boss of rock on the edge of the River Dee and was, unusually, pentagonal in plan, each of the five sides measuring about 50 ft. At four of the angles there were circular towers, apparently with turrets rising above them, and at the fifth a square tower. The entrance, without gatehouse, was in the middle of the side opposite the square tower. There were ranges of internal buildings, about 22 ft wide, against the curtain wall all round, leaving a central, open courtyard.

Although the pentagonal plan is unusual it is not unique. Morgraig Castle, described earlier (p. 47), was of a similar shape and resembled Holt in other respects also. It had four D-shaped towers at four of the angles and a rectangular tower at the fifth. As at Holt, the entrance, a simple gap through the curtain wall, was in the middle of the side opposite the square tower. The resemblance is quite striking and seems hardly likely to be mere coincidence. It is generally assumed that James of St George was involved to some degree with the design of the lordship castles, and the presence of turrets on top of the towers, as at Conway, may be an indication that this was also so at Holt. Morgraig was built early in the thirteenth century and must have been standing for fifty or sixty years when Holt was contemplated. Unless it is, indeed, mere coincidence, the most likely explanation is that Master James (or whoever else was responsible for the design) was familiar with, and presumably impressed by, Morgraig and decided to copy it when a new castle was needed at Holt.

Holt concludes the survey of Edwardian castle building in North Wales. In a relatively short period of time at the end of the thirteenth century, and in a relatively compact area, no less than seventeen castles were either built (or at least started) from new, or extensively rebuilt. In some cases building went on for a long time, and in a few cases castles were never finally finished. Nevertheless, in spite of these qualifications, Edward I's castle-building programme (including the 'lordship' strongholds) represents an unprecedented achievement in the annals of medieval castle building, and one that was never to be repeated. Building activities continued after Edward I, in the two remaining centuries of the medieval period (1307–1485), but it was now a different story, no less interesting, resulting in many impressive structures, but castles built for different times and different conditions.

5
Edwardian Castles Outside Wales

In spite of the spectacular nature of Edward's castles in North Wales, and the splendour of their visible remains, it would be wrong to assume that they represent the sum total of castle building in the period from 1272 to 1307 or thereabouts. There was a great deal of building activity throughout the British Isles during these years, both in the form of new castles and in additions to existing ones. About three dozen new castles were built (or so completely rebuilt as to be virtually new), more than twice as many as in North Wales, although they were spread over a much wider area, so that they do not make the same concentrated impact as the sites just described. Nevertheless, they include many large, spectacular, and well-preserved sites, a number of which were, like the North Wales sites, the work of Edward I, who must surely rank as the greatest castle-building king in English history. Outside North Wales his outstanding work was undoubtedly The Tower of London which, although originally built by William the Conqueror in about 1080, and added to by other hands, was brought substantially to its present shape, that of a concentric castle, as a result of the considerable rebuilding undertaken by Edward early in his reign, between 1275 and 1285.

The castle begun by William the Conqueror but completed after his death, probably by 1087 (William died in 1086), consisted of the great square keep with four tall corner turrets the 'White Tower', which still dominates the whole structure, standing within a bailey, two sides of which (the south and east) were formed by the still standing walls of Roman London. The two remaining sides of the bailey, to the north and west required a new wall but whether this was of earth and timber or of stone at this time is uncertain. The keep is a massive square structure (120 x 96 ft) with walls some 12–14 ft thick, rising over 90 ft high to the top of the main building with the turrets rising higher still. As originally constructed, the White Tower had three storeys (a fourth was inserted later), basement, entrance level, and main floor. Entry to the middle storey was by means of a forebuilding, now gone, although the blocked doorway is still visible. The basement was reached by a spiral staircase down from this level and similar staircases gave access to the upper storey and the battlements. The third, upper storey contained the principal rooms of the castle: the Great Hall (96 x 40 ft), the Great Chamber (a more private apartment, 65 x 28 ft), and the Chapel, a splendid structure with a gallery above the aisles and an apsidal or semi-circular east end.

Apart from its size and splendour, however, the White Tower was little or no different from other castles of the period, consisting basically of a keep and a bailey. It seems to have remained in this state for about a century, until the reign of Richard I (the Lionheart, 1189–99), on whose behalf, in Richard's absence abroad, his Chancellor, William Longchamp, spent nearly £3,000 on the castle, a very large expenditure even for a royal castle. Longchamp's work seems to have involved the digging of a defensive ditch on the north and west sides, the provision of a new or rebuilt curtain wall around the whole bailey, and the building of wall towers, only two of which can now be identified, the Bell Tower and the Wardrobe Tower. These additions brought the Tower up-to-date, but did not alter its basic layout which was still that of a keep-and-bailey castle. It was left to Henry III to begin, and his son, Edward, to complete, the work which transformed the Tower from its simple, early plan to the great concentric castle which exists today.

Henry's work on the Tower went on throughout his long reign (1216–72), and cost in the region of £10,000, a colossal outlay for a single building and more even than Edward spent on some of his North Wales castles, although spread over a much longer period. One of the major changes made by Henry was the extension of the castle to the east, beyond the line of the Roman wall which had since the beginning marked the eastern side of the bailey. Within the new enlarged bailey he built an inner bailey, more or less square in plan, between the keep (the White Tower) and the south curtain wall. The main bailey wall was equipped with circular, projecting, angle towers and regularly spaced D-shaped interval towers, all very much in the style one would expect in the middle decades of the thirteenth century. The entrance, on the western side, was almost certainly of the twin-towered type, again exactly in keeping with current styles. Thus by the end of Henry's reign the castle consisted of the White Tower (the keep), with a rectangular inner bailey on its south side, these two surrounded on three sides, west, north, and east, by the main bailey. The castle was surrounded on three sides by a wet moat and on the south side by the Thames.

Henry's work prepared the way for Edward's drastic reorganisation of the castle's defences. In spite of the huge cost of Henry's rebuilding, the castle basically remained much the same as it had been from the beginning. It was larger and stronger but not fundamentally different: a keep-and-bailey castle in which the curtain wall of the bailey was equipped with regular wall towers and a twin-towered gatehouse. Edward's work showed clearly his appreciation of concentrically planned castles, for the greater part of his effort was directed towards providing the Tower of London with outer defences which completely embraced those within. Edward's first task was to fill up the moat and transform it into the outer bailey. This was then surrounded by a new, plain curtain wall, more or less where the outer edge of the moat had been, between 50 and 100 ft beyond Henry's towered curtain wall, which thus became the inner curtain. Beyond the new outer curtain a much wider and deeper moat was built, between 75 and 125 ft wide, fed from the waters of the Thames.

These arrangements applied on the three landward sides of the castle, west, north, and east. On the south towards the Thames the arrangements were inevitably different. In Henry's time the waters of the Thames ran more or less immediately below the southern defences. In order to continue the concentric defences on all four sides of the castle more land

Previous page:
The nucleus of the Tower of London is the White Tower, the great rectangular keep built by William the Conqueror.

had to be taken in from the river. A wharf was built along the river front, with the Thames to the south and a moat to the north, between the wharf and the castle, continuous with the moat on the other three sides. On the north edge of the moat a curtain wall was built, completing the outer circuit and making the castle fully concentric. As completed by Edward the castle consisted of the keep (the White Tower), with the Inner Bailey immediately to the south, the Middle Bailey surrounding them on three sides, and the Outer Bailey, defined by Edward's new outer curtain wall and the moat.

In addition to the main defences Edward provided two new and elaborate entrances. Henry's entrance had been on the west side, in the position occupied by the present Beauchamp Tower which was completed in 1281 when Edward's new complex entrance came into use. Edward placed his entrance in the south-west corner of the castle; it was, in fact, a series of entrances, extending over a distance of nearly 600 ft, from the first drawbridge as far as the entrance to the Middle Bailey. This still left the Inner Bailey to be penetrated, and after that the keep. The first drawbridge led across to a D-shaped island (now gone) in a westward projection of the moat. From the island another drawbridge gave access to the second gate, a twin-towered structure standing in the moat. From here another bridge with a drawbridge led to the third gate, the twin-towered Byward Gate at the south-west angle of the outer curtain wall. The final stretch was the corridor formed between the inner and outer curtain walls from the south-west corner to the fourth gate, adjacent to the Wakefield Tower, which gave access through the inner curtain wall to the Middle Bailey. The whole arrangement imposed on an attacker a long and arduous approach to the interior, with a spaced-out series of obstacles, each or any of which would have seriously delayed, if not entirely halted, the impetus of the enemy. A similar, but simpler, entrance system exists at Goodrich Castle, to be described next. Edward also built an elaborate water gate, from the outer curtain across the moat to the wharf which was pierced at this point to allow access by water from the Thames to the area in front of the fourth gate mentioned above.

Of Edward's other works in England, Leeds Castle (Kent) has been dealt with already in the section on water defences (p. 68), and nothing now remains of Cambridge Castle, although Edward spent considerable sums on it and quite clearly saw it as of major importance. There had been a castle on the site since 1068, of the motte-and-bailey type, and this appears to have been maintained, with minor additions, until Edward's reign. He built a virtually new castle, incorporating the old one in it, although, in fact, his work was never finally completed. Edward's castle was typical of its period: quadrangular (more or less), with a round tower at each corner and a double-towered gatehouse in the centre of the south-west side, with a barbican in front of it. The motte, surmounted by a stone tower or keep, was on the south-east side. By 1441 the castle was in ruins and some of the stone was used in the building of King's College. The gatehouse survived longest, continuing in use as a gaol until 1842 when it was finally pulled down.

Goodrich Castle (Hereford and Worcester), mentioned earlier on, is one of the finest surviving examples of late-thirteenth-century military architecture, although there are remains of earlier works on the site. There

are records of a castle (called Godric's Castle) on the site as early as 1101 or 1102, nothing of which now remains. The earliest surviving structure is the fine keep (*c.* 30 ft square) which was built about the middle of the century (*c.* 1150), and which is now incorporated in the south range of buildings around the courtyard. This must originally have stood within a bailey defined (probably) by a timber palisade, standing above the natural defences on the north and west and a rock-cut ditch on the south and east. This ditch was probably a smaller, earlier version of the present very large rock-cut ditch and was presumably dug away when the latter was excavated. Fifty or sixty years later, at the beginning of the thirteenth century, the bailey was surrounded by a stone curtain wall, some remains of which are incorporated in the east curtain wall of the existing castle. Thus matters remained until the last decade or two of the century (1280–1300) when a completely new castle, in the current 'Edwardian' style, was built, sweeping away virtually everything earlier except the keep which is still a very prominent feature of the site.

The new castle was built by William de Valence, a half-brother of Henry III and therefore Edward's uncle. It would be difficult to believe that there was no contact between the two with regard to both the desirability and design of the castle, and indeed it seems a probability that Edward's advice and support were sought, together with that of his master builder, James of St George. Certainly it bears favourable comparison with anything built in North Wales at the same time. The castle is more or less rectangular (*c.* 150 x 125 ft), not counting the angle towers. The most noticeable variation in the plan is the south curtain wall which projects forward at the centre in a shallow V-shape, presumably to avoid the one surviving earlier feature on the site, the keep. There are boldly projecting circular towers on square bases at three of the angles, the one at the south-west corner being somewhat larger than the other two (*c.* 40 ft as compared with *c.* 33 ft). The fourth corner, the north-east, is occupied by the gatehouse although not one with the usual symmetrically placed twin-towers. There is a substantial

Above:
The south-east angle tower at Goodrich Castle, with the gatehouse beyond, at the north-east angle.

Opposite:
Caernarvon Castle. Looking across the River Seiont from the south.

U-shaped tower, housing the chapel, on the south side of the entrance passage, but only what amounts to a thickening of the curtain wall with a very small tower at the angle (*c.* 15 ft in diameter) on the north side. Between them they define an entrance passage some 55 ft long. This leads into the central courtyard with the remains of four ranges of buildings backing on to the curtain walls, including the Great Hall, the kitchen, and the solar, a more private apartment than the Great Hall, for the castle's owner and his family. Additional accommodation, on three floors each, was provided by the three angle towers.

In many ways the most striking aspect of Goodrich Castle, in spite of its splendid architecture, is its setting, and this owes a great deal to the great rock-cut ditch on the southern and eastern sides. The ditch is 60–70 ft wide and 20–25 ft deep, and provided a formidable obstacle to an attacker. In the entrance area, however, the defences were further reinforced by a barbican similar to, although rather less complex than, the one at the Tower of London described earlier (p. 117). A U-shaped ditch led off the main ditch in front of the gatehouse. This isolated a D-shaped barbican (*c.* 70 x 50 ft) reached by a drawbridge at one angle of the D. On the straight west side a stepped ramp led towards the gatehouse, but before this could be reached two drawbridges had to be crossed, although these have now been replaced by stone bridges. The barbican is later than the main part of the castle but was added within a decade or two, probably *c.* 1310–20, at the same time as the Outer Ward on the north and west sides which, because of the trend of the ground, is at the same level as the ditch bottom. The result is, in a sense, half a concentric plan. A complete concentric arrangement was not possible because of the pre-existing ditch on the southern and eastern sides.

Other Edwardian-type castles built in England during the years around 1300 included Beverstone (Glos.), and Skipton (Yorks.). Only a portion of Beverstone remains and in that portion the traces of the Edwardian castle are obscured by later rebuilding. The castle was probably quadrangular with circular towers at the corners, although only the western side now remains. Even here, however, the thirteenth-century circular towers have been replaced by later square towers. Much of the remainder of the site is occupied by a private house and the castle remains are not open to the public. However, they can easily be seen from the footpath which leads to Beverstone parish church from the main street of the village.

There was a Norman castle at Skipton (North Yorks.), possibly as early as 1080, and this, probably repaired and added to, was still in existence in 1284 when it was granted to Robert de Clifford. It was he who built what was virtually a new castle, before he was killed at Bannockburn in 1314. The structure appears to have been damaged in the Scottish wars and was restored, almost certainly on the same lines, by the third Lord Clifford who succeeded to the title in 1322. The castle has been almost continuously inhabited since then, and has fine internal medieval buildings. The most notable external addition is the house (built as a long gallery) to the east of the castle, added in 1536–7.

The Inner Ward or Bailey of the castle is D-shaped in plan with the straight side standing immediately above the cliff which forms the south bank of the River Aire. There is a circular tower at each end of this section,

Opposite top:
A general view of Carew Castle with three of the circular angle towers two of them on square bases.

Opposite bottom:
The nucleus of Kenilworth is the twelfth-century Norman keep.

and four other circular towers linked by short, straight sections of curtain wall in the roughly semi-circular section facing away from the river. Two of these form a twin-towered gatehouse, with a much later addition in front, added by Lady Anne Clifford during the castle's restoration in 1657–8. Internally, the main range of buildings (kitchen, great hall, and solar or retiring room) was built against the north curtain wall which forms the straight side of the D. The internal courtyard thus formed (the Conduit Court), was rebuilt towards the end of the fifteenth century when the fine residential buildings were added at the eastern end.

Inevitably, a considerable number of castles were built in South Wales around the end of the thirteenth century, matching, although in a less coherent way, Edward's programme in North Wales. Newport Castle (Gwent) was built about 1300, to a rectangular plan, although apart from foundations only the side towards the river is now preserved. This side, facing the River Usk, consists of two angle towers, semi-octagonal in shape on square bases, with a water gate in between. The lowest part of this, open at the front, was flooded at high tide and enabled boats to come in and unload under the cover of the tower above. The open front could be closed by a portcullis and double doors. The area of water enclosed was

The Conduit Court at Skipton Castle with the Norman entrance and the staircase to the domestic range.

Above:
Kidwelly Castle (Dyfed) is largely a work of the late thirteenth and early fourteenth centuries, although the great southern gatehouse is a later addition.

Bottom:
The rectangular Inner Ward at Kidwelly was built about 1280; about thirty years later the D-shaped Outer Ward was added, forming a concentric arrangement on three sides, but not on the east.

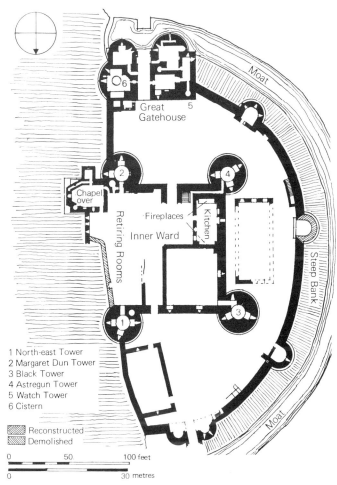

1 North-east Tower
2 Margaret Dun Tower
3 Black Tower
4 Astregun Tower
5 Watch Tower
6 Cistern

Reconstructed
Demolished

0   50   100 feet

0   30 metres

some 35 ft long and 20 ft wide. The inner end of the dock stepped up to an unloading platform and adjacent to this was a storeroom. From the storeroom there was a flight of steps up to the main courtyard. Although the lower part of the water gate is original the upper storeys were rebuilt in the fifteenth century, and there has been a certain amount of restoration in modern times.

Apart from Newport the remaining castles involved here are in Carmarthen and Pembrokeshire (both now in Dyfed). One of the most impressive is Kidwelly which was laid out on concentric lines, although because of the situation it is not fully concentric. It stands on the west bank of the River Gwendraeth Fach near the shores of Carmarthen Bay. The castle, as defined by the outer curtain wall, is D-shaped in plan, with the straight side of the D standing above the steep slope of the river bank. The semi-circle of curtain wall on the side away from the river is equipped with regularly-spaced D-shaped towers and two gatehouses, one at the north end, near the angle, of modest size, and one at the south angle of much greater dimensions, a massive keep-gatehouse of later date than the rest of the structure. This, some 90 ft wide and some 60 ft deep from back to front, was, in fact, added in the second half of the fourteenth century and is the most impressive surviving portion of the castle.

The Inner Ward conforms very closely to rectangular Edwardian planning, with four round angle towers (each *c.* 35 ft in diameter), linked by a curtain wall and defining an area some 90 ft square. The Inner Ward, however, is not completely surrounded by the Outer and the castle is not, therefore, truly concentric. Although the inner and outer curtains have a concentric relationship on the north, west, and south, on the remaining side the east curtain wall of the Inner Ward, in fact, coincides with the east curtain wall of the Outer Ward. The entrances to the Inner Ward, at the north and south, are fairly simple in character, with nothing like the gatehouses seen at some of the North Wales castles. On the other hand, as at Conway for example, the adjacent angle towers are so close anyway as to make separate gate towers superfluous. The Hall occupied the east side of the courtyard against the common curtain wall, with more private apartments at its southern end. The kitchen was in the south-western corner. A somewhat later addition was the chapel tower which projects beyond the east curtain wall at the south-east corner of the Inner Ward. The Inner Ward, the earliest part of the castle, was built about 1280 by the De Chaworth family, great servants of Henry III and Edward I. The Outer Ward was added some thirty years later (*c.* 1310), possibly about the same time as the Chapel tower was built. The great southern gatehouse, which presumably replaced an earlier, smaller structure, was probably added in the second half of the same century, between 1350 and 1400.

Carreg Cennen Castle, near Llandeilo, does not have much recorded history. It was certainly in existence early in Edward III's reign (1327–77), a possession of the Gifford family, and was probably built earlier in the century on the site of an earlier Welsh castle. The castle is almost square in plan with steep natural defences on the south and west and more gentle slopes on the north and east. There was a circular tower at the north-west angle and a large square tower (*c.* 30 ft square) with chamfered corners at the north-east. In between, at the middle of the north curtain wall, was a

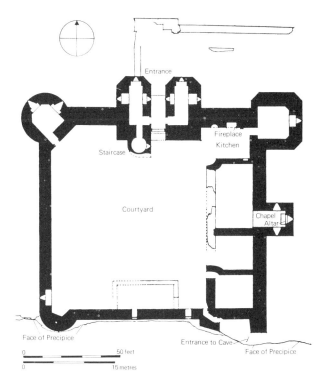

Carreg Cennen (Dyfed), built in the early fourteenth century, exemplifies the simpler type of rectangular Edwardian castle.

double-towered gatehouse, with two rectangular towers (*c.* 32 x 18 ft), each again with chamfered angles. About halfway along the east side was another projecting rectangular tower, housing a chapel. Because the south curtain wall was virtually on the cliff edge there was no room for projecting towers. At the south-west angle there was only a semi-circular turret and at the south-east an internal rectangular tower: that is, one built within the angle of the curtain wall rather than projecting beyond it. A postern gate opened beside this tower, giving access to the cliff top and allowing defenders to emerge and move around the east side of the castle, taking anyone attacking the main entrance by surprise. The main range of internal buildings was placed against the east curtain wall and included the kitchen, the hall, and the solar or withdrawing room, beyond which was the internal tower mentioned above. Because of the fall in the ground there was no direct approach to the main entrance. Instead there was a sloping ramp running across the front of the castle, from the north-east tower to the gatehouse, where anyone wishing to enter had to turn left through ninety degrees in order to pass between the twin towers.

The striking architectural remains of Laugharne Castle are the result of extensive rebuilding in the time of Henry VIII (1509–47). Only two round towers remain of the earlier castle built *c.* 1300. The castle stands near the mouth of the River Taf, a few miles from Llanstephan Castle (described earlier, p. 39), and about 10 miles from Kidwelly Castle. The medieval remains consist of two circular towers (35 ft and 30 ft in diameter) which are presumed to be the north-west and north-east angle towers of a rectangular or near-rectangular castle, similar to the Inner Ward of Kidwelly. Almost everything except these two towers was swept away in the major rebuilding carried out by Sir John Perrot during the reign of

Henry VIII. Sir John carried out a similar transformation at Carew Castle (p. 52). The most substantial remnant of the Tudor rebuilding is the four-storey gatehouse adjacent to the larger of the early towers and probably occupying the position of the original entrance.

As it now stands Llawhaden Castle is largely a work of the early fourteenth century and more in the nature of an ecclesiastical palace for the Bishops of St Davids than a true castle. There is an early mention of it in 1175 by the famous Giraldus Cambrensis (born at Manorbier Castle, *c.* 1146, below, p. 127); at that time the castle was probably a simple ringwork consisting of an earthen bank with a timber palisade on top enclosing a circular area about 150 ft in diameter, with an external ditch. The castle was destroyed in 1193 and appears to have been rebuilt in stone early in the following century, although much of the rebuilding is covered by the existing structures. Such remains as can be identified indicate a series of round towers, possibly four or five, linked by straight stretches of curtain wall, very much in the manner of Bolingbroke, Clifford, Morgraig, or White Castle, all of the early thirteenth century. The entrance was probably in the same position as the present one although whether it was a double-towered type or simply a gateway in the curtain wall is now difficult to say.

In turn this early-thirteenth-century castle was replaced by the structure which now occupies the site, probably early in the fourteenth century, by Bishop David Martyn who occupied the see of St Davids from 1293 to 1328. Virtually all the existing remains belong to this period; the major exception is the gatehouse which was extended forward about a century later. The new buildings follow, more or less, the existing circular plan; on the north and north-east, however, where the main block of buildings (the hall with its service and private rooms) was located, the projecting wings extended a long way out into the ditch. Quite clearly convenience and comfort took precedence over considerations of defence. As completed in the early fourteenth century the castle was D-shaped in plan, with a central

Manorbier Castle from the north-west, famous as the birthplace of the Welsh historian Giraldus Cambrensis (Gerald of Wales) who was born there in 1146.

courtyard. The gatehouse was placed in the middle of the curving section and there was an octagonal tower at the south-east angle with a semi-octagonal tower between. There was a range of buildings against the inner face of the curtain wall, including a chapel, although the bake house, in the north-west angle, was a somewhat later addition. The whole of the north-east side was occupied by the hall (c. 75 x 20 ft internally) over a vaulted undercroft, with large rectangular wings at either end, one for the kitchen and other services, and one for the Bishop's private apartments, both projecting into the surrounding ditch. The whole of the hall block is strongly built with walls nearly 10 ft thick and it is possible that the two wings, or the projecting portions of them, were carried up to form towers or turrets as part of the defensive apparatus of the castle. Whether this was so or not, it is noticeable that the only two unquestionably new towers were on the south-east side of the castle, between the gatehouse and the south-east angle. In the somewhat longer sector between the gatehouse and the north-west angle there are no new towers, only the foundations of the two round towers mentioned earlier as belonging to the first stone castle of the early thirteenth century. These, however, form a symmetrical arrangement with the two new towers in the other half of the castle, and it seems legitimate to ask whether these could not, in fact, have been retained, even if in modified form, in the rebuilt castle to provide cover along the north-west curtain wall, in the same way as the two new towers provided cover along the south-east. Although it was primarily used as an ecclesiastical palace, nevertheless at the time in question (the early fourteenth century), it could not afford to ignore defence considerations any more than a castle built for more conventional purposes.

Manorbier Castle (Dyfed, formerly Pembrokeshire), is famous as the birthplace of the Welsh chronicler, Giraldus Cambrensis (Gerald of Wales), born in 1146. Gerald's grandfather, Odo de Barri, who died in 1130, held the lordship of Manorbier and had a castle there, but his was almost certainly a timber-and-earthwork affair of which nothing can now be seen. The stone castle which replaced it appears to have been begun by his son, William de Barri, Gerald's father, between 1130 and 1153, when it was attacked by the Welsh, and most of the existing stronghold falls between that time and 1300, after which not many changes were made. The castle as it now stands cannot be attributed in its entirety to William de Barri; the two round towers, for example, must be of later date, probably around the turn of the century (c. 1200). Other than these and the rectangular gatehouse, the castle consists primarily of a curtain wall enclosing domestic buildings and this is in keeping with a pattern already noted in Chapter 2 at sites such as Grosmont and Chepstow (pp. 58/9). The first stone castle, built around the middle of the twelfth century, would therefore appear to have consisted of a plain curtain wall enclosure, roughly rectangular in plan (c. 250 x 150 ft), standing in a promontory position with the ground falling away on the north, west, and south. The entrance was in the east wall, facing the level approach and was probably housed in a square tower, as it still is; this may be, for the most part, the original tower. Internally, there was a range of buildings, probably along the southern and western sides of the courtyard, as again there still is, although the existing buildings (hall, chapel etc.) appear to date from about 1300, probably rebuilt from earlier structures with the same functions. The combination just described probably provided a perfectly adequate castle for the period and area in which it was built.

Inevitably, when it came to strengthening the castle, attention was focussed on the east front which faces more or less level ground. The main addition would appear to have been the two round towers at the north-eastern and south-eastern angles which, with their marked projection beyond the curtain wall, gave the castle a thirteenth-century look. A noticeable internal feature is the fact that their stairways rise concentrically with the tower in the thickness of the wall, as at Conisbrough (above, p. 23), instead of following the more common spiral form. This suggests a date for the towers around the year 1200. At the same time some addition may have been made to the central gatehouse tower. To the east of the castle was a larger Outer Ward, very little of which now remains, but it appears to have had one or two semi-circular towers which again suggest an early-thirteenth-century date. This may have been added at the same time as the circular towers, or be part of a later strengthening programme. Within the Outer Ward are the remains of a stone-built stable block. No doubt during this period (the thirteenth century) the internal domestic buildings were being progressively added to, improved, or rebuilt, to meet the growing demand for greater space, comfort and convenience.

Powys Castle (Powys, formerly Montgomeryshire) was built late in the thirteenth century, but was so heavily rebuilt in the late seventeenth century that only two sizeable portions are now easily recognisable. The site is bounded by a steep, in some places sheer, scarp to the south and the castle was built along this edge with man-made defences on the three remaining sides, the relatively narrow east and west sides, and the long northern side, parallel to the cliff. The castle consisted of an Inner Bailey (to the east of the surviving gatehouse), and an Outer Bailey (to the west). Of the Outer Bailey only the western section of the north wall survives, together with part of a D-shaped tower (*c.* 30 ft in diameter), a very small angle tower, and a very small section of the west wall. Most of the west side was probably occupied by a gatehouse but if so this was completely destroyed in building the existing gatehouse at the end of the seventeenth century. There was probably also a wall along the south side, above the cliff, although no trace of one now remains.

The east side of the Outer Bailey was formed by the west wall of the Inner Bailey, the most prominent feature being the double-towered gatehouse which is the most substantial remnant of the early castle. Linked to the southern tower is a surviving length of the original south curtain wall, here standing immediately above the steep natural slope. These remains are incorporated in the later buildings which occupy the whole area of the Inner Bailey. Possibly the north curtain wall as described above continued eastwards to form the north wall of the Inner Bailey also, with an east wall matching that on the west. The whole castle seems to have formed a large rectangle measuring 350 x 100 ft of which 150 ft to the east was Inner Bailey and 200 ft to the west Outer Bailey.

In 1296, with Wales subdued, Edward became embroiled in Scottish affairs. A dispute over the succession after the death of Alexander III (1286) and his successor, the Maid of Norway (1290), led Edward to intervene as (in his view) the overlord of Scotland. As a result of the intervention John Balliol became king in 1292. His acknowledgement of Edward as his overlord, however, did not last long, and by 1295 he had concluded a treaty with France, which was virtually a declaration of hostilities with England. The Scots began raiding in the north and in the following year (1296) Edward led an army into Scotland via Berwick on Tweed, and this was the beginning of a troublesome, expensive involvement in Scottish affairs which was to last until his death in 1307.

Caerlaverock Castle and Tibbers Castle, both in Dumfries and Galloway, seem to be a result of the growing troubles between England and Scotland in the last decade of the century (1290–1300). It is not known for certain who built Caerlaverock, the English or the Scots, although its position, reminiscent of the location of Edward's strongholds in North Wales, would appear to indicate an English origin. The castle is situated on a south-facing coast, guarding a natural landing place for traffic coming from the south, and this reliance on sea-borne supply suggests that it was built for English purposes, although possibly by a Scot, for a number took Edward's side in the conflict. One such was Sir Richard Siward, the builder of Tibbers Castle mentioned above.

Whoever built it, however, Caerlaverock was certainly in Scottish hands in 1300 when Edward laid siege to it. The siege is famous not so much as a very notable affair but because there is a contemporary account of it, in rhyme, written in French: *Le Siège de Karlaverock*. The description of the castle given there agrees closely with the existing remains, so that although Caerlaverock was destroyed (or at least badly damaged) several times, it looks as if in each case it was rebuilt on the same lines as before. The castle was first destroyed (or so badly damaged as to render it useless) in 1312. It was subsequently rebuilt: exactly when is not known, but it was certainly functioning as a castle in 1347, possibly having been rebuilt after the English victory at Halidon Hill in 1333. In 1356 or 1357 it was again destroyed by the Scots, but is known to have been functioning early in the following century so that presumably it had been rebuilt once more, probably towards the end of the fourteenth century. The fine, machicolated parapets which are such a feature of the site were added towards the end of the fifteenth century. The castle continued to figure in Border history in the sixteenth century, but the most notable structural addition was in the more peaceful period of the early seventeenth century when a fine range of Renaissance buildings was added along the east side of the central, triangular courtyard.

Throughout all these vicissitudes the castle remained, in its main outlines, what it had been in 1300, a triangular structure, with projecting towers at two corners and a double-towered gatehouse at the third. The unusual plan is dictated by the triangular shape of the outcrop of rock on which the castle stands, rising from an area of marshy land close to the coast. The water defences of the castle have been dealt with already (above, p. 71). The bank between the inner and outer moats may well have been surmounted by a timber palisade, turning Caerlaverock into a sort of concentric castle, albeit of a much simpler type than those encountered already. The angle towers at the south-west and south-east are quite small (*c.* 22 ft in diameter), and those forming the gatehouse not much larger (*c.* 28 ft). The triangle they define has sides 140 ft long internally, although the ranges of internal buildings (of various periods), reduce the courtyard to a triangle with roughly 70-ft sides. The oldest internal structures are those immediately behind the twin gate towers, dating from about 1300 (thus, from the first building of the castle), forming the gatehouse block which for a long time must have formed the nucleus of the castle, both for accommodation and defence.

Sir Richard Siward, mentioned earlier, began his castle at Tibbers, some 25 miles north of Caerlaverock, in 1298. This follows a much more conventional thirteenth-century plan, being more or less rectangular with four angle towers and a twin-towered gatehouse. As at Whittington (above, p. 69), one of the angle towers does duty as a gatehouse tower, an additional tower in the south curtain forming the opposite side of the entrance. The castle is quite small, approximately 130 x 100 ft overall, with the main internal buildings across the narrower north and south ends and a small courtyard (*c.* 60 x 40 ft) between.

In Ireland, one of the largest and best-preserved castles is Roscommon, begun around 1280, although on the site of an earlier and apparently smaller castle, built *c.* 1269 and twice destroyed, in 1272 and 1277. Roscommon is part of a large castle-building programme in Ireland around this time, a typically Edwardian approach to the problems of an unruly country. The main building work seems to have been carried out between 1280 and 1285, under the direction of Gregory of Coquile, although work on a smaller scale continued until the end of the century. Gregory seems to have been familiar with current fashions in military architecture for the castle bears a close resemblance to the Inner Bailey at Harlech Castle, which was, in fact, started three years later, in 1283. Roscommon, unlike Harlech, is not concentric but it does appear to have had two encircling moats (like Caerlaverock) which, with some strengthening of the intervening bank, could be interpreted as a simplified concentric arrangement.

Roscommon displays that regularity of plan which is typical of Edwardian castles when not restricted by natural features. It consists of a rectangular courtyard (162 x 130 ft), virtually the same size as Harlech, with four D-shaped angle towers, a double-towered gatehouse symmetrically placed in

The postern gate and angle towers on the south side of Roscommon (Ireland).

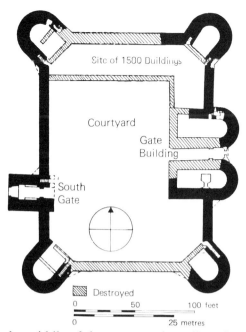

Site of 1580 Buildings

Courtyard

Gate
Building

South
Gate

Destroyed

0   50   100 feet

0   25 metres

Roscommon is an Irish
example of the rectangular
Edwardian plan and is
almost symmetrical in its
layout.

the middle of the east curtain wall, and a postern gate in a square tower in
the west curtain. Nothing now remains of the internal buildings. There is a
record of buildings against the north curtain, but these were of 1580,
although presumably earlier buildings, contemporary with the building of
the castle, were also placed against the curtain walls, leaving a central
courtyard. There is a reference to a hall early in the fourteenth century but
precisely where this was is not known.

If Roscommon resembles Harlech then Ballymote (Co. Sligo) certainly
resembles the Inner Bailey at Beaumaris, started in 1295. Ballymote was
begun around 1300 by Richard de Burgh and shows the same awareness of
current fashions as the previous castle. It was almost square in plan (c. 125
x 125 ft), with four three-quarter projecting angle towers (c. 35 ft in
diameter), a double-towered gatehouse at the centre of the north curtain,
D-shaped intermediate towers midway in the east and west curtain walls,
and (probably) a postern gate in the middle of the south curtain. The
resemblance to Beaumaris is quite striking and cannot be accidental. The
latter, too, is almost square in plan (c. 190 x 180 ft), and apart from the
larger size and an additional gatehouse is otherwise virtually the same as
Ballymote. The one is just a simplified version of the other, and there
seems little doubt that whoever designed Ballymote was well acquainted
with Beaumaris at first hand or with a detailed plan of it.

The two destructions of Roscommon mentioned earlier (in 1272 and
1277) were carried out by Hugh O'Connor as part of Irish resistance to
English rule. When work on Roscommon was almost complete, about
1300, the O'Connors built themselves a castle about ten miles away, at
Ballintubber, which they then held for several centuries. Ballintubber was
larger than Roscommon but was built on the same general lines. Its angle
towers, however, were polygonal rather than round. Since there was quite
clearly detailed information available locally about other North Wales
castles (for example, Harlech and Beaumaris), there is no reason why the

builders of Ballintubber should not have been aware of the latest fashions in castle architecture as exemplified by Caernarvon Castle and have decided to copy its polygonal towers in their new castle.

At least four other sites of this period conform to the quadrangular plan and another is trapeze-shaped, i.e. four-sided but wider at one end than the other in the manner of Skenfrith (above, p. 28). Quin Castle (Clare) is now heavily overlaid with the remains of a Franciscan monastery erected about a century and a half after its destruction in 1288. The castle had been built only a few years prior to that date (started 1278–80). However, it is clear from the remains that the original castle was square in plan with round angle towers. No trace remains of the entrance arrangements but there was almost certainly a gatehouse of the double-towered type, probably midway along one of the curtain walls.

Liscarroll (Cork) is oblong rather than square in plan. The long east and west sides had no flanking defences other than the angle towers at either end. The shorter north and south curtains had intermediate features, a square tower in the north wall (possibly housing a postern gate), and a strong oblong gate tower in the south, housing the main entrance. Portions of Dunluce (Antrim) have collapsed into the sea but there seems little doubt that the castle was originally four-sided and nearly if not precisely rectangular. It was built about 1300 possibly by Richard de Burgh, Earl of Ulster, although there may have been remains of an earlier castle on the site. The north-east and south-east angle towers and most of the south curtain are preserved. At the south-west angle there is a much later, rectangular gatehouse dating from about 1600. Kiltinane (Tipperary) was also quadrangular in plan but seems to have had only three angle towers. Kilkenny Castle belongs with this group although trapeze-shaped rather

Late thirteenth-century castle of Liscarroll, (Co. Cork).

than rectangular. It has been considerably altered over the centuries. Only three of the four original massive angle towers remain, pierced by modern windows, but the shape of the original castle of about 1300 is fairly clear.

Castleroche (Armagh) is of the same period, but is rather more irregular due to the nature of its situation. The site is triangular in plan with steep natural slopes below the north-west and south-west curtain walls which are unrelieved by wall towers. There are only three towers, all on the east curtain wall which faces more or less level ground. One tower was at the north end of the east curtain and the other two, forming a gatehouse, near the southern end. Immediately to the left on passing through the gatehouse was a large hall (60 x 40 ft). Within the triangular courtyard (c. 210 x 125 ft) are the remains of an earlier tower (c. 30 ft square), possibly a small keep.

The other probable late-thirteenth-century castles are notable chiefly for their entrances. Ballyloughan has a fine double-towered gatehouse in which, somewhat unusually, the round gate towers project for three-quarters of their circumference. The castle was not otherwise strongly defended and appears to have had low square towers at the angles. At Roscrea (Tipperary) the gatehouse is, in fact, rectangular, although there are two other towers which are D-shaped in plan. The plan of the castle as a whole is that of an irregular polygon. It was probably built about 1280, although the gables and chimneys on top of the gatehouse tower were added in the seventeenth century.

The castles considered so far in this chapter have all been new, or virtually new, constructions, exemplifying the latest ideas in fortification. But the same ideas had their effects on existing castles which, although they could not be completely rebuilt, could nevertheless be greatly improved in both strength and appearance by the addition of gatehouses, wall towers, additional baileys, and other works. In fact, as will appear

The major addition to Tonbridge Castle (Kent), was a great Edwardian-style gatehouse, on the lines of those at Harlech, Beaumaris, and Caerphilly, added around 1300.

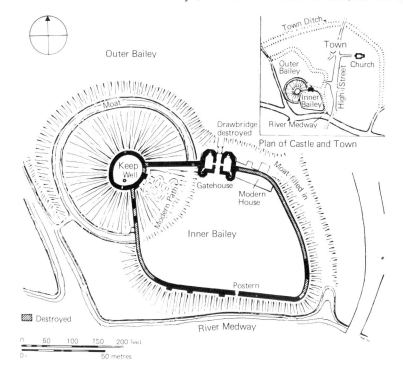

Outer Bailey

Town Ditch

Town

Outer Bailey

Church

High Street

Inner Bailey

Moat

Drawbridge destroyed

River Medway

Plan of Castle and Town

Keep
Well

Gatehouse

Modern House

Moat filled in

Modern Path

Inner Bailey

Postern

Destroyed

0   50   100   150   200 feet

0·   50 metres

River Medway

Rockingham (Northants) is
now mainly a Tudor
mansion. The principal
surviving remnant of the
castle is the twin-towered
gatehouse, seen here, added
by Edward I.

below, a great deal of attention was concentrated on entrances, and many
castles received new gatehouses at this time, similar to those already
described earlier in the chapter. It is this process of adding to existing
castles (to strengthen them, to bring them up to date, or simply to improve
their appearance) which is responsible for their great architectural variety
and which adds so much to their interest.

Tonbridge Castle (Kent) is a motte-and-bailey castle on the north bank
of the Medway, surrounded by an originally wet moat fed from its
waters. The existing remains are of a stone castle but this was almost
certainly preceded by a timber structure built in the first decade or two of
the Conquest. A castle at Tonbridge is recorded as being held by Bishop
Odo and his followers against William Rufus in 1088. As with so many
other timber motte-and-bailey structures the castle was rebuilt in stone
during the following century, probably in two stages. The oval shell-keep
(c. 80 x 70 ft) was probably built during the first half of the century and the
curtain wall of the Inner Bailey in the second half—roughly 1180. As in
many other castles of this type, the bailey walls do not end at the ditch
surrounding the motte, but continue across and up the slope to abut the
shell wall of the keep. The Inner Bailey (there is also an Outer Bailey to
the north) is situated to the east and south-east of the motte; it is roughly
oval in plan, being about 400 ft x 250 ft.

Around 1300 a new gatehouse, very much in the Edwardian style, was
added to the north wall of the Inner Bailey, immediately outside the ditch
surrounding the motte. It followed the main lines of such gatehouses as

Harlech, Beaumaris, and Caerphilly: two great D-shaped towers with the entrance passage between, with two smaller internal towers at the inner angles. The whole gatehouse was some 75 ft wide, 55 ft deep, and rose, in four storeys, to an original height of 75 ft. The arrangements in the entrance passage indicate quite clearly that it was conceived as a unit which could, if the need arose, survive independently of the rest of the castle. The outer end of the passage was defended by two sets of machicolations, a portcullis, and a two-leaved door. At the inner end the defences face the other way, against the Inner Bailey, and consist of a row of machicolations, a portcullis, and a two-leaved door. Thus the passage could be barred at either end to isolate the gatehouse, which is in effect a keep, from the rest of the castle. Between these two sets of defences were the entrances to the guard rooms on either side and these too were barred with portcullises and provided with arrow loops firing into the passage. Access to the upper floors was via the guard room so that it was important that these should survive as long as possible, even if the passage was taken by an enemy.

Rockingham Castle (Northamptonshire) is now, for the most part, a Tudor mansion, but it began as a very early timber motte-and-bailey castle under William the Conquerer. In the course of time this presumably became a stone shell-keep with an attached stone-walled bailey, probably on the same general lines as Tonbridge just described, although because of extensive later building not much early detail survives. Money was spent on the repair and maintenance of the castle over a long period, by Henry II, John, Henry III, and Edward I. It is to the latter that the most substantial surviving remnant of the castle, the gatehouse, must be attributed, probably between 1280 and 1290. Twin drum towers were added to an earlier gatehouse of about 1200, presumably rectangular in plan, bringing Rockingham in line with other castles being built from new with twin-towered gatehouses.

The twin-towered gatehouse added to St Briavel's Castle (Gloucestershire) was likewise the work of Edward I in the years 1292–3. This event is

The main Edwardian addition to St. Briavel's (Glos.) was the double-towered gatehouse (still occupied) which is now the most prominent feature of the site.

recorded in the accounts of the keeper of the castle, as is the cost of the work, £477 (*c.* £95,000 in modern terms). The surviving stone remains are those of a fairly simple castle consisting of a keep (little of which remains) and a curtain wall, surrounded by a ditch, probably built around the middle of the twelfth century. These structures may have been preceded by an earth-and-timber ringwork of the late eleventh or early twelfth century. Money was regularly spent on the castle by John and Henry III, but the principal surviving feature, the gatehouse, was added by Edward I, to bring the castle, at least in this respect, up to then modern standards.

Edward I also added a twin-towered gatehouse to the Outer Bailey at Corfe Castle (Dorset), but this was merely the completion of an extensive building programme started by John and carried on by Henry III. The nucleus of the castle is the square keep and pear-shaped Inner Bailey which occupy the summit of a natural mound in a gap in the long ridge formed by the Purbeck Hills. The bailey appears to have been built first, possibly before 1100, with the keep added in the early part of the following century, possibly about 1130. The next major addition was made under John (1199–1216) when the West Bailey was added. This was triangular in plan with an octagonal tower at the apex and two half-round towers, one in the north wall and one in the south, all reflecting the current fashion around 1200. Henry III's contribution was the greater part of the work on the large Outer Bailey which extends to the south-east of the earlier structures. This was enclosed by a strong curtain wall with regularly-spaced half-round towers, at least on the south-west side; on the north-east there was a steep natural slope below the curtain and, therefore, only two towers, with a long space between. This whole undertaking must have been nearly complete when Henry III died and the gateway must have been planned already. It was left to Edward I to execute it, but this was merely incidental. The work had to be completed to make any sense of the overall plan and it would probably have been completed in much the same way, whether by Henry III or by his son.

In the north not much now remains of the castle at Berwick-upon-Tweed (Northumberland), except for a length of curtain wall about 100 ft long and a semi-circular tower. However, a plan made in the Tudor period shows the outlines of the castle and the shape and position of its towers. A castle at Berwick is mentioned in 1174 when it was handed over to Henry II. At such a date, and in such a sensitive border area, one would expect a stone-built castle with a square keep and it is perhaps not too fanciful to see an indication of the position of such a keep in the square projection at the south-west corner of the castle as shown in plan. The western half of the castle is noticeably more irregular than the rest and this could well have been dictated by the shape of the original bailey. The eastern half of the castle shows clear evidence of rectangular planning and must represent thirteenth-century building, presumably added to the keep-and-bailey castle suggested above. The semi-circular wall towers, the boldly projecting angle towers (round and polygonal), and the semi-octagonal gate towers all tell the same story, and suggest that Berwick was enlarged and rebuilt, probably in the second half of the century. Edward I captured Berwick in 1296 and is known to have had considerable work done to strengthen the castle's defences. However, references to the work all seem to indicate

Opposite:
Powys Castle was built in the late thirteenth century, but was so heavily rebuilt in late sixteenth and seventeenth centuries that not much remains of the original castle.

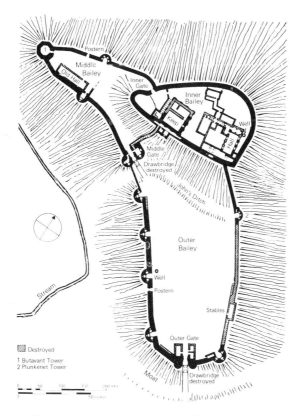

Opposite top:
Chirk Castle, with the southern range (left), built when the plan for a larger castle was abandoned.

Opposite bottom:
The approach to the gatehouse at Goodrich Castle with the chapel tower on the left.

Above:
The plan of Corfe Castle (Dorset) represents a long period of development, from before 1100 when the Inner Bailey surrounding the keep was built, to early in the reign of Edward I when the double-towered gatehouse was added to the Outer Bailey.

additional defences *in front of* the main entrance, so presumably the castle outlined in the Tudor plan was already in existence in 1296, and Edward simply added to what was there already. Nothing now remains of these additions, or indeed much of the castle to which they led, but an account of 1356 indicates the main features involved. In front of the main gate, and presumably forming an island in the ditch, stood the Douglas (later called the Percy) tower. This formed an outer entrance and had its own barbican in front of it. In order to enter the castle it was necessary to cross a drawbridge and pass through the barbican and the outer entrance formed by the new tower. Beyond this were three more drawbridges, obviously in a fairly long bridge, which had to be traversed before the main double-towered entrance, with its own defences (portcullises, machicolations, and double gates) could be reached. The whole arrangement is reminiscent of Scarborough (above, p. 54) where a not dissimilar range of outer defences was added about 1250.

A third Northumberland castle, Prudhoe, also received some additions at this time. The earliest surviving structures on the site are the square stone keep and the gatehouse, probably built around 1150. The remaining defences of this period were probably of earth and timber. During the thirteenth century they were replaced by a stone curtain wall with two boldly projecting round towers at the south-west end of the oval enclosure and a single rectangular tower at the north-east end. These additions are not precisely dated but they may well have coincided with work known to have been carried out in the keep about 1300. Such works may be connected with Edward I's activities in the north which began in 1296.

6
Later Medieval Developments

After the great castle-building activity of the Edwardian period there was almost inevitably a pause, which occupied the first half of the fourteenth century. By the end of Edward's reign castle building had been going on, more or less continuously, for some two and a half centuries, since the first days of the Conquest in 1066. Virtually all the stone castles ever built were still then in existence, even those in styles no longer fashionable (such as square keeps, for example), since a castle was too costly a possession to be given up simply on grounds of style. The net result of this very long period of building was that by the early fourteenth century there was, if not a saturation of castles, then at least a more than adequate supply for immediate needs. There was, in consequence, a very noticeable pause in the building of new castles which lasted, with only a handful of exceptions, for some fifty years after Edward's death, until about 1360. Even after that date there was nothing to match the castle-building activity of the thirteenth century. The period from Edward's death in 1307 to the end of the medieval period in 1485 was, in fact, the long twilight of the medieval castle. Although interesting and impressive castles would still be built, castle building had passed its peak in the Edwardian period. It never again commanded the same resources, either royal or baronial, and rarely achieved again the quality of such castles as Caernarvon and Beaumaris.

The differences between the Edwardian and post-Edwardian periods were not, however, simply those of quality and quantity, but also of type. If Edwardian standards were not achieved it was simply, for the most part, that the builders were not trying to build Edwardian castles. New times and new conditions produced different needs and requirements, and the differences between thirteenth-century castles and those of the fourteenth and fifteenth centuries are differences of type. The concentric plan, for example, so brilliantly shown at Beaumaris, was used only once more (at Queenborough in Kent, below, p. 152), and then in an unusual form which, unfortunately, no longer survives; nor was anything on the scale or strength of Conway or Caernarvon attempted again. The new, fourteenth-century objectives were different, and they inevitably produced new types of stronghold.

Among the factors which influenced castle building in the fourteenth and fifteenth centuries were the demands for greater domestic comfort and convenience, the desire for greater personal privacy, and, perhaps most important of all, the growth of what is known as 'bastard feudalism'. By the end of Edward I's reign the old, rigid, all-pervading feudal system as introduced by the Normans had begun to break down. Increasingly, services called for under the system were being replaced by cash payments.

As far as the barons were concerned it meant that they could now, among other things, hire mercenary troops for military service instead of relying on the limited service of their tenants. This provided them with a full-time professional armed force owing loyalty only to the man who paid them. This system of what were, in effect, private baronial armies is generally termed bastard feudalism, and it was the anarchy which it produced in the fifteenth century which finally put paid to the whole feudal system and led to the stronger central government under the Tudors (from 1485 onwards) which marked the end of the medieval period.

Bastard feudalism had its effect on castle architecture. Because their loyalty was up for purchase, and therefore suspect, mercenary troops were not the most reassuring company to have within the castle, no matter how useful they might be outside, terrorising the countryside or attacking a neighbouring castle on the baron's behalf. They were often simply thieves and cut-throats hired for their doubtful talents, who would have been thieves and cut-throats anyway, on their own behalf, had they not been hired for the purpose. The presence of such men within the castle walls must have led many a baron to fear for his life, his family, and his possessions, and the close proximity of wealth, or the signs of it, must have been a continual temptation to most of the hired soldiery. The result of this tension was a tendency, which became more evident in the second half of the fourteenth century, to isolate completely the baron's family quarters from those of his hired garrison. This meant the duplication of halls, kitchens, and other services so that the baron, and his family and immediate servants could survive independently of the rest of the castle should his mercenaries decide to take the law into their own hands.

This separation of family and retainers' quarters was achieved in various ways, depending on the castles involved. Such castles were based on a number of fairly clear-cut themes which summarise the main trends of castle-building in the fourteenth and fifteenth centuries. One such theme was the rectangular courtyard castle which obviously owes its origins to the rectangular Edwardian type. Another was the tower house, a self-contained residence in tower form, and these two themes will form the subject of the last chapter (7), in the years 1307 to 1485, and indeed beyond, albeit briefly, for both types overran the end of the medieval period. These two plans account for about two-thirds of the castles to be dealt with in the post-Edwardian period. The remaining castles, either new, or rebuilt, or added to, will be dealt with in the rest of the present chapter, covering the years 1307 to 1485. They too can be said to represent a theme, that of the gatehouse, which is a prominent feature in many of them, with links in certain cases with the tower-house type.

Both chapters will thus cover the same period, 1307 to 1485. In order to integrate them into a single coherent account the whole topic of castle building in the period will be summarised chronologically, in conjunction with a brief account of the historical background, beginning with Edward's son who came to the throne in 1307.

Edward II was a very different proposition from his able and energetic father. Weak and inept, he was regularly at odds with his barons and constantly under pressure from the Scots on the northern frontier where disaster followed disaster. Everything his father had gained was lost and

Previous page:
The north range of Doune Castle (Tayside) contains the Great Hall, the kitchen, and to the left, the gatehouse (the taller section) which is, in effect, an independent and self-contained tower-house.

England was raided as far south as Beverley in Yorkshire. Eventually he was deposed (1327) and subsequently murdered in Berkeley Castle (Glos.). Surviving remains from his reign can be summarised quite briefly. In Northumberland Dunstanburgh Castle was built from new and Alnwick Castle was extensively rebuilt. Elsewhere, additions were made to Ludlow Castle (Shropshire) and Pickering Castle (Yorkshire). Of the tower houses, Knaresborough (Yorks.), Dudley (Staffs.), and Caldicot (Gwent, formerly Monmouth) were provided with new towers, the latter in the form of a gatehouse. Of these works only Knaresborough was a royal undertaking, built for Edward's favourite, Piers Gaveston, at a cost of over £2,000. There was certainly work at other royal castles, but this is mostly a matter of written record rather than surviving visible remains.

Edward III, who reigned for fifty years (1327–77) once again provided England with an able military leader. Large sums were spent on fortification but for the most part it was a question of repairing and improving existing castles rather than building new ones. The most notable works of fortification came in the last two decades of Edward's reign from about 1360 on. Before that date there are only a handful of castles to be added to those built during Edward II's reign. Ford Castle (1338) and Chillingham Castle (1344), both in Northumberland, and Maxstoke Castle (Warwicks.) belong to the courtyard group. This amounts to only about a dozen castles, not all new, to fill the years from 1307 to 1360, a striking contrast to the almost feverish castle-building activity of the preceding, Edwardian period.

There is no question that the busiest post-Edwardian castle-building period was from about 1360 to 1400, during the later years of Edward III and the reign of his grandson, Richard II (1377–1399). By 1360 England was very much under the threat of invasion from France, and there was, in fact, a raid on the Sussex coast in 1359, and more raids, and worse, were feared. The danger increased during the last years of Edward's reign, culminating in an attack on the Isle of Wight in 1377, the year in which he died. It can be no coincidence that in these years there was a renewal of castle building, in noticeable contrast to the greater part of Edward's reign when repair and maintenance were the order of the day. In 1359, the year of the Sussex raid, the castle of Hadleigh on the Essex coast was extensively rebuilt, and two years later the Thames estuary was further reinforced by the building of Queenborough Castle in the Isle of Sheppey. Later in Edward's reign and in the reign of Richard II a number of new courtyard castles were built in southern England including Bodiam, Sussex; Donnington, Berkshire; and Farleigh Hungerford, Somerset. Nunney Castle (Somerset), a tower-house closely resembling the Irish towered keeps (above, pp. 33-5), and Old Wardour Castle (Wiltshire), another tower-house, were also built in this period. In the Midlands, Warwick Castle was extensively rebuilt, one of the major additions being an elaborate gatehouse.

Castle building in the last four decades of the century was not, however, confined to southern England. The threat from the French in the south was matched by one from the Scots in the north, sometimes deliberately matched, for the two were allied against England. The result was a period of castle-building activity concurrent with the one in the south. The courtyard castles of Ford (1338) and Chillingham (1344) were joined by

The earliest surviving portion of Carlisle Castle, the keep, built in the time of Henry II. One of the later features is the outer gate-house built between 1378 and 1383.

Bolton, Lumley, Wressle, Sheriff Hutton, and Raby Castles. Tower-houses were built at Hylton and Warkworth and new gatehouses at Carlisle, Lancaster, and Tynemouth. In Scotland new castles at Tantallon and Doune exemplify the gatehouse theme, but also have links with tower-houses, and indeed, in the case of Doune, with courtyard castles. Altogether, in south and north, something like half the castles of the post-Edwardian period (1307–1485) were built in the forty years from 1359 (when Hadleigh was begun) to 1399 when Richard II died, ending the long period of Plantagenet rule which began in 1154 with Henry II.

In the fifteenth century only a handful of castles were newly built or added to on any scale, although they include some very interesting, and familiar, sites. In the tower-house group there was new building at Ashby de la Zouch (Leics.), Tattershall, Buckden Palace, and Raglan Castle (Gwent), the latter of which was also a courtyard castle. There were other courtyard castles at Herstmonceux (Sussex) and Kirby Muxloe (Leics.). There was also a rebuilt castle at Tutbury (Staffs.) and a new castle of somewhat unusual design at Caister in Norfolk. To all of these must be added, of course, the numerous tower-houses in the border region of England, and in Scotland and Ireland, which were being built in the fourteenth and fifteenth centuries. These are not castles in the sense of the great royal and baronial structures considered so far, and they differ also, although to a lesser degree, from the miscellaneous group of English tower-houses mentioned above. They are, nevertheless, an integral part of medieval (and later) fortification and will be dealt with in Chapter 7, in so far as they fall into the medieval period.

As stated earlier, courtyard castles and tower-houses will be dealt with in Chapter 7. The remaining castles of the 1307–1485 period, in many of which the gatehouse is a prominent feature, will be considered in the present chapter, beginning with an entirely new castle at Dunstanburgh, in Northumberland. Dunstanburgh Castle stands on a rocky headland on the Northumberland coast and was begun in 1313. From 1255 on, the barony belonged to the famous Simon de Montfort, although at that time no castle existed on the site. He may have intended to build one, but the Barons' War in which he was prominently engaged led to his death in 1265, at the hands of Prince Edward, later Edward I, during the Battle of Evesham.

The then king, Henry III, granted the barony of Embleton, which included the site of Dunstanburgh, to his second son, Edmund, Earl of Lancaster. He died in 1296 and it was his son, Thomas, second Earl of Lancaster and High Steward of England who, in 1313, began work on the new castle of Dunstanburgh. The castle seems to have been substantially complete by 1316. The second Earl did not long enjoy his new possession. Always in opposition to Edward II, he was defeated and captured at the Battle of Boroughbridge in 1322 and subsequently executed

The principal defences were ranged along the south side of the castle facing down the coast. They consist of the great double-towered gatehouse, two square towers (The Constable's Tower and Egyncleugh Tower), a turret, and a linking curtain wall, covering a distance of some 450 ft with a rock-cut ditch in front. The defences on the three remaining sides are simpler. On the west above a steep natural slope there is a curtain wall

View of the inner side of the gatehouse at Dunstanburgh. Late in the fourteenth century the entrance passage was blocked up by John of Gaunt and the gatehouse became, in effect, a tower-house.

some 750 ft long with a turret and a square tower (Lilburn Tower), flanked by a postern gate. On the north there is a sheer basalt cliff, 100 ft high, surmounted probably by a wall, although no trace of such now remains. There is a long stretch of plain curtain wall (c. 1,000 ft long) along the east side, standing above a fairly gentle slope to a rocky beach. However, this whole side is further protected by a north-facing cliff at its southern end which runs from Egyncleugh Tower south-eastwards to the sea. Apart from Lilburn Tower, therefore, the main structural interest of the castle is centred on the south curtain wall and its associated features, principally the gatehouse.

The gatehouse is large by any standards (110 ft wide, much wider than either Harlech Castle or Beaumaris Castle, for example, although not as deep as either), and consists of two D-shaped towers, each 50 ft wide and 55 ft deep from back to front. There was originally a barbican in front of the entrance passage between them, the foundations of which still survive. The whole structure was three storeys high with the semi-circular front portions of the two towers rising another two storeys so that the external elevation of the gatehouse must have been much more imposing than the internal one, much of which is still preserved. The ground floors of the towers were used as guard rooms and the first floor, including a room from which the portcullis was worked, may also have been used for the garrison. The second floor, however, housed the hall, with service quarters at one end and a great chamber or more private, with-drawing room at the other.

An arrow slit from inside the gatehouse at Dunstanburgh Castle.

The Dunstanburgh gatehouse was quite clearly conceived on large and imposing lines. However, much of the interest in the structure arises from the changes made later in the century which transformed it from a gatehouse into a keep or tower house. In 1362 John of Gaunt succeeded to the barony of Embleton and in 1380 instituted a major programme of repairs and alterations, almost certainly as a result of incessant Scottish raiding in the area. He blocked up the entrance passage of the gatehouse and added a forebuilding, transforming the structure virtually into a single huge tower. Behind the 'new' tower he built a small Inner Ward (c. 100 x 60 ft) with a rectangular tower at its north-east corner protecting the entrance. Finally he provided a new outer entrance to the west of the old gatehouse. This was a quite different concept from the gatehouse idea, with its central passage between two large protective towers. It consisted basically of a long open-topped passage between the west curtain wall and a new wall (a mantlet), parallel to it, with a series of gateways and a right-angled turn into the final gatehouse in a tower, which gave access to the Outer Bailey. Anyone wishing to reach the Inner Bailey still had to pass along its north wall and turn right at the north-east angle tower and right again into the actual inner entrance. This still left the newly-contrived tower as the final refuge. In effect, John of Gaunt's changes imposed a series of formidable obstacles on an attacker, instead of the single major impediment represented by the gatehouse. Once the entrance passage of this had been breached the whole fortress lay open to an attacker. Under the new arrangement the castle had to be taken section by section.

The remaining structures on the south curtain wall are the Constable's Tower and Egyncleugh Tower (each c. 25 ft square and of two storeys), with a small tower or turret between. Attached to the Constable's Tower is the Constable's house, a rectangular structure some 60 ft square around a small courtyard. The Egyncleugh Tower which overlooks the north-facing cliff mentioned earlier is, in fact, a supplementary entrance, with (originally) a drawbridge in front crossing the ditch. This is probably the Water Gate to which there is a reference in 1368.

One of the best-preserved parts of the castle is Lilburn Tower on the west curtain wall, probably built for John Lilburn who was constable of the castle around 1325. This is some 30 ft square and three storeys high, with a solid stone plinth beneath and four solid turrets rising 18 ft above the roof level. It occupies the highest point of the site and commanded a view not only of the interior of the castle but also of much of its surroundings, particularly to the west and south. Lilburn Tower is, in fact, a tower-house, rectangular in plan, as are all the other towers on the site except the round-fronted gatehouse towers. This is in contrast to the circular and polygonal towers of most other thirteenth- and early-fourteenth-century castles. There was certainly a return to the rectangular form, always more convenient, in the late medieval period, and Dunstanburgh's towers may simply be an early anticipation of this. On the other hand, the preference for the rectangular form never really died out in the north. Round and polygonal towers were, on the whole, a southern phenomenon which never totally supplanted the rectangular form in northern regions. The tower-houses which began to appear in the border region in the early fourteenth century were also rectangular in plan, so that a northern builder would have found plenty of justification for using this form rather than round towers in any new building undertaken at this time.

While work was going on at the new castle of Dunstanburgh, Alnwick Castle, in the same county, was the subject of considerable improvement and rebuilding, including work on three gatehouses. The castle is a large one (7–8 acres in area), and probably started as a timber motte-and-bailey structure which was apparently rebuilt in stone by about the middle of the twelfth century. The castle then consisted of a polygonal shell-keep or inner bailey some 140 ft in diameter, standing at the junction of two

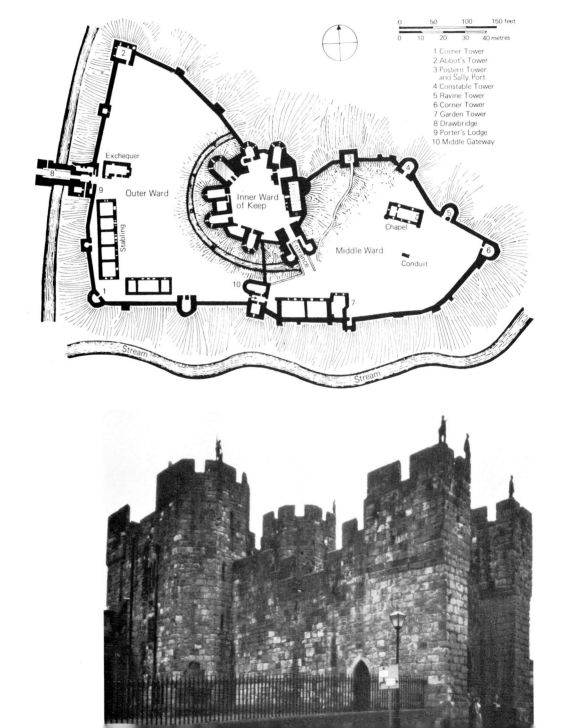

subsidiary enclosures, a middle bailey to the east and an outer bailey to the west, both defended by curtain walls.

In 1309 this castle came into the possession of Henry de Percy who, no doubt anticipating trouble from the Scots, set in hand an extensive reorganisation of its defences. First of all he added seven D-shaped towers to the Inner Bailey (the original shell-keep), together with a square-towered gatehouse. The effect was to transform this portion of the stronghold into a structure similar to a number of castles mentioned in Chapter 2: Bolingbroke, Clifford, Castell Coch, Morgraig, and White Castles, which consisted basically of polygonal enclosures with towers at

Opposite:
The existing plan of Alnwick is largely the work of Henry de Percy who received the castle in 1309 and almost immediately set in hand an extensive rebuilding programme. One of the results of his activities is the Outer Gateway.

Above:
About 1330 Rosamund's Tower (right) was added to the curtain wall of Pickering Castle (N. Yorks).

the angles. Some but not all of these had twin-towered gatehouses. Alnwick had a single rectangular tower with a central passage, but it has to be remembered that this was not an outer but the innermost of three successive gatehouses. In any case the existing pair of semi-octagonal towers was added about 1350 by Henry de Percy's son. In fact, both of the other gatehouses were also involved in the reconstruction (below). Many of the wall towers in the Middle and Outer Baileys were added at this time or shortly afterwards, bringing the castle more or less to its final medieval shape; the Inner Bailey was considerably altered, particularly internally, in the eighteenth century and again in the nineteenth century.

Of the two gatehouses not so far described, one stands between the Middle and Outer Baileys and one at the entrance to the Outer Bailey. The Middle Gateway is so placed as to control movement from the Outer Bailey to the Middle Bailey. It occupies the restricted space between the Inner Bailey ditch and main curtain wall of the castle. In fact, most of its

General view of Ludlow Castle (Shropshire) from the north.

southern tower projects beyond the curtain wall and is rectangular in plan. The northern tower is the more usual elongated D-shape. From its northern flank a wall runs across the ditch up to the wall of the Inner Bailey, so that the gatehouse could not be by-passed via the ditch.

The Outer Gateway, built between 1310 and 1314, is the largest and undoubtedly the most interesting of the Alnwick gates; even so, some of its outer features have probably been destroyed. It consists of two large towers, semi-octagonal at the front, which project some 40 ft forward from the west curtain wall. From the front of these, two high walls run forward again across the ditch to link on to two outer rectangular towers which flank the outermost gate. Between them these features define a narrow entrance passage nearly 100 ft long. There was a drawbridge in the passage in the section between the two linking walls and almost certainly another drawbridge and outer ditch in front of the rectangular towers, although there is now no surface indication of such. The Outer Gateway at Alnwick was a formidable structure comparable with later gateways at Tynemouth and Warwick Castles (below, p. 157), and with those in the York city walls (rebuilt in Edward III's time), only one of which, Walmgate Bar, retains its complete plan.

Apart from tower-houses (complete self-contained residences to be dealt with in Chapter 7), additions in this period included less specialised towers which simply added to the castle's range of accommodation. These allowed the provision of private rooms and suites which enabled members of the family and household to withdraw, when they so wished, from the largely communal life of the castle. Pickering Castle (Yorks.) and Ludlow Castle (Shropshire), in the first half of the fourteenth century, and Warwick

Castle (Warwicks. below, p. 158) in the second half, provide excellent examples of this type of addition. At Pickering Castle Rosamund's Tower was added about 1330 to an earlier motte-and-bailey castle of the twelfth century. The motte is crowned with a fragmentary shell-keep and is of the same date as the Inner Bailey. The Outer Bailey, surrounded by a curtain wall and towers (including Rosamund's Tower), was added about 1330. The tower is a three-storey square structure which projects beyond the curtain wall. The bottom storey is entered from the courtyard and has no connection with the two upper floors. These form a suite of rooms entered from the rampart walk. The lower room, possibly for a servant, has no fireplace, but the upper room would have formed a very comfortable apartment with a wide fireplace, windows in three walls, wall cupboards, and access to a private latrine via a door in the east wall. This is quite clearly not a tower-house. It has no kitchen or other resources to enable it to survive independently, and it was not conceived as such. It is simply additional accommodation to meet the growing need and desire for greater personal comfort and privacy. This was somebody's private suite in which he (or she) could get away from the close communal life of the castle and enjoy a measure of quiet and tranquillity in an apartment reserved for the occupant's exclusive use.

A whole set of such apartments was provided by additions to Ludlow Castle. A tall, four-storey tower (c. 40 x 20 ft) was added against the outer face of the inner wall when the Great Chamber block was built about 1330. The two lower floors are each divided into two apartments, but the two upper floors each contain a single, larger apartment. The smaller apartments consisted of a room about 10 ft square with a large window recess, opening to the north, in the 10-ft-thick wall of the tower. Each had its own private latrine. The upper apartments were more than twice the size of the others with two windows and a private latrine. These are quite clearly six specially-built private rooms for six members of the family or household, two of them on a grander scale than the others, indicating rank, seniority, or importance.

Queenborough Castle (Isle of Sheppey) no longer exists, but a plan survives. The castle, started in 1361, was circular and represents the final development of the concentric castle.

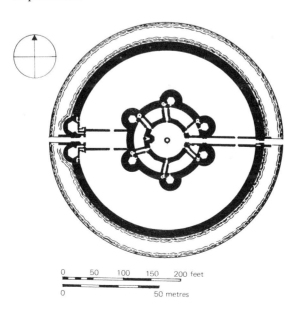

0   50   100   150   200 feet

0   50 metres

After Ludlow and Pickering there is not much to fill the gap between about 1330 and 1360 except the two courtyard castles of Ford (1338) and Chillingham (1344) to be dealt with in Chapter 7. Hadleigh Castle, on the Essex coast, marks the beginning of the period of fortification which occupied the last four decades of the century. Its purpose was the defence of the Thames estuary. Hadleigh was started in 1359, two years before Queenborough, but it was a rebuilding of an earlier stronghold and not an entirely new construction, which probably explains its somewhat old-fashioned plan. It consists of a single, polygonal bailey, some 350 ft from east to west and 150 ft from north to south, with round or half-round towers at the angles. The entrance was at the west end of the north curtain and was protected by an outer entrance or barbican. The two best-preserved towers are at the north-east and south-east angles where they project for three-quarters of their circumference. They are 36 ft in diameter and three storeys in height, with hexagonal interior rooms. On the south-west side of the castle are the remains of three square towers, possibly structures from the earlier castle incorporated in the rebuilding of 1359. The whole of the south side of the castle has slipped downhill some 40 ft but the main lines of its layout can be made out. It seems to have incorporated the main domestic buildings of the castle.

Queenborough Castle in the Isle of Sheppey (Kent), started in 1361, represented a further reinforcement of the defences of the Thames estuary against the possibility of French raids or invasion. Queenborough is particularly interesting because it looks back to the Edwardian period and must be regarded as the ultimate example of concentric planning. Combined with the concentric principle is a completely circular scheme which again can be seen as the ultimate stage of a process which began with quite irregular arrangements, progressed to polygonal plans, and then to trapeze-shaped, lozenge-shaped, rectangular, and triangular plans, leaving only the circular one to be explored. Circular features were not, of course, new. Circular keeps, shell-keeps, and wall towers had all been used in the past. What was new in the case of Queenborough was the rigid application of circular planning to the whole castle. Unfortunately, Queenborough was destroyed in the seventeenth century, but the plan of the site is known and there is also a very informative drawing of the castle, executed in the seventeenth century, by Wenceslas Hollar.

The outermost defence was a moat 25 ft wide, completely circular in plan, and nearly 400 ft in overall diameter. Within this was a massive curtain wall about 15 ft thick, also circular in plan and 330 ft in overall diameter, the same sort of size as Beaumaris, the outer curtain of which was approximately 330 x 330 ft. The main entrance, on the west side, was of the double-towered type, and on the diametrically opposite side, facing east, was a smaller, postern gate. Within it was the inner curtain, which formed, in effect, a shell-keep, 140 ft in overall diameter, with walls about 10 ft thick, leaving an 80-ft-wide space between inner and outer lines of defence. Attached to the inner curtain were six semi-circular towers, two of which, placed closer than the others, formed an inner double-towered gatehouse, on the side away from the main outer entrance. According to the Hollar illustration these towers and the inner curtain rose high above the rest of the castle and must have formed the most striking feature of the site. Within the keep the internal buildings formed a central, circular courtyard, again absolutely concentric with the inner and outer curtains.

The entrance arrangements of Queenborough were of some interest. They involved three gateways, two on the outer curtain and one on the inner. The main outer entrance, on the west side of the building, faced the back of the keep, the only entrance to which was on the opposite, eastern side, in line with the outer postern gate. From the main, outer gate parallel walls ran inwards, ending at the blank back wall of the keep. About half-way along each wall was another entrance and from these there was access to the main part of the Outer Bailey. To reach the inner part of the castle it was necessary to pass through one or other of these two entrances, around the north or south side of the Inner Bailey to entrances in another pair of parallel walls between the outer, postern gate and the inner main entrance. The arrangement imposed on an attacker a long, tortuous approach to the inner entrance over a distance of some 450 ft. It also meant that the two entrance corridors could be held, together with the Inner Bailey, even if the main part of the Outer Bailey fell to an enemy. Although, as stated earlier, Queenborough was the last flowering of the concentric castle, and nothing quite like it was ever built again, it does also in a sense look forward, in its preoccupation with circular planning, to the artillery castles of Henry VIII, although these are beyond the scope of the present survey.

Two Scottish castles built nearer the end of the century, Tantallon (Lothian, 1370), and Doune (Tayside, 1390) provide excellent examples of keep-gatehouses, but now in basically rectangular form, like the tower-houses which were appearing in increasing numbers in Scotland. Tantallon stands in a coastal promontory position with precipitous natural defences on the north, east, and south and the main, man-made defences across the western approach, the sub-rectangular area thus defined being about 270 ft x 150 ft. Immediately beyond the curtain wall was a great rock-cut outer ditch, with the Middle and Outer Baileys beyond, defined by elaborate earthworks. The Outer Bailey at least is a later work and the Middle Bailey in its present form may also be later than the stone castle. However, it seems not unlikely that the original structure consisted of an Inner Bailey (the surviving stone castle), and an Outer Bailey (now the Middle Bailey), running from cliff to cliff, which may have been strengthened at a later time.

The stone defences along the west side of the castle consist of a massive curtain wall, 12 ft thick and nearly 60 ft high, with a D-shaped tower above the cliffs at the south end, a massive circular tower (*c.* 45 ft in diam.) in a corresponding position at the north end, and an originally square gatehouse (*c.* 40 ft square) in the middle, the whole complex extending over a distance of 320 ft. Although the gatehouse is the principal feature of interest, the great size of the north tower is worthy of note. With a diameter of 45 ft and a probable original height of about 90 ft this is of keep-like proportions and in an earlier castle might well have been one. However, since this function is here performed by the keep-gatehouse, the north tower at Tantallon may be presumed to have been similar to the tower at Ludlow (above, p. 151) and to Guy's and Caesar's Towers at Warwick Castle, all three of which provided several storeys of private rooms, each with a latrine, fireplace, and other comforts. The main suite of internal buildings abuts the tower at one end and occupied the north side of the castle at the head of the cliff; it contains a first floor hall, over a vaulted undercroft and a range of domestic offices including a kitchen and bakehouse etc.

The centrepiece of the castle, both visually and functionally, was the gatehouse which also formed a keep, or perhaps more accurately at this date, a tower-house. As originally constructed the gatehouse was a rectangular tower at base, which about halfway up its estimated 90-ft height, blossomed into twin circular turrets of the front angles. The structure was five storeys high, the first storey (the ground floor), housing the entrance passage, a guard chamber and a staircase. Apart from the passage, the projecting part of the tower was solid at base level. Within the passage was a formidable array of defences designed to isolate the tower not only from enemies without but also from possible traitors within. Facing the exterior were four portcullises, followed by two sets of two leaved doors. At the inner end of the passage was another portcullis with double doors behind, facing the interior and intended to prevent access from that side also. Above the entrance passage were four superimposed floors of living rooms forming a self-contained residence for the lord of the castle. The Tantallon entrance has been described as a keep-gatehouse and in so far as it resembles the Edwardian keep-gatehouse this term is admissible. But the resemblance to the Scottish tower-house is clear, and in the geographical and chronological context of Scotland in the 1370s this link needs to be acknowledged, even if the alternative term 'tower-house-gatehouse' is too cumbersome for general use.

Doune Castle (Tayside) is roughly rectangular in plan, with a plain curtain wall for most of the circuit and, originally, ranges of buildings forming a central courtyard, although the buildings on the south, east, and part of the west sides have been destroyed. The north range is very well preserved. In the north-west quarter are the great hall and kitchen with a service room between. However, it is the remaining section of the north range which is of the greatest interest. In this north-east corner stands a great rectangular gatehouse rising high above the rest of the castle. In spite of a half-round tower (c. 25 ft in diameter) on one side of the entrance the gatehouse is much more like a conventional Scottish tower-house than Tantallon and also much more ingenious. The gatehouse is a slightly irregular rectangle (60 x 40 ft), with walls c. 7–8 ft thick. It is of four storeys, the upper three of which are isolated from the gateway below and from the adjacent Great Hall. The entrance passage running through the middle of the block is some 45 ft long with a machicolation and a still-preserved iron yett (a two-leaved openwork metal gate) at the outer end and (originally) a two-leaved door at the inner end, closing against the courtyard. On the right of the passage is a guard room with a prison opening off it. On the left are storage rooms and a well chamber, housed in the circular tower. Both stores and water were accessible from the rooms above by means of hatches in the floor of the Baron's Hall and the first floor of the half-round tower.

The three upper storeys of the gatehouse form a self-contained tower-house, accessible only by means of a staircase from the courtyard. On the first floor was the Baron's Hall, only marginally smaller than the adjacent Great Hall, and illustrating the duplication of facilities mentioned already

which was becoming a common feature in fourteenth- and fifteenth-century castles. The two upper floors were reached by a spiral staircase up from the Baron's Hall: immediately above was the Great Chamber, similar in size to the Great Hall, forming a more private family apartment, and the top floor housed smaller rooms, presumably providing that personal privacy which again was an increasingly common feature in castles of the time.

In England, Warwick Castle was extensively rebuilt in the second half of the fourteenth century. The reconstruction was started by Thomas Beauchamp, Earl of Warwick, and was still unfinished when he died in 1369. It was completed by his son in 1394. The most prominent features of the rebuilt castle (which have survived largely intact) are the gatehouse (with barbican), and the two great angle towers, Guy's Tower and Caesar's Tower, which on their many floors provided a large amount of additional accommodation. At the same time the Great Hall and associated buildings were added on the south-eastern side of the bailey, against the curtain wall. Warwick was one of the very early group of castles erected by William the Conqueror between 1066 and 1071. It was of the motte-and-bailey type, although the motte and its structures were of little significance by the fourteenth century. Presumably it began as a timber structure, to be replaced in the twelfth century by a stone shell-keep with a stone curtain wall around the bailey. As defined by its existing walls the castle was a large one, with a bailey 400 ft long and nearly 300 ft wide, lying to the north-east of a motte some 250 ft in diameter, surmounted by the remains of an irregularly polygonal shell-keep measuring 70 x 60 ft. The castle is surrounded on three sides by a large moat and on the fourth by the River Avon.

The north-east front of the castle consists of two great towers mentioned above, Guy's Tower and Caesar's Tower, at the angles, with the gatehouse mid-way between them. The outer part of the entrance, the barbican, projects well into the ditch and originally had a drawbridge in front of it, now replaced by a stone bridge. The entrance passage runs between two semi-octagonal towers and forms the lower of three storeys. The two upper storeys and the battlements could not be reached directly from below but only via a sloping passage (in the east linking wall) which started inside the courtyard. On the inner side of the barbican was a gallery or balcony, overlooking the middle section of the entrance passage, from which attackers who had managed to get through the barbican could be assailed from the rear. The walls linking the barbican to the gatehouse proper are 7 ft thick and 35 ft high topped by battlements, leaving the middle section of the passage open to the sky, and to attack from all sides. The gatehouse rose twice as high as the barbican and linking walls, standing nearly 70 ft above the interior of the castle. It is five storeys high in the flanking towers and four storeys in the central portion over the entrance passage. The flanking towers are circular to the front but octagonal where they project into the courtyard to the rear.

Prudhoe Castle (Northumberland) was strengthened, possibly by Edward I, when a new curtain wall was built equipped with round towers.

Impressive as the Warwick gatehouse is, it is overtopped by the two great angle towers which form the end pieces of the castle's north-eastern facade. Caesar's Tower is 85 ft high above the courtyard and 133 ft high from the bottom of the massive plinth on which it stands outside the curtain wall. It is tri-lobed in plan with overall dimensions of 40 x 32 ft. Two tiers of battlements at the top give the tower a very distinctive outline; the first

Top:
The gatehouse, with barbican, at the centre of the east front of Warwick Castle, with Caesar's Tower in the background.

Bottom:
Corresponding to Caesar's Tower at the south-east angle is Guy's Tower, at the north-east.

tier is a machicolated gallery, with the second tier rising above and within it. Caesar's Tower is six storeys high, the two uppermost forming a guardroom and ammunition store. The bottom storey, below courtyard level, was a prison. The three remaining storeys provided three suites of apartments, each consisting of a large, rectangular room (*c.* 20 x 15 ft) with two windows and a fireplace, another chamber in the thickness of the wall, and a latrine in the thickness of the opposite wall.

Guy's Tower (*c.* 40 ft in diameter) is similar in height to Caesar's, but simpler in plan. It is a multi-angular structure (12-sided) with only a single tier of battlements. It is five storeys high, the top storey being a guardroom. Below are four suites of apartments very much the same as those in Caesar's Tower, that is a large central room (*c.* 25 x 18 ft) with a mural chamber on one side and a latrine on the other. Between them the two angle towers provided seven spacious suites of rooms (in addition to space in the upper part of the gatehouse and in the main domestic block along the south-east curtain wall), and are outstanding examples of the fourteenth-century practice of catering for extra space and privacy by means of additional towers.

A gatehouse-with-barbican was added to Tynemouth Castle late in the fourteenth century, but following the rectangular style of Alnwick (above p. 148) and Carlisle (below, p. 160), rather than Warwick with its round and octagonal towers. Tynemouth is both a monastery and a castle and there are extensive remains of the church and monastic buildings within the curtain walls. These seem to have been built about 1295, including no doubt the gatehouse which preceded the one to be described. This was built by Prior John de Whethamstede around 1390 and was almost certainly based on, or at least strongly influenced by, the outer gatehouse at Alnwick described above.

The barbican consisted of two oblong towers (*c.* 32 x 12 ft) with the vaulted entrance passage between them, situated on the outer edge of the

The original entrance (*c.* 1295) at Tynemouth was replaced late in the fourteenth century by the existing gatehouse with barbican.

ditch which ran in front of the gatehouse. There was probably an outer ditch, with a drawbridge, in front of the barbican, as (originally) at Alnwick, but all trace of any such feature there has now gone. The lower storeys of the oblong towers formed outer guardrooms on either side of the entrance passage. The barbican towers are linked to the main gatehouse towers by a wall on the north side and a narrow building on the south side, both running across the main ditch, forming a middle section of the entrance open to the sky, and enclosing a drawbridge in front of the gatehouse proper. As at Warwick and Alnwick this stood high above the outer features. However, unlike these with their twin towers, Tynemouth consists of a single rectangular block or tower (*c.* 60 x 35 ft), housing the vaulted entrance passage with (inner) guard chambers, symmetrically disposed on either side, occupying the whole of the ground floor. The two upper floors at Tynemouth were occupied by the Great Hall (first floor) and Great Chamber (second floor), with the kitchen and other services housed in an additional wing attached to the south-east corner of the gatehouse.

The outer gatehouse at Carlisle was rebuilt between 1378 and 1383 to a somewhat unusual plan. The two-storey building formed a square (44 x 44 ft) but instead of the entrance passage running through the middle, it formed the eastern side of the block. Further, this side was divided into two parts, the outer of which was, in fact, a barbican, open to the sky. The walls on the south and east sides of this space (*c.* 12 ft square) were 6 ft thick and had parapets at front and rear. The outer gate was in the south wall of the barbican and anyone passing through it could be attacked from the wall above and the wall to the east. Beyond the barbican was the vaulted entrance passage with a portcullis and gate at its outer end and another gate at its inner end.

Another notable gatehouse built around this time was the one at Lancaster Castle, probably started under Henry IV (1399–1413, formerly Duke of Lancaster), as soon as he came to the throne, after the overthrow of the last of the Plantagenets, Richard II. The earliest surviving portion of the castle is a square keep, probably of the twelfth century. King John is known to have done considerable work on the castle, probably adding an outer ditch, a curtain wall, and round wall towers, and the castle appears to have been maintained more or less in this state throughout the thirteenth and fourteenth centuries. The most prominent feature of the existing structure, the gatehouse, was added, as indicated above, at the beginning of the fifteenth century. It consists of two tall towers, semi-octagonal to the front, rising over 60 ft to strongly projecting battlements carried on corbels, with square upper towers or turrets on each, giving an overall height of some 80 ft. Between the towers a great archway, 15 ft wide and 20 ft high, with the arms of Henry IV and his son (created Duke of Lancaster in 1399) above, leads into the entrance passage. Presumably the whole structure was fronted by a ditch, crossed by a drawbridge, but if so all trace of these outer features has now gone.

Tutbury Castle (Staffs.) was also the property of the Duke of Lancaster and most of the surviving remains are of works carried out under the Lancastrian kings, beginning with Henry IV. Tutbury was one of the castles built within a few years of the Conquest, and was of the motte-and-

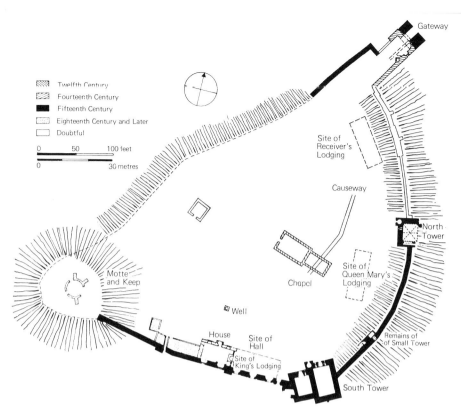

Twelfth Century
Fourteenth Century
Fifteenth Century
Eighteenth Century and Later
Doubtful

0   50   100 feet
0   30 metres

Gateway

Site of
Receiver's
Lodging

Causeway

North
Tower

Motte
and Keep

Site of
Queen Mary's
Lodging

Chapel

Well

Remains of
of Small Tower

House   Site of
                     Hall

Site of
King's Lodging

South Tower

The original Tutbury (Staffs.), a motte-and-bailey castle, was built between 1066 and 1071. The existing remains are mostly of the fifteenth century.

bailey type, with the motte originally surmounted by a shell-keep, presumably preceded by timber structures and now replaced by an eighteenth-century folly. The bailey, which forms the existing castle, was D-shaped in plan, and there are remains of a much larger earthwork enclosure to the south, protecting the village or township associated with the castle.

The building work initiated by Henry IV began in 1400 and went on intermittently for the next sixty years. The surviving remains (mostly fifteenth-century, with some fourteenth in the gatehouse), consists of the curtain wall forming the curving part of the D-shaped plan and a short straight section on the north-west side, two square towers (North Tower and South Tower), and the gatehouse at the north angle. The main part of the gatehouse is fourteenth-century, added to the castle in the years 1313–14, but the two rectangular towers which now flank the outer entrance passage are part of the fifteenth-century additions. The North Tower, four storeys high, was about 40 x 30 ft although the outer wall is now missing. It was apparently one of the last main features to be added, being built between 1446 and 1461. A noticeable feature is the spiral staircase housed in a small projecting wing at the north-west corner of the tower. This is a feature found in many pele towers and Scottish tower-houses, and suggests that the tower was, in effect, a tower-house, a suggestion supported by the date, the dimensions, and the number of storeys.

The South Tower is a much larger affair and less regular in shape. In plan it consists of two main rooms, the larger of which is 55 x 35 ft externally; a smaller room on the west side is 40 x 25 ft externally. The spiral staircase which served both was again housed in a projecting wing, at the junction between the two parts. The overall dimensions of this composite structure were more than 60 x 60 ft, so that it is quite clearly something more than a defensive wall tower, and the large windows tell the same story. Again one must think in terms of the contemporary tower-houses built in the north of England and Scotland at this time. The South Tower was begun about 1441 and appears to have been completed by about 1450, probably before the North Tower was started.

The last post-Edwardian castle to be considered here, Caister Castle, Norfolk, is both interesting and unusual. It was built by Sir John Fastolf, on whom Shakespeare's Falstaff was based, although the original Sir John was a much more redoubtable character than the buffoon of *Henry IV*. He was born around 1378 in a moated manor house at Caister which preceded the present castle, begun in 1432. In the context of the castles considered so far, Caister is unusual in being built of brick, although a number of castles to be dealt with later (Herstmonceux, Tattershall, Kirby Muxloe), were also built of this material. Caister was by no means the first use of brick, but it was only in the fifteenth century that it came into common use. Another unusual feature was the gun-loops in the tower and elsewhere in the stronghold, reflecting the growing use of firearms in warfare in the fifteenth century. The tower is a lofty affair, nearly 100 ft high, which dominates the surviving remains and must have dominated the original castle. The building was an elaborate affair in plan, with the main structure (to one corner of which the tall tower was attached) in the form of a rectangular courtyard castle. As such it could perhaps have been dealt with in the next chapter, but it does not appear to belong to the straightforward courtyard type. As will appear below it is something of an anomaly and as such it is perhaps best dealt with here.

The nucleus of the castle was a trapeze-shaped rather than strictly rectangular curtain wall, with ranges of buildings on all four sides (although to different depths) forming a somewhat irregular courtyard. Overall, but not counting the projecting towers, this inner structure measured 165 x 145 ft, very close to both Bodiam (150 x 140 ft) and Bolton (170 x 130 ft). Like Bodiam there were gatehouses on opposite sides and a moat about 40 ft wide around the whole structure. The Caister gatehouses were on the east and west sides and it was on these two sides, beyond the moat, that Caister differed from other English courtyard castles. On both eastern and western sides there were large, walled forecourts in front of the entrances. The eastern forecourt (*c.* 200 x 120 ft) had a curtain wall on three sides (north, east, and south) with three ranges of internal buildings and round towers at the two angles. It was surrounded by a moat, linked to the moat around the nucleus of the castle. The open side of the forecourt faced the castle and from the middle of this side a bridge and drawbridge led across the moat to the east gatehouse. Access to the forecourt from the exterior was via another bridge on the north side of the forecourt. The western forecourt was generally similar but not so completely isolated by water, although it seems to have acted as a water gate. From it an arched passage gave access to a 'barge ditch' or canal linked to the River Bure, and this seems to have been the means of conveying goods to and from Caister.

Apart from this elaborate plan the other striking feature of Caister is, of course, the tower which survives at very nearly its original height. The impression of height is strengthened by its relatively small diameter, only 23 ft. The tower proper was 90 ft high (walls 4 ft thick), with the attached hexagonal stair turret running 8 ft higher. Internally there were five storeys of hexagonal rooms. Four of these were provided with windows and fireplaces and were presumably personal rooms for members of the household. To that extent the Caister Tower fulfils the same function as Guy's, Caesar's, and other towers in providing extra, private accommodation within the castle. The topmost storey at Caister had a window but no fireplace and presumably, therefore, had some other function.

The combination of a courtyard plan, elaborate forecourts, and a lofty tower make Caister an unusual castle in an English setting and prototypes have been sought abroad, most particularly for the tripartite plan of the buildings. Douglas Simpson has, in fact, demonstrated that Caister is based on the *Wasserburg* of the Rhine area in Germany. *Wasserburg* means literally 'water castle' and denotes a castle in which water plays a prominent part in the defences, although not in the Caerphilly or Leeds Castle manner. The Rhenish castles are very much like Caister with a rectangular nucleus and rectangular or near-rectangular forecourts, separated from each other and the exterior by a series of wet moats fed from an adjacent river. The unusual form of Caister Castle presumably represents Sir John Fastolf's personal choice, possibly based on what he had seen in his military service abroad. In any case, the castle's position on the East Anglian coast placed it in an area which was inevitably in trade contact with the Lower Rhine area, and architectural indications of such contact need come as no surprise.

Caister Castle (Norfolk) was built by Sir John Fastolf (Shakespeare's Falstaff). The tower, nearly 100 ft high, must always have dominated the castle.

7
Courtyard Castles and Tower-Houses

The courtyard castles built in the period from 1307 to 1485 have been mentioned already. Two of the finest examples are Bodiam (Sussex) and Bolton (N. Yorks.), and these illustrate a noticeable difference between southern and northern types. In the south the circular angle tower persisted, as at Bodiam, Farleigh Hungerford, and Donnington. In the north, on the other hand, the rectangular type was preferred, as at Bolton, Lumley, or Sheriff Hutton. Entrance arrangements also tended to differ. In the south elaborate, twin-towered gatehouses persisted. In the north, the design was generally simpler. At Bolton Castle, for example, access was via a vaulted passage through the east range of buildings, immediately adjacent to the south-east angle tower.

The main group of courtyard castles was built in the second half of the fourteenth century, in response to threats on both northern and southern flanks, from Scotland and France respectively. It is perhaps an indication of the longer-term unsettled conditions in the north, however, that both courtyard castles and pele towers (below) appear there in the first half of the century. Ford Castle (Northumberland) was built in 1338 by Sir William Heron and has been occupied more or less continuously ever since. During that time it has inevitably been subjected to a great deal of alteration and rebuilding, the last occasion being as recently as 1938, six hundred years after its original foundation. Nevertheless, a considerable part of the early castle survives and the main lines of the plan are clear.

As originally constructed in 1338 Ford Castle followed a simple rectangular plan with four square towers at the angles, projecting boldly beyond the curtain wall which was some 7 ft thick. The two surviving towers, at the north-west and south-west angles, are five storeys high. The south-east tower is completely gone and the one at the north-east is now buried in later buildings. There is no surviving indication of a gatehouse and the entrance was probably a vaulted passage as at Bolton Castle (below). Nor is there any indication of the four ranges of buildings around the courtyard, found in so many later castles, and it may be that at Ford they were timber-built, although there is some slight evidence which may indicate a stone-built hall against the east curtain wall.

Chillingham Castle (also Northumberland) was started by Sir Thomas de Heton some six years after Ford, in 1344. It appears to have been very much the same type of building although it too has been extensively altered over the centuries and can be discussed now as a castle only in its broad outlines. It consisted of four more-or-less square angle towers linked by a curtain wall. If the existing structure is any indication then the towers had

One side of the hexagonal keep-like tower at Raglan Castle isolated by its own moat from the rest of the castle.

four storeys and possibly a basement as well, the same arrangement as at Ford. The ranges of stone buildings around the courtyard are fifteenth- and early-sixteenth-century but there is just a possibility that their lowest portions may be earlier, indicating stone-built internal buildings from the beginning. If this is not so, the internal buildings must have been of timber, as at Ford Castle. The stronghold was extensively remodelled in the seventeenth century (1625–35) and Chillingham owes most of its present appearance to this work.

About four years after Chillingham was begun work started at Maxstoke Castle in Warwickshire (1348). Appropriately, situated as it is midway between northern and southern groups, Maxstoke has neither round nor rectangular towers but octagonal ones. The castle, of red sandstone, was built by William de Clinton, Earl of Huntingdon, and has been lived in continuously ever since. It is still surrounded by its original wet moat. The castle is fairly simple in plan: four projecting octagonal towers are linked by a plain curtain wall; there are no intermediate towers or turrets. In the middle of the east front is the gatehouse, a rectangular block projecting in front of the curtain wall, with two tall octagonal towers at its outer angles, the same arrangement as at Donnington (below). The north-west angle tower (The Lady's Tower) is both taller and wider than the other three towers. Internally there are ranges of stone buildings on the west and part of the north sides. If there were original buildings on the remaining sides then presumably they were of timber, as suggested for Ford and Chillingham.

In the second half of the fourteenth century work at Bolton Castle (N. Yorks.) began, in 1375. The castle, built for Lord Scrope, Chancellor to Richard II, is based on a rectangular and nearly symmetrical plan. Four rectangular towers (c. 45 x 35 ft), each five storeys high, are linked by a high curtain wall, with ranges of internal buildings, three storeys high, on all four sides, defining a central courtyard 90 ft long and 50 ft wide. The internal ranges are between 30 and 40 ft wide. There are small rectangular intermediate towers midway in the longer north and south curtain walls. The entrance is a vaulted passage through the east range, immediately north of the south-east tower, with a portcullis at either end. The five doorways in the courtyard which give access to the internal buildings were also equipped with portcullises.

In the layout of the internal buildings there is a duplication of rooms, which divided the castle into two independent parts. There is, for example, a kitchen in the north-east tower, and a hall in the north range, with another kitchen and hall, both smaller, in the south-east angle. The larger versions of each were for the garrison as a whole. The smaller versions formed part of what was virtually a self-contained residence in the key south-eastern corner of the castle where the entrance was situated. This special section of the stronghold consisted of the south-east tower, the entrance passage and the rooms above to the north and a section of the south range as far as the chapel to the west, forming an L-shaped block of rooms. These were cut off from the rest of the castle at every floor by blank walls, with access only from the entrance at ground level, as if the section were, indeed, a free-standing tower. At ground level the section consists of the main entrance passage, the guardroom (occupying the south-east) tower), the entrance from the courtyard, guarded by a portcullis, with a spiral staircase to the rooms above, and a store in the south range. On the first floor there was a portcullis room above the entrance passage which meant that the entrance to the castle was always under the lord's control. Above the guardroom was the lord's hall, and above the store the lord's kitchen. On the second floor were his solar and camera (the more private rooms), and the two remaining floors of the tower were probably also given over to private and smaller rooms. Even though it constitutes less than a quarter of the castle as a whole the isolated section still forms a very commodious dwelling, with five storeys of accommodation in the tower section and three elsewhere.

Raby Castle (Co. Durham) has been considerably altered since it was first built in 1381. Nevertheless, the main lines of the courtyard castle from which the present structure developed are reasonably clear. The structure was built or at least started, by John Neville who became fifth Lord of Raby in 1367. The plan of the existing building is irregular and complicated by much later building. However, there is still a central rectangular courtyard and this may be presumed to be the courtyard (or part of it) around which the original castle was built. There are five named towers, four of which (however rebuilt), are in positions which would fit with a courtyard plan. The external elevations are probably more informative than the plan. On the east front Bulmer's Tower (north-east angle) is five-sided rather than rectangular and projects boldly beyond the adjacent walls which were clearly built later. At the north-east angle Mount Raskelf is rectangular but hardly projects at all. Between the two towers is the Chapel Gateway, with two slim rectangular turrets. However, altered and adapted, this looks like the main framework of one side of a courtyard castle of Bolton type. Both Bulmer's and Mount Raskelf towers have thick walls and therefore presumably belong to the earliest period of building.

The west front tells a broadly similar story. The Watch Tower and Joan's Tower occupy the north-western and south-western angles respectively with a twin-towered gatehouse (the Neville Gateway) between. These are largely thin-walled structures and probably represent reconstructions, and probably enlargements, of the original structures, the names of which they bear and preserve. Nevertheless, this appears to be the skeleton of one side of a courtyard castle. Joan's Tower projects a long way to the west, but this is simply an enlargement of an originally smaller angle tower, the upper portion of which can still be seen from the south.

The two fronts (east and west) as described above could well have formed the two shorter sides of an oblong courtyard castle, the longer northern and southern sides of which are respresented by the existing north and south ranges. The thin walls of the south range appear to be of later date, but thicker walls in the north range could indicate an intermediate tower made necessary by the greater length of this side. There would presumably have been a similar tower in the south range. Although this does not take account of all the structures at Raby, none the less all the elements of a thoroughgoing courtyard castle are present: a rectangular plan (long axis east and west) with four angle towers, two intermediate towers on the two long sides, and entrances in the middle of the two shorter sides. The same formula would fit both Bolton and Bodiam Castles

1 Gatehouse
2 Clifford's Tower
3 Bulmer's Tower
4 Joan's Tower
5 Watch Tower
6 Mount Reskelf

Kitchen

Courtyard

Nevill Gateway

Chapel Gateway

Entrance Hall

Small Drawing Room

Library

Dining Room

Octagon Drawing Room

with only minor variations, and there seems little doubt that Raby was originally conceived in the same terms.

The last of the five towers mentioned earlier presumably did not form part of this plan. If the hypothesis outlined above is correct, Clifford's Tower was originally a free-standing tower to the north-west of the early castle, incorporated in the main structure by later building in the intervening space. As a free-standing tower, just inside and therefore virtually controlling the gatehouse, it must be regarded as (originally) a tower-house, a self-contained residence probably for the owner. Perhaps at Raby this is how the separation of the lord's quarters and those of the mercenaries was achieved.

Another courtyard castle in the same county, Lumley Castle, near Chester-le-Street, was started about ten years later, around 1390. It was built by Ralph, Lord Lumley, on high ground above the River Wear. Although there have been later alterations, most notably by Sir John Vanbrugh in the early eighteenth century, the main lines of the original castle are very much clearer than at Raby. There are four rectangular towers at the angles linked by ranges of internal buildings forming a rectangular courtyard with a gatehouse in the middle of the east side. The angle towers (all with vaulted basement and three upper storeys) have their long axes east and west and they all project boldly in these directions; the projection to north and south is only slight. The north-east tower housed the chapel while the larger north-west tower contained the kitchen. The corners of each tower were carried up to form turrets in tower-house fashion which is, in essence, what each one was, in shape if not in function.

The east front was symmetrical about the entrance with flanking rectangular turrets. This gave access to the courtyard (120 x 75 ft) with the hall block (the west range) on the far side. All the ranges surrounding the courtyard were made up of vaulted basements and two upper storeys. There was a good deal of internal alteration in the early eighteenth century, particularly in the south and west ranges, but the exterior of the castle was not affected to the same extent.

The three remaining northern courtyard castles (Sherriff Hutton, Wressle, and Middleham, all in Yorkshire) can be dealt with more briefly. There was a castle at Sherriff Hutton (about 10 miles north-east of York) from about 1140, but not on the present site; the early castle is presumably represented by the motte-and-bailey earthwork south of the parish church. The existing structure was begun in 1382 by the same John Neville who built or at least started Raby Castle in 1381. Nikolaus Pevsner described Sherriff Hutton as 'almost a copy of Bolton Castle' started a few years before in about 1375. Its four oblong angle towers (55 x 35 ft) were in three cases four storeys, and in the fourth (the north-west tower) five storeys high. The linking ranges, probably consisting of vaulted basements with two storeys above, formed a central courtyard 120 x 100 ft. Access was via a gatehouse on the eastern side of the castle.

Wressle, about 6 miles east of Selby, is also of what may be described as the Bolton type although only two angle towers and the intervening range survive, together with a fragment of the east range containing the entrance. Of the two surviving towers the western one was of three storeys while the eastern one was of four and contained the chapel. The intervening range

Opposite top:
The plan of Raby Castle (Co. Durham), is complicated by later building, but the main lines of the original, rectangular courtyard castle (built 1381) are clear.

Opposite bottom:
The east front of Raby Castle with the Chapel Gateway in the centre.

(the south range) contained the hall. The castle was built by Sir Thomas Percy who started it around 1380.

Middleham Castle, about 10 miles south of Richmond, was not originally planned as a courtyard castle and, strictly speaking, never became one. Nevertheless, the forces which shaped the other northern courtyard castles were quite clearly at work here as well. The existing stone castle, with a rectangular keep (105 x 78 ft), was started about 1170. A keep such as this must have stood within an enclosing bailey but nothing of such an early date survives in the existing curtain which is mostly of the late thirteenth century. This curtain wall is rectangular in plan (c. 220 x 180 ft) and more or less equidistant (c. 50 ft) from the keep on all four sides. In the fourteenth and fifteenth centuries ranges of buildings were built against the

Bodiam (Sussex), often described as the most picturesque castle in England.

curtain wall on three sides (north, west, and south), but because of the limited space they were relatively narrow, *c.* 25–30 ft overall, leaving a slightly wider space between them and the keep. In the same period rectangular towers (*c.* 35 x 25 ft) were added to three of the angles (one of them on the north-east forming a gatehouse), and a D-shaped projecting bastion on the south-west was heightened to form an angle tower of the same shape. Thus virtually all the features of a courtyard castle were present at Middleham. Also present, however, was the great rectangular keep which must always have dominated the scene. Most courtyard castles were built from new, thus giving the builders an entirely free hand. At Middleham the earlier structures had to be taken into account and this is why it could never be transformed into a full-scale courtyard castle.

The entrance at Middleham (N. Yorks), at one corner of the rectangular curtain wall of the fourteenth century.

While these courtyard castles were being built in the north a corresponding group was under construction in the south of England, the most notable of which was Bodiam Castle, Sussex. Bodiam's extensive water defences were dealt with at the end of Chapter II. Its most noticeable difference from the castles considered above are the four circular angle towers. Even so, the intermediate towers on the east, south, and west curtains and the gatehouse towers on the north are solidly rectangular, indicating that rectangularity was not entirely a northern preference. The castle was built by Sir Edward Dallingrigge, who was granted the licence to build in 1385 by Richard II. England was beset with troubles at this time: control of the Channel had been lost and raids on south coast ports were frequent—at one stage the Isle of Wight was occupied. In granting to Sir Edward, a distinguished soldier under Edward III, a licence to build a castle in Sussex Richard had very much in mind the protection of the adjacent countryside and provision of a formidable obstacle in the case of a full-scale invasion.

The castle follows the standard courtyard formula. Four circular angle towers (c. 30 ft in diameter) are linked by two-storey ranges of buildings forming a central courtyard c. 90 x 80 ft. Access was via an imposing rectangular-towered gatehouse on the north side with a formidable range of obstacles in its vaulted entrance passages. At the outer end were a portcullis and two-leaved gate, and this pattern was repeated halfway along the passage. A third portcullis and gate were placed at the inner end, but this time facing the courtyard: that is, with the portcullis on the courtyard side, so that the gatehouse could, if the need arose, be isolated from there as well. There were rectangular towers halfway along the three remaining sides, the one on the south with a vaulted passage through forming a postern gate.

Left:
The only surviving portion of Donnington Castle (Berks.), apart from foundations, is the gatehouse.

Right:
Farleigh Hungerford Castle (Somerset), showing the two best-preserved circular angle towers.

As at Bolton Castle, there is a clear division of the internal accommodation separating the lord's quarters from those of his hired soldiery. The larger section (the lord's) occupies the south and east ranges and half of the north, including the whole of the gatehouse. Since the postern gate was also in his section he could control all movement in and out of the castle at critical times. At one end of the lord's suite was the kitchen, separated from the retainers' hall by a blank wall. From the kitchen a passage led eastwards to the lord's hall and from the hall a doorway led into the west range containing more private apartments and the chapel. In the north range it is noticeable that all access to the upper parts of the gatehouse is on the lord's side. On the retainers' side, to the west, there is only a blank wall between their quarters and the entrance passage.

The retainers' quarters form an L-shaped suite on the west and part of the north side of the castle, contained as it were between two blank end walls, the one just mentioned, and the one referred to above on one side of the lord's kitchen. From the latter the retainers' hall runs northward, with the second kitchen beyond. Beyond the kitchen again the remaining L-shaped portion probably provided sleeping and storage accommodation for the garrison. The retainers' quarters were thus strictly contained while the lord's section included three of the four angle towers, the gatehouse, and two of the three rectangular towers (one of them a postern gate), enabling him to exercise a reassuring degree of control over his necessary but potentially unruly mercenaries.

In the same year (1385) as he granted a licence for Bodiam, Richard II also granted a licence for Donnington in Berkshire, presumably for the same reasons. The castle was built by Sir Richard Abbenbury. Unfortunately, apart from foundations, little of the building is preserved except for the imposing gatehouse. The foundations indicate a somewhat irregular, quadrangular plan with small, projecting round towers at the angles and the usual ranges of internal buildings. In the middle of the east front is the surviving gatehouse. This consists of a three-storey rectangular block projecting forward from the curtain wall, with tall, three-quarters projecting round towers at its two outer angles with the entrance passage between. The towers rose one storey higher than the main block and a spiral staircase in the south tower provided access to the battlements. The remains of a barbican-like structure on the front of the gatehouse indicate again that this was a castle intended for war, even if the impressive scale of the building did not already tell the same story.

Farleigh Hungerford Castle (Somerset) was built by Sir Thomas Hungerford, one-time Speaker of the House of Commons (1377), who bought the estate of Farleigh in 1370. He was responsible for the main part of the castle; the Outer Court was added by his son early in the following century. Sir Thomas's building consisted of a rectangular curtain wall (190 x 170 ft) with four circular angle towers (no two of which are exactly alike), and a double-towered gatehouse in the middle of the south curtain wall. There is a ditch along this side and along the west curtain, but on the north and east there was a steep natural slope and no ditch was required.

Farleigh Hungerford displays a number of differences from the sites considered so far. Its walls are comparatively thin (c. 5 ft) and its towers somewhat irregular in size, one of them hardly projecting at all (at the north-west angle). The main difference, however, is in the internal layout, which although providing a courtyard, does not do so in the manner of Bodiam or Bolton. Instead of a clear, open space defined by four surrounding ranges, Farleigh Hungerford had a building range (in effect a manor house) built across the courtyard from the east range to the west, dividing it into a smaller courtyard to the south and a space to the north containing a garden and one or two subsidiary domestic buildings. This pattern of a domestic block with courts on both sides is not uncommon in domestic architecture, one of the advantages being that it allowed windows on both sides of the hall, and may be indicative of the status of Farleigh Hungerford, that of a fortified manor house. This is supported by the lightness of the structure mentioned above and the generally less formidable appearance (as far as one can judge) as compared with the other courtyard castles.

It may have been this lack of strength which led to the additions of the following century, of a type not normally found in courtyard castles. Around 1425 Sir Thomas's son, Sir Walter Hungerford, built the Outer Court on the south side of the existing castle. At the same time a barbican was added to the double-towered gatehouse. The Outer Court included the existing parish church of St Leonard (*c.* 1350 and the earliest structure on the site), which thus became the castle chapel. The polygonal curtain wall of the Outer Court was surrounded by a ditch and strengthened with round towers, one of which (the South Tower) survives today. Not much remains of the west entrance but the east gate has a square, two-storeyed tower with the Hungerford arms above the archway.

The courtyard theme is continued in the following century, most notably at Herstmonceux (Sussex) started by Sir Roger Fiennes in 1441. Herstmonceux is brick-built with stone dressings and this as much as anything else contributes to a somewhat less military (although still architecturally very impressive) appearance than its neighbour in Sussex, Bodiam, built over fifty years earlier. The castle is large (over 200 ft square) with four octagonal angle towers and three semi-octagonal towers on each of three sides (north, west, and east). The middle tower on the north side houses a postern gate. On the south front there are two semi-octagonal towers with a very imposing double-towered gatehouse between. The flanking towers are semi-octagonal below, semi-circular above, surmounted by a heavily machicolated parapet. Within the parapet the towers are continued upwards as turrets, providing two tiers of firing positions at the top of the gatehouse.

The original internal buildings have been destroyed but fortunately good plans were made before the demolition work took place in 1777. The most interesting aspect of these is that they recall the arrangement at Farleigh Hungerford, with the hall range running across the courtyard. There were also the usual ranges against the curtain walls (here of two storeys) and given the size of the castle the five ranges must have provided a very large amount of accommodation. The hall range ran east to west, dividing the internal space into two oblong courtyards, north and south. These were further sub-divided (forming four courts in all) by ranges of buildings running north and south from the hall block, probably added at a slightly later date.

The main entrance of Herstmonceux (Sussex), an imposing double-towered gatehouse in the south front.

Kirby Muxloe Castle (Leics.) was also built of brick with stone dressings, although unlike Herstmonceux it was never completed. It was begun in 1480 by the first Lord Hastings, but after his sudden execution by Richard III in 1483 work soon came to an end. The castle was intended to be large (*c*. 250 x 200 ft) and the remains still stand within a rectangular moat *c*. 350 x 300 ft. There was, in fact, an earlier (fourteenth-century) manor house on the site and this was retained in the projected castle, producing the same effect as at Herstmonceux and Farleigh Hungerford, a range across the courtyard in addition to the four surrounding ranges. Apart from foundations nothing survives but the three-storey south-west angle tower and the gatehouse. Although the gatehouse, like Herstmonceux, is flanked by semi-octagonal towers, the other towers in the plan were all rectangular, in the northern fashion, although at this date the shape may be more a matter of convenience than regional preference. The one surviving angle tower is 27 ft square and in the region of 70 ft high to the top of the flanking turrets, and the other three were the same, in plan at least. It was intended that there should be intermediate towers, one each in the middle of the north, east, and south sides, but few details have survived. On the west side the only other upstanding portion is the gatehouse, two of the three storeys of which survive. It is basically rectangular in plan, with semi-octagonal towers at each end of the long sides, both external and internal, producing a plan not unlike the contemporary tower-houses of Tattershall and Buckden (below, p. 189).

The last flourish of the courtyard castle was Thornbury in Gloucestershire, a product of the last flourish of bastard feudalism early in the sixteenth century under the Tudor monarchs. Edward Stafford, third Duke of

Above:
Kirby Muxloe was never completed. Only the gate-house and the south-west angle tower survive.

Opposite:
At Thornbury (Glos.) the buildings around the huge outer court were planned as a barracks for the private army of the third Duke of Buckingham.

Buckingham, had all the characteristics and leanings of an old-style great baron, believing himself capable of defying the king, and getting away with it. His execution in 1521 by Henry VIII proved him wrong and his great baronial castle at Thornbury remained unfinished. The castle consists of two main parts. First, there is, or was intended to be, a normal, if architecturally sumptuous, courtyard castle, about 200 ft square—about the same size as Herstmonceux. There were octagonal towers at the north-west and south-west angles, and a central gatehouse with flanking semi-octagonal towers, together with smaller intermediate semi-octagonal interval towers. The one completed angle-tower is massive and businesslike and shows that whatever architectural pretensions Thornbury possessed, it was also conceived in serious military terms. If Buckingham intended to defy the king then he also intended to have the means of doing so.

It is, however, the second part of the complex, the greater outer court, which is such an astonishing part of Thornbury and so clearly indicative of Buckingham's intentions and aspirations. Although incomplete it was clearly intended to be over 300 ft square, with ranges of buildings on three sides, north, west and south, the east side being formed by the entrance front of the castle proper. These ranges, equipped with defensive towers and a double-towered gatehouse, were, in fact, a great barracks for Buckingham's armed retainers. The ground floor contained stables and the floors above, reached by outside staircases, were living quarters for the hired army with which Buckingham intended to assert his independence.

Just how many men would have been involved is difficult to say, but it must have been many hundreds and possibly more than a thousand. Thornbury is the courtyard castle on a grandiose scale. Instead of two sets of accommodation (the lord's and the retainers') disposed (but separated) around a single courtyard, there are now two courtyards, one within a palatial rectangular castle, and a much larger one within what is virtually a military establishment in its own right. Thornbury was a formidable concept and a potential threat to the country's stability, a fact clearly recognised by the king, whose action, in disposing of the Duke of Buckingham, resulted in the castle's unfinished state.

The story of the courtyard castle has been followed from 1307 to 1521 when Buckingham's execution brought work at Thornbury Castle to an end. The second major theme of this period is the tower-house. There are large numbers of these in Scotland and Ireland and in the border regions of Cumbria and Northumberland, displaying a high degree of uniformity in plan and elevation. There are, in addition to these, about a dozen sites scattered widely throughout England and Wales which, although still coming under the heading of tower-houses, display a great deal of variety, again in both plan and elevation, and these will be dealt with first. In addition to their wide geographical spread the small number of English and Welsh sites are also of greatly varying dates within the period under review, so that they are a sporadic phenomenon, unquestionably of great interest, but different from the geographically and chronologically compact pattern of Border, Scottish, and Irish tower-houses. These, both in their numbers and their style, represent a separate topic from castles proper and cannot be fully dealt with here; they will, in consequence, be summarised in

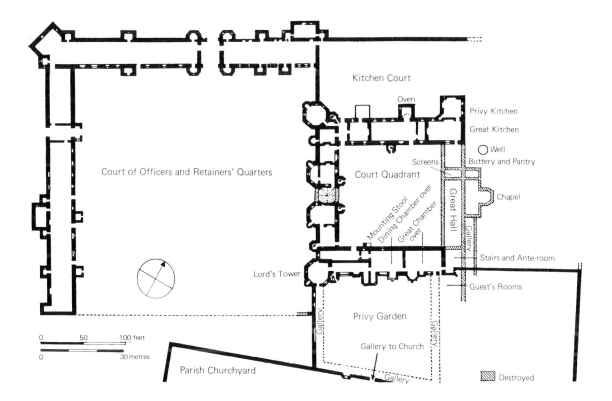

three groups rather than fully described, after the English and Welsh examples have been dealt with.

One of the few notable royal works of Edward II's reign was the new tower at Knaresborough Castle (Yorks.), started in the first year of his reign for his favourite Piers Gaveston. Knaresborough occupies a promontory position, with natural defences on the north, west, and south and a ditch on the east. Not much of the curtain wall is preserved but it appears to have been about 40 ft high and was probably strengthened with semi-circular towers. The castle was divided into two baileys, east and west, divided by a north/south cross wall, which has disappeared. The new Knaresborough tower was placed at the north end of this wall, at its junction with the north curtain wall. It was basically rectangular (64 x 52 ft) but with the north-east and north-west angles chamfered, so that from the exterior it was semi-octagonal. It had four storeys, one of them a basement below ground level, reached by a flight of steps down from the Inner Bailey to the west. At ground-floor level there was a kitchen and above that a hall. The top storey was the solar or private family room although little of it survives in the existing remains. There was also reported to be a chapel and watch towers, presumably turrets at the angles, rising higher than the rest of the building.

The new tower at Knaresborough formed what, in fact, can be described as a tower-house—a large keep-like tower within a castle forming a self-contained residence which can survive independently of the rest of the stronghold. As such it exemplifies the principle seen already in many of the castles just described where the separation of quarters was achieved around the courtyard by means of intervening blank walls. Tower-houses such as Knaresborough are another sign that, increasingly in the fourteenth and fifteenth centuries, it was desirable for the owner of the castle to have quarters separate from, and independent of the rest of the garrison. Knaresborough illustrates one difference between English tower-houses and those further north. The English towers tend to be additions to existing castles. In the Border region, and in Scotland and Ireland, on the other hand, tower-houses tend to be independent structures (whatever they became later) with only a small, walled yard attached to or surrounding them. Many tower-houses eventually became quite elaborate structures, but the additions are clearly later and the original, free-standing tower is easily identifiable.

Knaresborough is not the earliest example of an English tower-house. At Chepstow Castle (Gwent, p. 59) the fine D-shaped tower (Marten's Tower) has a great deal in common with Knaresborough, and was probably built in the latter part of the previous century. Like Knaresborough it is of four storeys, the basement being below courtyard level. The entrance was protected by a portcullis and a door, and the tower was clearly conceived as a self-contained unit. The ground floor was evidently the kitchen with the first floor forming the hall and the second floor the solar. This is a tower-house in very much the same way as Knaresborough and must be included in any survey of such structures in England. Nor should the Eagle Tower at Caernarvon Castle (built about the same time as Marten's Tower) be overlooked in this context (p. 98). It was almost certainly intended to be the self-contained residence (in other words, a tower-house) of the constable of the castle, Sir Otto de Grandson.

Opposite:
One of the few surviving royal works of Edward II's reign is the tower, virtually a tower-house, built at Knaresborough Castle (Yorks.).

Overleaf:
Warwick, one of the greatest and best-preserved English castles seen from across the River Avon.

Dudley Castle (Staffs.) provides the first example of an English tower-house built on the lines of the Irish towered keeps mentioned earlier (pp. 33-5). Dudley was built about the same time as Knaresborough by Sir John de Somery, who has been described by W. Simpson as a 'baronial thug', who terrorised the Staffordshire countryside with a gang of hired villains, during his tenure of Dudley from 1300 to 1321. The original castle at

Opposite top:
The nucleus of Cawdor Castle (Highland) is a rectangular four-storey tower-house.

Opposite bottom:
The north range at Doune Castle (Tayside), built *c.* 1390, with the gatehouse at the far end.

Above:
At Caldicot Castle (Gwent) a large rectangular gatehouse (right), virtually a tower-house, was added to the earlier (circular) keep-and-bailey castle.

Dudley was of the motte-and-bailey type and the timber superstructure seems to have remained in use until the early fourteenth century. However, between 1300 and 1321 Sir John de Somery built a tower-house on the motte of the earlier castle. Unlike most other tower-houses Dudley was of only two storeys, but it nevertheless formed a self-contained residence which could be isolated from the rest of the stronghold. It was oblong in plan with round towers at the angles and the upper storey consisted of a hall, with two smaller chambers at the west end and service rooms (pantry and buttery) at the east end. The kitchen and servants' quarters were at ground-floor level. There was a portcullis defending the entrance and an embattled parapet along the top of the wall. At the same time as the work on the motte, work proceeded on new domestic buildings in the bailey. These included another kitchen, another hall and solar, and another chapel. The reasons for this expensive duplication are the same as for Bodiam, Bolton etc. The tower-house on the motte provided Sir John de Somery with a safe and self-contained residence within the castle where he could secure himself, his family, and his possessions in the event of relations with his followers turning sour.

The early-fourteenth-century gatehouse at Caldicot Castle (Gwent, formerly Monmouth) would also appear to belong to, or at least have been influenced by, the tower-house. At this date one might have expected a twin-towered Edwardian structure, but not so. Caldicot was designed on lines which immediately suggest a tower-house. The gatehouse takes the form of a great oblong tower with one of the long sides to the front, and the vaulted entrance passage running through the middle. At the narrow ends

are two square latrine towers which rise higher than the main structure. The two floor levels above the entrance passage provided spacious domestic accommodation and it is presumed that the gatehouse took the place of the round keep as the residence of the owner. As such it shares the characteristics of a tower-house, and can thus be included in this section.

Nunney Castle in Somerset (started 1373) is the successor of Dudley in plan if not elevation and bears a very close resemblance to the Irish towered keeps considered earlier (pp. 33-5). It was built by Sir John de la Mare, a veteran of Edward III's French campaigns. The tower-house now stands alone, surrounded only by its moat, which is about 30–40 ft wide, but originally it stood within a large more or less rectangular bailey (c. 400 ft square), of earlier date, with a curtain wall on three sides (north, west, and east), and Nunney Brook to the south.

The tower-house consists of a basically rectangular tower, 80 x 40 ft, with boldly projecting round towers (c. 30 ft in diameter) at the four angles; at the narrow ends the wall is reduced to a narrow strip between the two towers. Internally there are four storeys (as compared with two at Dudley), each consisting of a large room in the main part of the tower and four smaller, circular rooms in the four towers. Entry was at ground-floor level, via a drawbridge across the moat, and this led into the kitchen and associated domestic offices. From one side of the entrance passage a straight staircase in the thickness of the wall led up to the first floor where the principal room was the common hall. From here a spiral staircase led up to the lord's hall on the second floor, with the solar or private withdrawing room on the third floor. This was very much a self-contained, self-sufficient residence, its independence emphasised by the surrounding moat.

On one side at least (the south) the structure is preserved at very nearly its full height, apart from the actual roof. At the top of the walls was a continuous machicolated parapet and within each angle tower was a narrower upper portion rising one storey higher. The towers were crowned with tall conical roofs as is made clear from a sketch made in 1644 by a Cavalier officer. They must have given the tower a very French appearance and this, no doubt, was Sir John's intention, arising from his close acquaintance with France during his service under Edward III.

The tower-house at Warkworth Castle (Northumberland) is quite unlike anything described so far. A castle at Warkworth is first mentioned in 1158, and this was almost certainly of the motte-and-bailey type with a timber superstructure. During the late twelfth, the thirteenth, and the early fourteenth centuries these timber defences were progressively rebuilt in stone and a stone keep was built on the motte; the bailey eventually had a stone curtain wall, with a double-towered gatehouse in the middle of the south face. Internally there were domestic buildings along the three curtain walls, including a handsome hall range on the west side.

Nunney Castle (Somerset), of the late fourteenth century, bears a close resemblance to the Irish towered keeps of the early thirteenth century.

In 1332 Warkworth was granted by Edward III to Henry, second Lord Percy of Alnwick, and it was under the Percys that the great tower-house for which Warkworth is chiefly renowned was built, probably in the years 1380–90, replacing the earlier keep. The plan consists of a square tower (75 x 75 ft) with four subsidiary towers or wings, one in the middle of each wall. The towers on the west, north, and east are about 25 ft wide and project about 18 ft. The tower on the south is of the same width and projects for the same distance (25 ft) to allow room for the entrance. This unusual plan creates twelve salient angles and at Warkworth all of them are chamfered, further adding to the unique nature of the design. Another unusual feature is the lantern or light well which runs through the centre of the tower from top to bottom, providing light to the inner ends of many rooms.

Warkworth Castle (Northumberland), came into the possession of the Percy family in1332, and it was they who built the magnificent tower-house.

Because of its spacious plan, many of the important rooms at Warkworth could be placed side by side on the same floor, adding greatly to the comfort

and convenience of the occupants. On the ground floor there are cellars, storerooms, a guardroom, a prison, and other facilities within a 10-ft-thick wall. The main accommodation was on the first floor. An ante-room in the south wing led into a service passage with the Great Hall to the right, and the buttery and pantry to the left. One doorway led to the kitchen in the north-west quarter of the tower and another to the Great Chamber, with another large room beyond in the north wing. Opening from the Great Hall was a spacious chapel. A generous provision of staircases completed what was virtually a manor house accommodated on a single floor within a

Warkworth is the result of more than two centuries of building, starting *c.* 1158 with a simple motte-and-bailey castle.

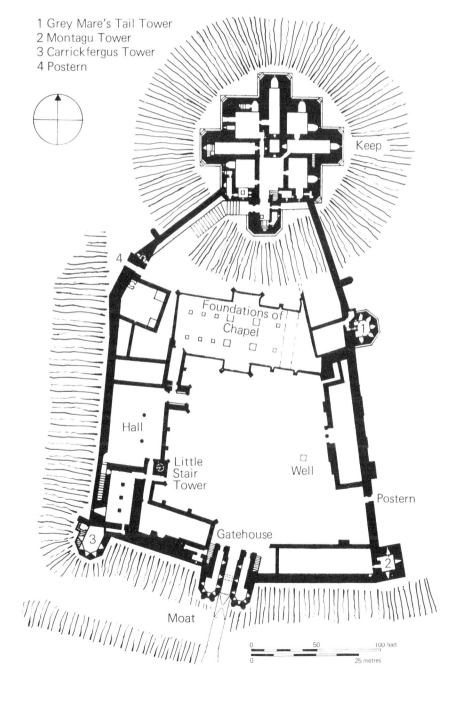

1 Grey Mare's Tail Tower
2 Montagu Tower
3 Carrickfergus Tower
4 Postern

Keep

Foundations of Chapel

Hall

Little
Stair
Tower

Well

Postern

3

Gatehouse

2

Moat

0   50   100 feet

0   25 metres

tower-house. The Great Hall, the kitchen, and the east end of the chapel rose through two storeys. The rest of the third storey was occupied by additional rooms providing more private and personal accommodation. All in all, the Warkworth tower formed a very spacious and comfortable residence by any standards, tower-house or otherwise.

The tower-house at Old Wardour Castle (Wilts.) is an even more extraordinary structure than Warkworth. The front (east) elevation is about 70 ft wide and still stands nearly 60 ft high. It consists of two rectangular flanking towers and a recessed centre section with the entrance passage in the middle. Thus far it looks like a simple tower-house with rectangular towers at the angles. However, the two front towers are not matched by two at the back. Instead, there is a five-sided structure attached to the rear of the main building, with a central hexagonal courtyard, reached via the entrance passage. The site is thus a combination tower-house and (hexagonal) courtyard castle, making it unique in British castle planning. The hall is on the first floor, above the entrance passage, and is lit by a pair of handsome windows on the east side and a matching pair overlooking the courtyard. There are more floor levels in the tower (four) than in the hall section and a similar number in the ranges around the hexagonal court. The kitchens were in the south ranges at ground-floor level. The upper levels in all ranges must have contained a great deal of private and personal accommodation. In spite of the courtyard (*c*. 30 ft across), which is in a sense simply an enlarged version of the Warkworth lantern, Wardour is probably better classed as a tower, but one of unique design, further adding to the variety found already in the small group of English tower-houses.

The east side of Wardour was, in effect, a gatehouse and one or two other tower-houses were also built as gatehouses. Hylton Castle (Co. Durham) is one such tower-gatehouse, begun in the last few years of the fourteenth century by Sir William Hylton who succeeded to the barony in 1376 and died in 1435. The tower has been extensively altered and rebuilt on a number of occasions and the existing windows are a nineteenth-century addition. However, the main lines of the structure have been made clear as a result of work by the Department of the Environment in the last twenty years.

The tower is basically rectangular in plan (70 x 37 ft) and some 70 ft high. On the west (outer) front there are four buttresses, two at the angles and two flanking the entrance, which rise above the general roof level as rectangular turrets, with octagonal superstructures. There are smaller angle turrets on the east face and a larger central rectangular turret or tower which again rises above general roof level. There was a central entrance passage, barred by a portcullis, with guardrooms on either side and possibly some private accommodation as well in two other rooms. The first floor contained a centrally placed hall, with kitchen, buttery, and pantry at one end, a chapel to one side (east) and a private chamber at the other end. The hall was very tall and rose from first-floor to roof level, but there were at least six additional rooms, some of them large (*c*. 25 x 15 ft) on the second and third floors. Hylton was a carefully planned and self-contained tower-house (with its own well, in one of the guardrooms), designed to act as a gatehouse. The implication of such a battlemented structure in gatehouse form is that it stands in front of a full-scale castle. But no such structure ever existed at Hylton, as far as is known. The tower-house is the castle. Presumably the thinking is the same as that which placed the entrances at Bolton and Bodiam courtyard castles firmly under the control of the lord. At Hylton the only structure being built was a tower-house and therefore it needed to be in gatehouse form to control movement in and out of whatever enclosure existed at the time.

There was certainly no associated castle at Thornton (Humberside, formerly Lincolnshire), where the tower-gatehouse forms part of the precinct of Thornton Abbey. It was built about 1382 and bears a general resemblance to Hylton. It is basically rectangular in plan (60 x 30 ft) with octagonal and semi-octagonal buttresses at the angles and flanking the entrance passage. The hall appears to have occupied the whole of the first floor apart from the surrounding wall passages. The solar was on the second floor and it too occupied the whole of the area apart from a small room over the large oriel window in the hall below. The whole arrangement is thus both smaller and simpler than Hylton and clearly less self-contained. Its association with an abbey leaves it even more isolated from the military sphere than Hylton where there was only a tenuous link anyway. The answer may be that architectural style and fashion played a bigger part in the conception of Thornton than military precaution, and the same may be true of other tower-houses as well.

The English tower-house tradition is continued in the fifteenth century at such outstanding sites as Tattershall (Lincs.), Raglan (Gwent), and Ashby de la Zouch (Leics.). The great tower at Tattershall (c. 120 ft high) was built between 1432 and 1445 by the first Lord Cromwell, one-time Treasurer of England (1433–43). The first castle on the site, built about 1231, had a polygonal curtain wall with round towers at the angles, probably very much on the lines of nearby Bolingbroke Castle (above, p. 40). The great brick tower which is Tattershall's chief claim to fame was added some two hundred years later. The structure is of the same general type as Nunney (above, p. 185), that is, a basically rectangular tower with four boldly projecting angle towers. Internally there is a basement below ground level, and four storeys above (six in the angle towers). At each floor-level there is a single large room with smaller rooms in three of the towers and the staircase in the fourth, together with a number of chambers and passages contrived in the thickness of the wall. Nowhere, however, is there any indication of kitchen, buttery, pantry, chapel, and other domestic rooms which might have been expected in such a prestigious building, and it is the lack of these facilities which provides the most important clue to the function of the Tattershall tower.

As it now stands one of the most noticeable features of the tower is the generous provision of doors (no less than three) at ground-level. Above the doors, on the east front, there is also clear evidence that the tower was attached to existing buildings. The evidence takes the form of two rows of sockets for the timbers of a two-storey corridor linking the tower to already existing buildings. This means, of course, that the three doors were not external doors at all but internal; it also means that the tower, despite its martial appearance, was not an independent, self-sufficient structure. The right-hand of the three doors leads into the ground-floor room of the tower

The pitched stone court at Raglan Castle (Gwent), looking towards the gatehouse.

which was simply a parlour for the adjacent buildings, while the middle door leads down to the basement below. The left-hand door led to a spiral staircase in the south-east angle tower and this provided access to the first, second and third floors. The room at first-floor level was a hall, the room above an audience chamber, and the third floor a large bed chamber. This was all spacious, handsome accommodation but it did not constitute a tower-house in the same way as Nunney or Warkworth. It was simply an extension of the then existing buildings which must have contained all the necessary services which were missing from the great brick tower. Tattershall could never stand alone nor was it intended to. It was simply an imposing architectural addition to the castle in tower-house form, a splendid showpiece, which indeed it remains today.

A very similar tower, quite clearly based on Tattershall, was built about 1460 at Buckden Palace (Hunts.), a residence for the Bishops of Lincoln, again acknowledging that domestic comfort and show rather than security were the primary considerations. The Buckden tower is of only four storeys and simpler in arrangement, lacking Tattershall's mural passages and chambers, but externally it has the same oblong plan with four octagonal angle towers, and the structure is again of brick. One of the great advantages of building in tower form is that it can provide a greater degree of privacy than is generally possible in (say) buildings grouped horizontally around a courtyard, and this may be one of the motives underlying the type. The Buckden tower was apparently considered a suitable residence for a king, for Henry VIII is known to have stayed there, almost certainly in the tower itself, and this is perhaps an indication of the social status of the tower form of building, whether of the Tattershall/Buckden type or of the more formidable, independent, self-sufficient tower dwelling.

The great tower at Raglan Castle (Gwent, formerly Monmouth) adds another dimension to the pattern of English tower-houses. it is hexagonal in plan and perhaps more keep-like than anything considered so far. It forms part of a large and complex castle with two imposing courtyards, the Fountain Court and the Pitched Stone Court. Like so many other castles, Raglan started as a motte-and-bailey, probably in the twelfth century, the tower marking the position of the motte and the two courtyards probably indicating the area of the original bailey.

The reconstruction of the early castle was started by Sir William ap Thomas, a wealthy and politically ambitious man, an adherent of the Duke of York who led the opposition to Lancastrian rule which eventually developed into the Wars of the Roses, although by this time ap Thomas was dead (1445). The castle was completed by his son, the first Earl of Pembroke, probably in the years 1461–69. Later work, mainly in the late fifteenth and early sixteenth centuries, did not affect the overall pattern of the castle as completed about 1469.

The tower (the Yellow Tower of Gwent) is a regular hexagon in plan, 65 ft wide (across the angles) with 10-ft-thick walls, still standing four storeys high on one side and probably originally of five storeys. The tower tapers noticeably towards the top and would have been crowned with machicolations and battlements in the same way as the other surviving hexagonal towers in the castle. Access was at first-floor level, originally via a wooden bridge and drawbridge, later by a stone bridge and a fore-building. This led into a small lobby with access to the spiral staircase communicating with the other floors, each of which consisted of a single room. Below was a room which was, or at least could be used as, a kitchen, with a large fireplace and a well. The room at entry-level was a hall or main living room while the one above was the lord's camera or private apartment. The fourth floor was a bedroom, and likewise the fifth, if one existed. The tower was surrounded by a low apron wall of the same shape with semi-circular turrets at the angles and this in turn was (and still is) surrounded by a wet moat.

The remainder of the castle (and it is a substantial remainder) consists of two courtyards and their surrounding ranges of buildings. The Fountain Court to the north-west of the tower is slightly irregular in plan, probably because it follows the shape of the original bailey. The larger Pitched Stone Court is much more regular in plan although it is trapeze-shaped rather than rectangular. These courts are surrounded by ranges of buildings providing extensive accommodation for the castle's retainers. There is an imposing gatehouse with flanking hexagonal towers and there are large hexagonal towers at the angles. Between the two courts is a large hall range which apart from the hall itself (c. 60 x 30 ft) contained an audience chamber with (probably) a parlour below and a chapel with a buttery and passage at the far end, leading to the north-west range and the pantry with another passage leading to the north tower which housed the kitchen. Raglan was undoubtedly one of the most elaborate castles built in the post-Edwardian period, and the question which inevitably arises is why did the first Earl of Pembroke, who was responsible for it, need, or choose, to build on such a grandiose scale?

There are, in fact, two questions to be answered: the purpose of the great tower, and the purpose of the castle as a whole? There is no doubt about the clear physical separation of the tower from the rest of the castle, but is this a result of bastard feudalism or simply a desire for greater privacy? The traditional view, that it was another manifestation of bastard feudalism, has been challenged recently, and the castle as a whole has been seen in terms of the struggle between the two factions in the Wars of the Roses, although without adopting the alternative view of the tower, that it was built for comfort, convenience, and privacy. This, on balance, is the writer's view, in spite of the very martial appearance and the surrounding moat. By means of the bridge the tower is closely linked with the apartments at the upper end of the hall and forms a natural extension, allowing the Earl and his immediate family to withdraw absolutely from the main part of the castle to a comfortable private retreat. The Earl of Pembroke was new to the nobility and the building of a keep-like tower on an early motte may have been simply a token of his new rank, suggesting a greater antiquity to his noble status than he could actually lay claim to.

As far as the castle as a whole is concerned the keep would appear to be in a relatively weak position if it was conceived as a full and integral part of the castle's defensive apparatus. Rather than drawing strength from any surrounding walls, it stands outside the perimeter of the castle proper so that it could be attacked separately from one side. If the keep is left out of account, except as a showpiece and private retreat, then the rest of the castle falls into place in the context of courtyard castles of the fourteenth and fifteenth centuries. Rather than the castle of a local baron it is seen in larger political terms as the stronghold of an ambitious supporter of Edward IV holding South Wales for the Yorkist cause in the protracted struggle of the Wars of the Roses.

The last tower-house to be considered in this section is Ashby de la Zouch (Leics.) built by the same Lord Hastings who built, or at least started, the nearby courtyard castle of Kirby Muxloe. The licence to crenellate Ashby was granted in 1474. Although the tower was an addition, it was an addition not so much to an existing castle as to a manor house. This had stood on the site since the twelfth century, although it had been rebuilt in the fourteenth and it is the stone-built fourteenth-century remains which now form much of the site. Lord Hastings surrounded the whole of the existing structure with a high curtain wall and in the middle of the south front he placed the tower-house which, in spite of its partial destruction in 1648, still dominates the site.

The tower is rectangular in plan (48 x 41 ft) with a projecting square wing on the east side. It was originally 90 ft high and is, in fact, only a little short of that today. At the top there was a machicolated parapet and at the angles there were projecting octagonal turrets carried through the two upper storeys and richly decorated. The whole tower was a handsome architectural composition. Internally there were four storeys in the main tower and seven in the square wing. Access was at ground-floor level via a doorway protected by a portcullis and this led into a vaulted storeroom. The room above, also vaulted, was a large kitchen. Above this was the main living room, the hall, and on the top floor the great chamber or withdrawing room. There was a small chapel off the hall, in the north-west

Arnside Tower (Cumbria), a northern pele tower built around 1330.

turret and there were, of course, additional rooms in the square east wing.

As a self-contained tower, capable of surviving independently of the rest of the castle, Ashby could be interpreted as another manifestation of bastard feudalism with the same duplication of services as seen elsewhere. However, as with Raglan, it has been suggested that the rebuilding of what was originally only a manor house had wider political implications. Like Sir William Herbert (Earl of Pembroke), Lord Hastings' fortunes were very much bound up with the Yorkist side of the Wars of the Roses and it is suggested that Ashby de la Zouch and Kirby Muxloe were intended to secure the Midlands for the York faction as Raglan attempted to secure South Wales. Lord Hastings completed Ashby de la Zouch but, as described earlier, work at Kirby Muxloe was still far from complete on his sudden execution at the hands of Richard III in 1483.

This year is close to the nominal end of the medieval period (1485), and therefore of the medieval castle, although already the account has strayed a little beyond this limit in respect of Thornbury (Glos. above, p. 175). Tower-houses in Scotland and Ireland carry the story even further beyond 1485, although, as pointed out earlier, it is now no longer the story of great royal and baronial castles but of structures fulfilling a humbler social role. These tower-houses are, in fact, manor houses up-ended—for reasons of security—with their rooms stacked vertically in tower form rather than horizontally around a courtyard. They were not, as in most of the examples considered so far, additions to existing castles; they normally stood alone, with only a small walled yard or barmkin attached to one side, although many of them were added to later and developed into very elaborate buildings, often in courtyard shape.

In the same category as the Scottish and Irish towers are the pele towers of northern England, located mainly in Cumbria and Northumberland. For

about three centuries (1300–1600) the northern counties of England were very much a frontier zone, under the constant threat of Scottish raids and invasions. The result of these unsettled conditions was the building of local manor houses in the form of towers, known as pele towers, which were essentially the same as the Scottish and Irish towers. There are about two hundred such towers (or remains thereof) in Cumbria, Northumberland and adjacent areas and their numbers are indicative of their modest status and only local importance, as compared with the great royal and baronial castles which, although relatively few in number, were of great regional and even national importance.

Sizergh Castle (Cumbria, and a pele tower despite its name) is an excellent example of the type. The tower, built about 1350, measures 60 x 40 ft and stands nearly 60 ft high, with a small turret rising 10 ft higher. At basement level the walls are 9 ft thick and there are three storeys above. As first built the tower stood alone, probably surrounded by a wet moat, but there have been considerable additions over the centuries and the whole complex now surrounds three sides of a courtyard. There is a broadly similar complex at Yanwath Hall (also Cumbria). The original nucleus is a tower (38 x 30 x 55 high) with a vaulted basement and two storeys above, and four corner turrets rising above the battlemented parapet. The tower was built early in the fourteenth century and in the following century a great hall and kitchen range were added to the east side and subsequent additions enclosed a courtyard on three sides. Other Cumbrian sites in this category include Catterlen Hall with a fifteenth-century tower and extensive additions enclosing a courtyard, and Askham Hall, with a fourteenth-century tower given new windows around 1685–90 and with the battlements restored in Victorian times.

Unlike Sizergh or Yanwath there are no structures other than the original tower at either Arnside or Dalton. Arnside, built about 1330, now stands gaunt and isolated on a small hillock a mile or so outside the village. One half of the structure has fallen away. The tower, some 50 ft high, was 45 x 31 ft in plan, with a large turret, approximately 13 x 12 ft, at the north-west corner. Dalton Tower, in the village of Dalton-in-Furness, is intact, although much altered internally. It was built about the same time as Arnside and measured 45 x 30 ft in plan. Shank Castle, near Stapleton, is in a similar state to Arnside. It is 52 x 29 ft in plan and was originally about 45 ft high. Other Cumbrian towers include Dacre Castle (early-fourteenth-century), Strickland's Tower (fourteenth-century) in Rose Castle, and Dacre's Tower (fourteenth-century) in Naworth Castle.

In Northumberland an excellent example of an early tower (*c.* 1300), unencumbered by later additions, is provided by the Vicar's Pele in Corbridge on the south side of the churchyard. As its name implies, it was simply the vicar's house, built as a matter of course in the tower style because of the troublesome border conditions. Apart from angle turrets and battlemented parapet the exterior is quite plain, with only a ground-floor doorway and a few window slits. There are Vicar's peles of similar form at Alnham, Elsdon, Embleton, Ford, Ponteland, and Whitton.

Chipchase Tower (fourteenth-century) now forms part of a Jacobean mansion added about 1631. It is larger than Corbridge, 51 x 34 x 50 ft high, with another 10 ft for the original height of the circular angle turrets. There

Vicar's pele, Corbridge, stands in Corbridge churchyard, and was simply the priest's house, built in tower form.

Threave Castle (Dumfries and Galloway), built c. 1380, consists primarily of a five-storey tower-house with an outer rectangular curtain wall with angle towers, added in the following century.

is a vaulted basement (at ground level) and three further storeys above. At Belsay Castle (c. 1340) the vaulted ground-floor basement formed the kitchen and there were two storeys above, one housing the hall and the one above the chamber or private apartment. There were two small additional rooms on each floor provided by two wings on the west side. Langley Castle (also of the fourteenth century) is rather more elaborate in plan. It consists of an oblong centre block, providing one main room on each floor, and four large rectangular angle towers, providing four additional rooms on each floor. Other Northumbrian towers worth noting are Halton Tower, Feather-stone Castle, Cocklaw Tower, Preston Tower, Etal Tower, and the Moot Hall and Prison, both in Hexham and both of the pele-tower type in spite of their names.

In England the tower-house is a localised regional type, made necessary by particular circumstances in the border counties in the years 1300–1600. In Scotland, on the other hand, in whatever circumstances it began, the tower-house came to be a universal type, found throughout the country, from the border to Shetland and from the east coast to the Western Isles. Although more elaborate shapes developed later, the earliest towers, as in England, were rectangular in plan, as at Threave (Dumfries and Galloway), Drum (Grampian), Cawdor (Highland), and Crichton (Lothian). Threave (60 x 40 ft) still stands about 70 ft high and is of five storeys, with entry at first-floor level where the kitchen is situated. Above were the hall and chamber with the top floor, immediately below the battlements, occupied by the armed guardians of the tower. Drum, near Aberdeen, is of similar dimensions (53 x 40 x 70 ft high), and likewise of five storeys, with access at first-floor level. It has rounded corners and the exterior is quite plain, apart from the battlements at the top. Cawdor Tower (45 x 44 ft) was originally of four storeys, although a fifth was added in the seventeenth century. Other additions and alterations in the fifteenth, sixteenth, and seventeenth centuries produced the existing plan, with ranges of buildings and courtyards on all sides, the whole surrounded by a moat on three sides and a stream on the fourth. The tower house at Crichton was added to in a similar way, although only one courtyard was involved there.

Although the simple rectangular tower always remained a basic type there were inevitably moves to provide more space, beginning in the latter part of the fourteenth century. One method of achieving this was to build an L-shaped rather than a rectangular tower. An early example (c. 1374) is Craigmillar Castle (Edinburgh) which is a rectangular tower (52 x 38 ft) with an additional tower or wing (c. 30 x 10 ft) added to one of the long sides, forming a squat L-shape in plan. This allowed at least some of the rooms to be alongside each other rather than superimposed. Although it originally stood alone Craigmillar now forms part of a complex of buildings added in later centuries. Many other castles of the late fourteenth and the fifteenth century were built on the L-plan. Glamis Castle (Tayside), much added to and rebuilt in later centuries, almost certainly contains an original nucleus in the form of an L-shaped tower of the late fourteenth century. Other examples are Dunottar (Grampian) of the fourteenth century, and Affleck (Tayside) of the fifteenth century. Another fifteenth-century example is Dundas (Lothian), originally this was an L-shaped

Although much altered and added to in later centuries Glamis Castle (Tayside) began as a fairly simple L-shaped tower-house in 1376.

tower to which a second wing or tower was added to increase the accommodation.

The alternative method of providing more space was to make use of the thickness of the walls above ground level. Elphinstone Tower (*c.* 1440) retains the simple rectangular plan (50 x 35 ft), but in addition to the main room on each of five floors, there is a whole series of smaller chambers contrived in the thickness of the walls which must have added greatly to its comfort and convenience. The tower-house at Comlongon (Dumfries and Galloway) is of the same date as Elphinstone and follows the same plan and arrangement.

The majority of Scottish tower-houses of the fourteenth and fifteenth centuries conform to the rectangular L-shaped plan. In the same period, however, there are a few examples of tower-houses built on a more elaborate plan. Borthwick Castle (Lothian), built around 1430, consists of a large main tower (75 x 47 ft x 100 ft high), with two additional towers or wings (each *c.* 30 x 20 ft) on the west side, rising to the same height. The walls are up to 12 ft thick, but there is still a great deal of accommodation on each of the five floors. The double-wing plan allowed the hall (50 x 24 ft) on the first floor to have the kitchen at the same level in one wing, and the solar or withdrawing room in the other.

Hermitage Castle (Borders) is even more elaborate in plan. Originally built as a manor house (*c.* 1360) it was, late in the century, converted into a rectangular tower-house. Shortly afterwards (*c.* 1400) four rectangular angle towers were added, resulting in Hermitage's present striking appearance. The main central tower measures 75 x 45 ft. The additional towers mask the angles and are all of different sizes, the smallest at the north-east being 23 ft square, the largest at the south-west being 56 x 32 ft. At the eastern and western ends the gaps between the towers are bridged across at fourth-storey level. There is a generally similar tower-house with four angle towers at Crookston (Strathclyde) and another is known from excavation at Braemar (Grampian), the castle of Kindrochit.

Tower-houses of the types described above fall within the early period of Scottish tower-house building from about 1330 to 1480, and therefore within the medieval period. After 1480 there was a noticeable slowing down in building activity for about eighty years, which ended with the return of Mary Queen of Scots from France in 1561. Within a few years another great period of tower-house building was under way, but now on a much more ambitious scale, including many which are deservedly well-known and in many cases still occupied. This second phase of Scottish tower-house building lasted from about 1560 to 1670, although in the last few decades tower-houses were being superseded by purely domestic, non-Scottish types of house with no pretensions to military strength and security. However, apart from noting the continuation of the tradition after 1480 the matter of Scottish tower-houses in the second phase cannot be pursued here.

The tower-house building period in Ireland was somewhat shorter than in Scotland, from about 1400 to 1650, although the results, in terms of numbers built and surviving visible remains, are no less impressive. As in Scotland the basic type is the simple rectangular tower. Clara Castle (Kilkenny) is a well-preserved example of the type, built late in the

Clara Castle (Kilkenny), a well-preserved, late fifteenth-century, Irish tower-house with a small bawn or walled courtyard attached to one side.

Dunsoghly (Co. Dublin), one of the more elaborate Irish tower-houses, with a main rectangular tower and four square angle towers.

fifteenth century. The tower (34 x 27 x 70 ft high) has five storeys plus an attic. There is a walled courtyard or bawn in front of the entrance which is at ground level. Burnchurch Castle (also in Kilkenny) is broadly similar in size and layout to Clara but differs in one respect. The gable-end walls are carried up one storey higher than the other two walls and form two elongated turrets with their own rampart walks at the highest part of the building.

Included in the towers of simple rectangular plan are the so-called 'ten-pound castles', built as a result of a statute of Henry VI in 1429. This was designed to encourage the building of tower-houses in the counties of Dublin, Meath, Kildare and Louth (the counties of the English pale), by offering a subsidy of £10 for each tower built. The offer seems to have been successful for in 1449, only twenty years later, a limitation was imposed on the number of towers to be built. The tower-house at Donore (Meath) provides a good example of the type. It is 28 x 22 ft in plan and four storeys high. It has rounded angles and a stair turret at one corner.

As in Scotland, the simplest variation of the rectangular plan was the provision of a second smaller tower or wing producing an L-shaped plan. Probably the best-known example of this type is Blarney Castle (Co. Cork), built about 1446, famous for its Blarney Stone. The main tower is massive, 85 ft high with walls 12 ft thick, and has five storeys. Abutting one side is a smaller, lower tower containing a staircase and some smaller rooms. At Roodstown (Louth) the staircase is housed in the same way, leaving space in the main tower for a single uncluttered rectangular room. There is a second smaller tower or wing at the diagonally opposite corner. This had four storeys and was about 45 ft high.

The Irish towers include one or two of somewhat more ambitious plan. Kilclief (Co. Down) has two additional towers projecting from one face of the main tower, as at Borthwick (Lothian, above, p. 199). The space between the towers is spanned by an arch at fourth-storey level. Bunratty Castle (Co. Clare) is even more elaborate in plan. It consists of a main tower (c. 64 x 43 ft) with four rectangular flanking towers, one masking each angle, with arches spanning the gaps high up on the north and south sides. The main block is of three storeys, the corner towers of six storeys each. Dunsoghly (Co. Dublin) also has four angle towers, although the whole structure is on a smaller scale than Bunratty.

Circular tower-houses form a type for which there is no parallel in Scotland or England, although apart from the circular plan such towers perform exactly the same function as rectangular towers. Ballynahow (Tipperary) is of five storeys and in spite of its external appearance the main rooms are more or less square. Another round tower, Reginald's Tower, in Waterford, forms part of the city walls, but is otherwise the same as the free-standing towers. There are other circular tower-houses at Synone (Tipperary), Balief (Kilkenny), and Newtown (Clare).

This concludes a brief survey of tower-houses in northern England, Scotland, and Ireland which carry the story of the medieval castle, or at least medieval fortification, up to and beyond the end of the medieval period and the medieval castle proper. In the areas in which they occur the tower-houses form an intermediate type and stage between the castle and the purely domestic, undefended home. Elsewhere, there is no such clear-cut intermediate stage. As the great royal and baronial castles became fewer in number so the purely domestic, undefended houses became more and more numerous, until the one had completely replaced the other except for certain limited administrative, military, and penal functions.

This ends our survey of some 300 years of castle building in the British Isles. In historical terms the period coincides closely with the rule of the Plantagenet kings. The earliest signs of new trends in military architecture appeared in the reign of the first Plantagenet king, Henry II (1154–89), and by the end of the dynasty (1399), the story was largely over. Only a handful of castles (as opposed to tower-houses) were built after that date, and those that were built were on lines already well established in the previous century. For all practical purposes the major developments in the later medieval castle took place within the 250 years of Plantagenet rule, from 1154 to 1399, and within that period royal castle building was of particular significance. The character and personality of the Plantagenet kings was of no little importance in this development. A less energetic king than Henry II might not have produced Dover or Windsor, and although the innovations represented there would eventually have appeared anyway, they would have appeared later and in different circumstances and the story of the medieval castle would have been thereby greatly altered. A less determined king than Henry's great-grandson, Edward I, might have adopted a different solution to the North Wales problem, or have been deterred from completion of the programme by the vast expense, and again, the story of the medieval castle, if not the whole history of North Wales, would have been very different.

Much of this final chapter has been devoted to tower-houses, which are defended by means of elevation, and elevation—the use of the tower—is one of the basic themes of all fortification, in any period and in any area. The second basic theme is that of enclosure, the protection of an area, large or small, by means of a curtain wall. These two considerations, either separately, or more often in varying combinations, together with the exploitation of natural features, account for virtually all defence works built by man. They certainly account for all the medieval castles in the British Isles, both the later examples as described here and early ones built in the century or so after the Conquest. The development of the two themes can be followed separately.

In the early period of castle building, from 1066 until about 1180, the tower in the form of the square keep was the dominant theme. Thereafter there was a dual development, castles with keeps in polygonal and circular form, and castles without keeps, and both types persisted up to the threshold of the Edwardian period. Nor was this the end of the story. The tower as a separate entity had a place in the repertoire of James of St George, as exemplified by Flint, Hawarden, and Caernarvon. Moreover, by this time the twin-towered gatehouse had developed into a solid keep-like structure, designed to survive independently of the rest of the castle. Marten's Tower (in Chepstow Castle), Knaresborough, and Dudley carry the story from the late thirteenth to the early fourteenth century, and these are followed by a long series of tower-houses which continue it to the end of, and beyond, the medieval period. What this means, in fact, is that the tower theme never died out. The independent tower, be it keep or tower-house, was not always dominant, and did not exclude other themes, but it did persist throughout the medieval period. In a real sense the wheel had gone full circle. Although they occupied different geographical regions, and although the political, social, and economic circumstances were different, the tower-houses of the border region and of Scotland and Ireland represented the same answer to turbulent times as that provided by the great keeps of the Norman period: elevation in the form of free-standing, or at least independent, towers.

There is no doubt that in the early period the curtain wall was a subordinate element, and followed no particular plan. Wall towers, where they existed at all, were rectangular and haphazardly placed. Dover, Framlingham, and Windsor Castles introduced regularly-spaced towers, still in rectangular form, at the end of the twelfth century, to be followed shortly by circular towers. At this stage the keepless castle became a regular type and although the keep (in round form) was very much alive in one group of castles, in a parallel group the emphasis was now on a strong enclosing wall with interval towers. The punctuation provided by wall towers led to the polygonal plan, with straight stretches of curtain wall between each tower. By the second half of the thirteenth century rectangular planning had appeared with the emphasis on boldly projecting angle towers. The ultimate development of the enclosure theme was the concentric castle with two curtain walls, one enclosing the other. In the fourteenth and fifteenth centuries the enclosure tradition was continued by the series of courtyard castles described in the early part of this chapter. Alongside them were, of course, the various tower-houses described in the later part, so that both traditions were running parallel, although for geographical and political reasons tower-houses survived longer, so that the story ended where it began, with the tower and an associated but subordinate enclosing wall.

There is no question that the high noon of medieval castle building was the reign of Edward I, represented by the works of his master builder, James of St George, in North Wales, described in Chapters 3 and 4. In this period the medieval castle reached its peak of development, not only in the British Isles but in Europe as a whole. In terms of architecture there is little or nothing to rival Caernarvon, and in terms of technique there is nothing to match Beaumaris. They and the other Edwardian sites stand at the mid-point of the later castles. Before them is a century of development (1170–1272) represented by castles with round keeps (the old tradition), and castles without keeps (the new tradition). After them is not so much the long twilight, as suggested earlier, as the long afternoon of the medieval castle in which, although Edwardian influence and tradition is clear, there were new aims and new principles which meant that the fourteenth- and fifteenth-century castles could never be the same as those of Edward and his master builder.

In a very real sense the pre-Edwardian and post-Edwardian castles have provided the setting in which the North Wales castles can be seen in their true context. The thirty-five years of Edward's reign and his great castle-building programme are very much the centrepiece. What went before was a long prelude, important in its own way, but always heading in the same direction. What followed was an even longer postscript, again significant, but only emphasising the heights which the preceding Edwardian castle had reached. Those heights were never scaled again and the castles of Edward I and James of St George in North Wales remain one of the greatest achievements in the world of medieval military architecture.

Select Bibliography

Braun, H., *The English Castle* (3rd ed.), London, 1948.

Brown, R. A., *English Castles*, London, 1976.

Clark, G. T., *Medieval Military Architecture in England* (2 Vols.), 1884.

Colvin, H. M., *The History of the King's Works*, Vols. I & II, HMSO, 1963.

Cruden, S., *The Scottish Castle*, Edinburgh, 1960.

De Breffny, B., *Castles of Ireland*, London, 1977.

Forde-Johnston, J., *Castles and Fortifications in Britain and Ireland*, London, 1977.

Gascoigne, B. & C., *Castles of Britain*, London, 1975.

Hogg, G., *Castles of England*, Newton Abbot, 1970.

Hughes, Q., *Military Architecture*, London, 1974.

Johnson, P., *The National Trust Book of British Castles*, London, 1978.

Leask, H. G., *Irish Castles and Castellated Houses*, Dundalk, 1951.

Mackenzie, W. M., *The Medieval Castle in Scotland*, London, 1927.

Renn, D. F., *Norman Castles in Britain*, London, 1973.

Simpson, W. D., *Castles in England and Wales*, London, 1969.

Sorrell, A., *British Castles*, London, 1973.

Stalley, R. A., *Architecture and Sculpture in Ireland 1150–1350*, Dublin, 1971.

Thompson, A. H., *Military Architecture in England during the Middle Ages*, Oxford, 1912.

Toy, S., *The Castles of Great Britain*, London, 1953.

Warner, P., *The Medieval Castle*, London, 1971.

Index